CONTRA KEYNES AND CAMBRIDGE

F. A. HAYEK

THE COLLECTED WORKS OF

F. A. Hayek

CONTRA KEYNES
AND CAMBRIDGE

Essays, Correspondence

F. A. HAYEK

Edited by Bruce Caldwell

Liberty Fund

INDIANAPOLIS

Contra Keynes and Cambridge is volume 9 of The Collected Works of F. A. Hayek, published by The University of Chicago Press.

This Liberty Fund paperback edition of *Contra Keynes and Cambridge* is published by arrangement with The University of Chicago Press and Taylor & Francis Books, Ltd., a member of the Taylor & Francis Group.

Library of Congress Cataloging-in-Publication Data

Hayek, Friedrich A. von (Friedrich August), 1899–1992.
Contra Keynes and Cambridge: essays, correspondence/F. A. Hayek; edited by Bruce Caldwell.
p.   cm.— (The collected works of F. A. Hayek)
Includes bibliographical references and index.
ISBN 978-0-86597-744-0 (pbk.: alk. paper)
1. Keynesian economics.   2. Keynes, John Maynard, 1883–1946.   I. Caldwell, Bruce, 1952–   II. Title.
HB99.7.H35   2009
330.15'6—dc22   2008028282

Liberty Fund, Inc.
8335 Allison Pointe Trail, Suite 300
Indianapolis, Indiana 46250-1684

THE COLLECTED WORKS OF F. A. HAYEK

Founding Editor: W. W. Bartley III
General Editor: Stephen Kresge
Associate Editor: Peter G. Klein
Assistant Editor: Gene Opton

Published with the support of

The Hoover Institution on War, Revolution and Peace,
Stanford University

Anglo American and De Beers Chairman's Fund, Johannesburg

Cato Institute, Washington, D.C.

The Centre for Independent Studies, Sydney

Chung-Hua Institution for Economic Research, Taipei

Engenharia Comércio e Indústria S/A, Rio de Janeiro

Escuela Superior de Economia y Administración de Empresas
(ESEADE), Buenos Aires

The Heritage Foundation

The Institute for Humane Studies, George Mason University

Instituto Liberal, Rio de Janeiro

Charles G. Koch Charitable Foundation, Wichita

The Carl Menger Institute, Vienna

The Morris Foundation, Little Rock

Verband der Österreichischen Banken und Bankiers, Vienna

The Wincott Foundation, London

The Bartley Institute, Oakland

CONTENTS

CONTENTS

EDITORIAL FOREWORD

I

The task which W. W. Bartley III, the founding editor of the Collected Works of F. A. Hayek, set for the editors of each volume was not only to assemble the writings of Hayek in a comprehensive and readable order, but to provide a theoretical, critical, and historical context in which the full significance of Hayek's work could be understood. *Contra Keynes and Cambridge*, volume 9 of the collected works and the fourth volume in order of publication, recreates the original debate between Hayek and John Maynard Keynes, which began on the pages of *Economica* in 1931 and which, in its implications for both economic theory and policy, has yet to be resolved.

The inclusion in this volume of the replies of Keynes and Piero Sraffa to Hayek's provocative review of Keynes's *A Treatise on Money* provides a new opportunity to examine the argument as it moved from similar premises to differing conclusions and on to altogether dissimilar premises and to conclusions that we ourselves must provide. The Hayek essays in this volume have not been previously collected, and his introductory essay, "The Economics of the 1930s as Seen from London", is published here for the first time.

II

Returning to the Hayek-Keynes debate after the events and controversies of over fifty years is not unlike stepping from the noise and bustle of the High Street into the measured precinct of a Cambridge or Oxford college court. And, like eager undergraduates, refusing to be intimidated by those august structures, we cannot help asking the question John Hicks asked: Which was right, Hayek or Keynes?

"Why was it right of Drake to play bowls when he heard the Armada was approaching, but wrong of Charles II to catch moths when he heard that the Dutch Fleet had entered the Medway? The answer is, 'Because Drake won'....We must take a larger view of the past than of the present, because when examining the present we can never be sure what is going to pay". So wrote E. M. Forster in 1920 from somewhere just off the High Street before his return to rooms just off the central court at Kings College.

Was Keynes right because he captured the professional economists and policymakers? Was Hayek wrong because it took much longer than he, or anyone, could have expected for certain of his predictions to be fulfilled? And could either eventuality have occurred in the same con- ceptual and political world in which it was initiated?

Neither Hayek nor Keynes was unmindful of the cultural and political consequences of their economic theories. They shared similar objectives: To preserve where possible and defend where necessary the values of prewar European liberal civilization. This was a world in which national identities mattered less than standards of conduct, which were not yet presumed to be amenable to government control; a world in which, for example, Ludwig Wittgenstein (Hayek's cousin), although fighting on the opposite side in 1915, could write to Keynes, in a letter posted from the K.u.K. Feldpost 186, "I am very interested to hear that Russell has published a book lately. Could you possibly send it to me and let me pay you after the war?...You're quite wrong if you think that being a soldier prevents me from thinking about propositions. As a matter of fact, I've done a good deal of logical work lately....The war hasn't altered my private feelings in the least (thank God!!)...." Civilization, for Keynes, was Cambridge and Bloomsbury, and he found himself pulled and prodded into increasingly nationalist positions (on tariff policy, for example, and the gold standard) and would not live long enough to reverse the severe nationalist measures that 'Keynesian' economics led to.

Hayek remained an internationalist to the end, more faithful to the values of the Cambridge halls than the ardent native. Hayek may have lost every battle except the last, but he kept alive for a new generation the possibility of discovering for themselves an answer to the persistent question, Which was right?

III

I would like to express my appreciation to Bruce Caldwell for accepting the perilous task of editing this volume and for remaining undaunted to its completion and to Gene Opton for preparing the text. We are grateful to Penelope Kaiserlian of the University of Chicago Press and Alan Jarvis of Routledge for their patient care in seeing this volume into print. Blackwell Publishers, *The Economist*, *The Journal of Modern History*, the Macmillan Press, and the Provost and Scholars of King's College, Cambridge, have kindly granted permission to reprint various of the essays and letters here included.

I would like to thank the sponsors of the Collected Works of F. A. Hayek for their support of the project, and I am most grateful to Mr. Walter Morris of the Morris Foundation, without whose help and counsel the editorial labour of the project would have neither commenced nor continued. He, above all, can share no blame for our mistakes.

Stephen Kresge
Oakland, California

INTRODUCTION

In early 1927, Friedrich A. Hayek, a young Austrian economist who had not yet even begun his university teaching, sent a request to the most famous living British economist. John Maynard Keynes answered the query with a postcard dated February 24. It contained the single sentence, "I am sorry to say that my stock of *Mathematical Psychics* is exhausted".[1]

In early 1946, Hayek saw Keynes for the last time; their conversation would haunt him for years. Hayek asked Keynes whether he was concerned about what certain of his followers were making of his theories. The ever-confident Keynes replied that one must not worry about such things, that should those who called themselves 'Keynesians' ever become dangerous, he could turn public opinion against them in an instant. In the closing sentences of his review of Roy Harrod's *The Life of Keynes*, Hayek remembered the moment: "[H]e indicated by a quick movement of his hand how rapidly that would be done. But three months later, he was dead".[2]

In the nineteen years between the postcard and the conversation, twentieth-century economics was transformed, and the battle between Hayek and Keynes was central to the transformation. Sir John Hicks put it this way:

> When the definitive history of economic analysis during the 1930s comes to be written, a leading character in the drama (it was quite a drama) will be Professor Hayek. Hayek's economic writings—I am not concerned here with his later work in political theory and in sociology—are almost unknown to the modern student; it is hardly remembered that there was a time when the new theories of Hayek were the

---

[1]Postcard, Keynes to Hayek, February 24, 1927. In the Hayek collection, The Hoover Institution Archives, Stanford, Calif.

[2]F. A. Hayek, "Review of R. F. Harrod's *The Life of John Maynard Keynes*", *The Journal of Modern History*, vol. 24, June 1952, pp. 195–198, reprinted as chapter 10, this volume.

principal rival of the new theories of Keynes. Which was right, Keynes or Hayek?[3]

Our goal in this volume is to recount the story, one that can be seen as part cautionary tale, part morality play, and (as it remains even now) part riddle. Though they first met in the late 1920s, the active exchange between Hayek and Keynes actually began in 1931. We will begin by tracing the sequence of events that brought each to his position in the ensuing debate.

Keynes

John Maynard Keynes was born in Cambridge on June 5, 1883, the first child of John Neville and Florence Keynes. Neville Keynes taught logic, but had been an early student of Alfred Marshall's and would become famous for publishing in 1891 an influential book on the methodology of economics. Maynard studied mathematics as an undergraduate. In 1905, he briefly took up economics to prepare for the Civil Service Examination. From 1906 to 1908 he worked in the India Office, then accepted a lectureship financed by A. C. Pigou in economics at Cambridge. Keynes was elected a Fellow of King's College in 1909 to continue his work on probability theory. He also continued to teach economics, and made his mark relatively quickly within the small circle of Cambridge economists. He took over editorship of the *Economic Journal* from F. Y. Edgeworth in 1911 at the age of twenty-eight and became secretary of the Royal Economic Society two years later. During the war he held a post in the British Treasury. His work there earned him a seat at the Paris Peace Conference as the chief Treasury representative. He was to resign in protest over the severity of the 'Carthaginian Peace' that, despite his best efforts, he saw emerging from the talks. Prior to his resignation, Keynes's successful efforts to ensure the avoidance of mass starvation in Austria had made him a hero among Central Europeans. But in the late summer, after leaving Paris, he penned the book that would bring him truly international fame, *The Economic Consequences of the Peace.*[4] Keynes became a hero to idealists and

---

[3]John Hicks, "The Hayek Story", in *Critical Essays in Monetary Theory* (Oxford: Clarendon Press, 1967), p. 203.

[4]J. M. Keynes, *The Economic Consequences of the Peace* [1919], reprinted as vol. 2 (1971) of *The Collected Writings of John Maynard Keynes*, Austin Robinson and Donald Moggridge, eds, 30 vols (London: Macmillan (for the Royal Economic Society), 1971–89). All further references to Keynes's writings will be to the relevant volume in *The Collected Writings of John*

internationalists around the world. His main thesis was not that the terms of the treaty were unjust, though he thought that they were. It was rather that the huge amounts of reparations demanded, intended to punish Germany and prevent her from ever becoming a power again, could potentially lead to the collapse of civilization in Europe. His prescience about the consequences of the peace increased Keynes's reputation as time passed.

Keynes and the Gold Standard

A central theme of *Economic Consequences* was that the war had transformed Europe, that relations among states were categorically different from those that had existed before, and that the new age demanded new policies. Keynes gave concrete form to his vision when he joined the debate over the return to the gold standard a few years later.

For two generations preceding the war, England had been the world center for trade and finance. The gold standard was widely credited at the time with keeping international financial markets orderly and thereby ensuring the steady growth of commerce and capital investment. It was thought to work this way: Whenever the British bought more goods from foreigners than they sold to them, gold would flow out to make up the difference. The gold outflow would, through various channels, cause the Bank of England to raise Bank Rate (the interest rate under its control) in response. As other interest rates were pushed upwards, economic activity would slow. The slowdown would bring about a general deflation, a forcing down of domestic prices and wages, which was usually accompanied by increased unemployment as well. The lowering of wages and prices was painful but restorative medicine. Lower British prices would reduce domestic demand for relatively higher-priced imports while stimulating foreign and domestic demand for British goods. This would lead to a restoration of balance of payments equilibrium.

Recent scholarship asserts that many of the beliefs prevalent in the interwar period about the workings of the gold standard were myths. The relative success of the standard in the late nineteenth century is now attributed less to the vigilance and power of the Bank of England, and more to the cooperation of a number of central banks and to the credibility of their joint responses to crises. World War I ended both the ability and willingness of the banks to act in concert. Indeed, the attempt to reestablish and maintain the standard in the new environ-

Maynard Keynes.

ment was one reason that the 'Slump of 1930' turned into a worldwide Great Depression.[5] The central point for our purposes, however, is that at the end of the First World War many in government thought that a return to gold was a necessary condition for the reestablishment of stability in international commerce and finance.

In Britain, an embargo on gold exports imposed during the war became embodied in an Act in 1920, but was set to expire in 1925. If no further action were taken, on expiration the pound sterling would again be exchangeable against the dollar at the prewar exchange rate of £1 = $4.86. Though the pound was worth considerably less than $4.86 following the war, the embargo provided some breathing room during which, it was hoped, its value might rise towards prewar parity. A recession in Britain in 1920–21 helped move sterling in the right direction against the dollar. But the unemployment rate also soared, reaching a high of 22.4 per cent in July, 1920, and remaining in the 10 per cent range for the next three years.

It was in his 1923 book, *A Tract on Monetary Reform*, that Keynes began to speak out against the "barbarous relic" of the gold standard.[6] He began the book by detailing the adverse effects of an "unstable value of money" on both distribution and production. He analyzed both inflation and deflation, and summarized their effects as follows: "Thus inflation is unjust and deflation is expedient. Of the two perhaps deflation is, if we rule out exaggerated inflations such as that of Germany, the worse; because it is worse, in an impoverished world, to provoke unemployment than to disappoint the rentier".[7]

If England were to decide to return to the gold standard, Keynes (at least in 1923) was willing to take a wait-and-see attitude about whether it should be at the prewar rate or at a lower one. More controversially for the times, Keynes argued that a return to gold at a fixed convertibility rate, no matter what the value, would be a mistake. It was here that his vision of a changed world came into play. The gold standard may have provided stability for international markets when England dominated world trade. But its time had passed. European markets were in shambles; socialist, reactionary, and nationalist movements competed for influence in both long-established and newly formed nations; most

---

[5]See Barry Eichengreen, *Golden Fetters: The Gold Standard and the Great Depression, 1919–1939* (New York and Oxford: Oxford University Press, 1992).

[6]J. M. Keynes, *A Tract on Monetary Reform* [1923], reprinted as vol. 4 (1971) of *The Collected Writings of John Maynard Keynes*, op. cit., p. 138.

[7]*Ibid.*, p. 36. *Rentiers* are owners of financial capital and other property. In Germany, hyperinflation had wiped out the savings of the middle- and upper-class *rentiers* who had bought bonds to support the war effort.

importantly, the United States had replaced Britain as the world centre of commerce and finance. A return to gold would require that the US Federal Reserve system, only a decade old and buffeted by domestic political influences, should avoid errors and coordinate its actions with the Bank of England. Keynes doubted that such coordination could be achieved on a sustained basis. His policy recommendation was that the monetary authorities of Britain and the United States should make the internal stability of the value of money their first priority. Rather than fixing the exchange rate, he recommended that a form of the "crawling peg" system be instituted in which the exchange rate would move to preserve internal price stability. If the central banks of the United States and Britain were able to coordinate their actions, exchange rate stability would also result. But internal stability should be the first priority of policy.

Again his advice went unheeded. On March 17, 1925, Chancellor of the Exchequer Winston Churchill held an unusual dinner party. Two months earlier, he had distributed a memorandum that made the case against a return to gold, to which he invited a response. (Given its similarity to a school examination, the memo became known as "Mr. Churchill's Exercise".) Over dinner, Keynes and former Chancellor Reginald McKenna debated the merits of the case with two top Treasury officials. Churchill listened, occasionally offering comments of his own. In the end, the Chancellor decided to return to the gold standard at a fixed prewar parity of £1 = $4.86.[8]

The Evolution of Keynes's Policy Views

Harry Johnson called the return to gold at $4.86 "an act of blind traditionalism", and Churchill's error was indeed a consequential one.[9] Increased foreign competition had begun to undermine England's industrial, manufacturing, and commercial sectors even before the war. The disruption of trade during the war years exacerbated longstanding problems. In the best of circumstances, the 1920s would have been a painful period of structural realignment for England. The upwards

---

[8]For accounts of the fateful dinner party, see D. E. Moggridge, *British Monetary Policy 1924–31: The Norman Conquest of $4.86* (Cambridge: Cambridge University Press, 1972); and P. J. Grigg, *Prejudice and Judgment* (London: Cape, 1948). The latter was written by Churchill's private secretary for matters of Finance and Administration, who had attended the dinner.

[9]Harry Johnson, "The Shadow of Keynes", in *The Shadow of Keynes: Understanding Keynes, Cambridge and Keynesian Economics*, Elizabeth Johnson and Harry Johnson, eds (Chicago: University of Chicago Press, 1978), p. 176.

movement of the value of sterling towards prewar parity prior to 1925, and efforts to sustain that exchange rate afterwards, kept interest rates high, battered export industries, and held the unemployment rate in the 10 per cent range for the rest of the decade.

Even more crucial for our story is Keynes's response to the stagnant economic conditions of the 1920s. Though he did not deny the effects of both structural changes and policy missteps, Keynes ultimately concluded that a more fundamental change had occurred, that the whole system of laissez faire capitalism required re-examination.[10]

In Keynes's colorful prose, the unemployment rate had become "stuck in a rut"[11] at an unusually high level: something had caused the equilibration mechanism to stall. As noted above, one of the consequences of the return to gold was high interest rates. Such rates attracted savings. Unfortunately, the level of savings became too high; there were insufficient profitable domestic investment opportunities available. As a result, British funds were drawn to finance investments overseas. Looked at another way, British industry was no longer competitive.

Normally such a situation should not persist. High unemployment should cause British prices and costs to drop, and this should eventually restore a competitive edge. But it was here that an additional problem surfaced. Due to the growing political strength of Labour, it was more difficult to force wages, and hence costs, downwards.[12] Nor was a cut in real wages via inflationary monetary policy an option, since inflation would only serve to exacerbate the exchange rate problem.

It was in considering this dismal situation that Keynes hit upon another solution, one that went beyond the nostrums of laissez faire, one that he himself thought constituted a "drastic" remedy.[13] The state should coordinate savings and investment, undertaking an extensive program of public works (such as the construction of roads, housing, and electrical plants) that would create jobs to make use of the unemployed labour. This would reverse the flow of savings out of the

[10]That Keynes's goal in the interwar period was "to save a capitalist system he did not admire" (p. xv) is a dominant theme in Robert Skidelsky, *John Maynard Keynes: Volume Two, The Economist as Saviour 1920–1937* (London: Macmillan, 1992).

[11]J. M. Keynes, "Does Unemployment Need a Drastic Remedy?" [1924], reprinted in *Activities 1922–1929: The Return to Gold and Industrial Policy*, ed. Donald Moggridge, vol. 19, part 1 (1981), of *The Collected Writings of John Maynard Keynes*, op. cit., p. 220.

[12]Though it was to last only ten months, the first Labour government was formed in 1923 with Ramsay MacDonald at its head. Keynes's prognostications received further confirmation when a bitter dispute between workers and owners in the coal industry led to a General Strike in 1926.

[13]J. M. Keynes, "Does Unemployment Need a Drastic Remedy?", op. cit., pp. 219–223.

country, would add to the domestic capital stock, and best of all, once such projects were under way, it would be discovered that "*prosperity is cumulative*".[14] The happy effects on labour are described by Keynes as follows:

> [W]e must seek to submerge the rocks in a rising sea,—not forcing labour out of what is depressed, but attracting it into what is prosperous; not crushing the blind strength of organized labour, but relieving its fears; not abating wages where they are high, but raising them where they are low.[15]

Over the next few years, Keynes developed and promoted these ideas, both in his popular writings and in a series of Liberal Summer Schools, open to the public, held in alternate years in Oxford and Cambridge. In 1928, his ideas formed the basis for a number of themes in the Liberal Party publication *Britain's Industrial Future*, dubbed the 'Yellow Book'. Lloyd George, the Liberal Party leader, embraced the proposals in his manifesto, *We Can Conquer Unemployment*, published prior to the 1929 General Election.

The most outspoken opponent of Keynes's new views was neither another political party nor a body of academic economists, but the Treasury. In his budget speech in April, Churchill stated a position that soon became known as the 'Treasury View': "It is the orthodox Treasury dogma, steadfastly held, that whatever might be the political and social advantages, very little additional employment and no permanent additional employment can in fact, and as a general rule, be created by State borrowing and State expenditure."[16] This was followed by an official Treasury White Paper defending from Liberal criticisms various actions that the Treasury had taken. The Liberals placed third in the election. Ironically, neither Labour (which won) nor the Conservatives had any truck with the new ideas. Keynes's impression of the matter is recalled by Elizabeth Johnson:

---

[14] *Ibid.*, italics in original, p. 221. Note the suggestion of the notion of the multiplier in this phrase. Keynes's biographer Roy Harrod observed that this article contains "the outline of the public policy which has since been specifically associated with his name". See his book *The Life of John Maynard Keynes* (New York: Harcourt Brace, 1951; New York: Norton, 1982), p. 350.

[15] *Ibid.*, p. 220.

[16] The evolution of the Treasury View from a theoretical to a pragmatic argument against public works as a policy to fight unemployment is carefully documented in Peter Clarke, *The Keynesian Revolution in the Making, 1924–1936* (Oxford: Clarendon Press [1988], 1990), chapters 3 and 7. Churchill's quote may be found on p. 67.

Both Conservative and Labour governments—in the "fatalistic belief that there can never be any more employment than there is", as Keynes had expressed it in 1929—sat tight during the 1920s and 1930s, instructed by the civil servants of the Treasury school whom he later characterized as "trained by tradition and experience and native skill to every form of intelligent obstruction".[17]

As usual, Keynes did not give up. Debate over the issue would continue in deliberations of the Macmillan Committee on Finance and Industry, a group set up to investigate the effects of the financial and monetary systems on the state of industry, which met from November 1929 through May 1931. Keynes both offered his own evidence and, as a member of the committee, played the role of interrogator when Treasury and Bank of England officials appeared.

The evolution of Keynes's thought on policy during the 1920s has necessarily been simplified in this account, but in broad outline it was as follows: The return to gold at a fixed and overvalued rate kept interest rates high, and it also effectively eliminated monetary policy as a stabilization tool. The emerging strength of the Labour party meant that cuts in nominal wages could be resisted. As such, the deflation necessary to bring the system back into equilibrium would take a very long time to work and would be accompanied by unacceptably high levels of unemployment. Increased spending on public works held out the promise of at least putting some people back to work. If prosperity indeed turned out to be "cumulative", it might be able to do much more. All of this was contained in Keynes's popular writings and governmental papers; it had yet to work its way convincingly into his theoretical tracts in economics.

A final episode provides additional insights into Keynes's views on policy, and into his personality as well. When Keynes was writing in the 1920s, the unemployment rate in Britain was 10 per cent. By 1931, it was in the 20 per cent range. As early as the summer before, Keynes began reluctantly to advocate that protectionist measures be undertaken to help fight unemployment and stem the flight of gold. He did this privately, in deliberations of government committees and in letters to government officials. But finally on March 7, 1931, he publicly en-dorsed a revenue tariff in an article printed in the weekly *The New Statesman and Nation*. This was followed by a more popular version the following week in *The Daily Mail*.[18]

---

[17]Johnson and Johnson, op. cit., p. 19.

[18]See his "Proposals for a Revenue Tariff", reprinted in *Essays in Persuasion*, vol. 9 (1972) of *The Collected Writings of John Maynard Keynes*, op. cit., pp. 231–238; also see the

Prior to the 1930–31 period, Keynes had been an advocate (and sometimes an outspoken one) of free trade. Indeed, earlier in the 1920s, he had lambasted a proposal put forward by Conservatives to use protectionism to reduce unemployment. His reversal brought an outcry from Lionel Robbins and a number of others in the academic community.[19] Exchanges in the form of letters to the editor appeared in papers and weeklies in March and April. As summer approached, the economic situation deteriorated. Problems faced by an Austrian bank (the *Credit-Anstalt*) in May led to a gold drain from English banks by July. In August, the Labour government led by Ramsay MacDonald collapsed, and a "National Government" coalition with MacDonald at its head took over. The gold standard was finally abandoned on September 21, 1931. Since his dalliance with protectionism was tied to preserving the standard, once it had been given up, Keynes withdrew his support for the tariff.[20] The political damage had already been done, however. The first move of the National Government was to institute a general protective tariff.

The situation facing England in the summer of 1931 was a complicated one, and Keynes, like others, was desperately seeking a solution for it. While calls for protection from foreign competition can always be heard, they become particularly vociferous, as well as politically attractive, in times of high unemployment. At such times, economists are often the only group consistently willing to articulate the case for free trade, and, if their arguments are persuasive, this may keep politicians from giving in to protectionist pressures. When the most famous and articulate British economist supports first one policy, then another, the making of economic policy very quickly becomes subservient to political concerns, and principle yields to expediency. At least this was the way that Keynes's opponents saw it, and in this case it seems that they were right.

---

materials in *Activities 1929–1931: Rethinking Employment and Unemployment Policies*, ed. Donald Moggridge, vol. 20 (1981) of *The Collected Writings of John Maynard Keynes*, op. cit., pp. 488–515.

[19]Robbins wondered how the internationalist who had written *Economic Consequences of the Peace* could succumb to "the petty devices of economic nationalism". Quoted in Donald Winch, *Economics and Policy: A Historical Study* (New York: Walker, 1969), p. 150.

[20]It was doubtless his flip-flop on the tariff that led to the following version of the old joke about the propensity of economists to disagree: "Where five economists are gathered together there will be six conflicting opinions, and two of them will be held by Keynes." See Thomas Jones, *A Diary with Letters, 1931–50* (London: Oxford University Press, 1954), p. 19.

Hayek

Friedrich A. Hayek was born in Vienna on May 8, 1899, making him Keynes's junior by sixteen years. After serving in an artillery battery in the First World War, Hayek entered the University of Vienna, where he took courses in a variety of fields, including psychology, law, and economics. His first degree (in law) was awarded in November 1921. While working towards a second degree under Friedrich von Wieser (one of the 'second-generation' Austrian economists), Hayek took a job at a temporary government agency that had been set up to resolve private international debts incurred prior to the war. Ludwig von Mises was a director at the agency and soon became Hayek's mentor. Mises was a staunch anti-inflationist, and had made a name before the war as a monetary theorist with his book *Theorie des Geldes und der Umlaufsmittel.*[21] In the year following Hayek's appointment, Mises finished his next major work, *Die Gemeinwirtschaft: Untersuchungen über den Sozialismus.*[22] According to Hayek, this book "gradually but fundamentally altered the outlook of many of the young idealists returning to their university studies after World War I".[23] This group included, of course, Hayek himself.

Hayek's Trip to America

In the spring of 1922, the American economist Jeremiah Jenks passed through Vienna. He was planning to write a book on Central Europe and promised Hayek a job as a research assistant if he came to the United States the following year. In March 1923, immediately upon finishing his second degree, Hayek left for a fourteen-month stay in the United States. He worked briefly for Jenks, then enrolled on scholarship as a student at New York University. While there, he worked collecting business cycle data for Professor Willard Thorp. He did his research at the New York Public Library, often sharing a table with B. H. Beckhart, who was writing a book on the Federal Reserve System. In his spare time, Hayek 'gate-crashed' courses at Columbia, including Wesley Clair

---

[21]Ludwig von Mises, *Theorie des Geldes und der Umlaufsmittel* (Munich and Leipzig: Duncker & Humblot, 1912), 2nd edition translated by H. E. Batson as *The Theory of Money and Credit* (London: Cape, 1934; reprinted, Indianapolis, Ind.: Liberty*Classics*, 1981).

[22]Ludwig von Mises, *Die Gemeinwirtschaft: Untersuchungen über den Sozialismus* (Jena: Gustav Fischer, 1922), 2nd edition translated by J. Kahane as *Socialism: An Economic and Sociological Analysis* (London: Cape, 1936; reprinted, Indianapolis, Ind.: Liberty*Classics*, 1981).

[23]Hayek, Foreword to Mises translation, *ibid.*, p. xix.

Mitchell's class on the history of economic thought and J. B. Clark's final seminar, in which Hayek gave the last paper.

Hayek also did some travelling. Joseph Schumpeter had been an exchange professor at Harvard before the war and provided Hayek with letters of introduction to a number of famous economic theorists, among them Clark, E. R. A. Seligman, Henry Seager, Thomas Carver, Irving Fisher, and Jacob Hollander. But the young visitor quickly learned that the ideas of many of the grand old men who had formulated much of economic theory were considered passé in the 1920s.

> I must confess that from my predominantly theoretical interest the first impression of American economics was disappointing. I soon discovered that the great names that were household words to me were regarded as old-fashioned men by my American contemporaries, that work on their lines had moved no further than I knew already, and that the one name by which the eager young men swore was the only one I had not known until Schumpeter gave me a letter of introduction addressed to him, Wesley Clair Mitchell. Indeed business cycles and institutionalism were the two main topics of discussion.[24]

Hayek spent some of his stay in the United States learning about economic forecasting. It was a popular new topic at the time, with institutes like the Harvard Economic Service (which regularly published a set of 'economic barometers' on the state of the economy) springing up everywhere. (Most of these institutes died out after failing to foresee the coming Depression.) His education consisted of learning some simple statistical techniques for smoothing times series data. Though suspicious of the value of empirical work for the scientific study of complex phenomena, Hayek always acknowledged that such techniques had practical uses. They also helped him land a job. When he returned to Austria, Hayek worked a while longer at his previous post. When the agency finally closed, Mises tried to get Hayek a position at the Chamber of Commerce. Failing this, Mises was able to obtain private funding to set up a business cycle institute in January 1927 with Hayek at its head. More significant for his later research, while in the United States Hayek also learned a considerable amount about the workings of the new Federal Reserve System. As he was later to recall, "it was in the studies

---

[24]"The Economics of the 1920s as Seen from Vienna", which is the Prologue to *The Fortunes of Liberalism*, ed. Peter G. Klein, being vol. 4 of *The Collected Works of F. A. Hayek* (Chicago: University of Chicago Press and London: Routledge, 1992), pp. 35–36.

of my descriptive work on American monetary policy that I was led to develop my theories of monetary fluctuations".[25]

One can see the broad outlines of Hayek's reaction to his trip to America in one of his first published papers, "Die Währungspolitik der Vereinigten Staaten seit der Überwindung der Krise von 1920" ["The Monetary Policy of the United States after the Recovery from the 1920 Crisis"].[26] The Federal Reserve System had been established in 1913 in the hope that centralized cash reserves might help mitigate financial panics of the types that had plagued the American economy in previous decades. By the 1920s, certain American economists had more ambitious goals: not merely to counteract crises already under way, but "to prevent cyclical and crisis phenomena from evidencing themselves at all".[27] Hayek thought that this was too ambitious an aim. Though it might be possible to restrict the cycle to narrower bounds than before, achieving its total elimination required more knowledge than then existed or might ever exist. The dangers with holding such unrealistically high expectations seemed evident to Hayek, too. If the goals were not met, political intervention might occur. Then the credit system "would constitute a source of continuous disturbances of economic life, instead of exerting a stabilizing influence upon it".[28]

Hayek also offered a brief but telling reaction to institutionalism. He praised the institutionalists for clarifying the complex relationships among the data in a typical cycle, in particular for identifying rising consumer prices and an excess stock of capital goods as characteristics of the onset of the crisis stage. (For Hayek, these were the 'facts' that a theory of the cycle had to explain.) But he also faulted them for foreswearing an explicit theoretical framework, calling their work a type of "symptomatology" which is "of little help when what is at issue is not

---

[25]F. A. Hayek, Introduction to *Money, Capital, and Fluctuations: Early Essays*, ed. Roy McCloughry (Chicago: University of Chicago Press and London: Routledge, 1984), p. 2.

[26]"Die Währungspolitik der Vereinigten Staaten seit der Überwindung der Krise von 1920", *Zeitschrift für Volkswirtschaft und Sozialpolitik*, N. S. 5, in two parts, sections 1–3, 1925, pp. 25–63; sections 4–6, 1925, pp. 254–317. Section 6 has been translated and appears under the title, "The Monetary Policy of the United States after the Recovery from the 1920 Crisis", in McCloughry, ed., op. cit., pp. 5–32.

[27]*Ibid.*, p. 5. Those responsible for directing Federal Reserve policy were more conservative in their aims; the ones with greater ambitions for government control included institutionalists like John R. Commons.

[28]*Ibid.*, pp. 22–23. Given their experiences following the war, this latter point would have struck his German-language audiences as rather obvious.

detailed interconnections but the cause of cyclical fluctuations in general".[29]

In any event, the burning question of the day for the American economics profession was a characteristically pragmatic one: What actions if taken by the central monetary authority hold the best chance of eliminating the cycle? Though different schemes were offered, stabilization of the general price level emerged as the favoured policy. If the price level (as measured by a statistically constructed index number) rose beyond a certain point, the Federal Reserve would raise the discount rate (and possibly also sell bonds in the open market to reduce the amount of currency outstanding; such "open market operations" were then still controversial in the United States) in an effort to slow economic activity. If the price level fell, the opposite procedure would be followed.

It was this apparently commonsensical approach to the control of credit that Hayek found objectionable.

> The objection that appears to us to be much more serious is that the cyclical movement finds its initial expression not in the behaviour of the general price level but in that of the relative prices of the individual groups of commodities. Hence an index of the general price level cannot yield any relevant information as to the course of the cycle nor more importantly can it do so at the right time.[30]

Hayek argued that if American institutionalist economists had only had a better theoretical grasp on the causes of the cycle, they would not have been misled by their statistics into making wrong-headed policy recommendations. And indeed, behind Hayek's criticisms lies a particular theory of the business cycle, one that had its origins in the monetary

---

[29]*Ibid.*, pp. 6–7. Hayek's response to institutionalism was typical for someone who was trained in the Austrian tradition. For nearly forty years, the principal adversaries of the Austrians had been Schmoller and members of the Younger German Historical School, for whom data collection (albeit usually absent the sort of statistical analysis that the institutionalists advocated) was the method of the social sciences. Hayek's reaction was not altogether fair. Mitchell was no simplistic inductivist. Nor was institutionalism simply a transplanted historicism: It contained pragmatic and scientist elements as well. Though many Americans had fallen under the spell of the Historical economists when they studied overseas in the 1880s and 1890s, the lessons that they drew were varied.

[30]*Ibid.*, p. 17.

writings of the Swedish economist Knut Wicksell,[31] and which was further developed in the second (1924) edition of Mises's book on money.[32] Hayek would spend the next few years articulating his own version of this Mises-Wicksell theory of the cycle.

Hayek's Theory of the Business Cycle[33]

For Hayek, any adequate theory of the business cycle must be consistent with what he called "equilibrium theory". This theory states that in a free-market system, changes in underlying conditions of demand and supply bring about adjustments in relative prices, adjustments that continue until demand and supply in all markets are equalized. So long as relative prices are free to adjust, the price mechanism coordinates the actions of agents on both sides of any market.

One such market is the market for loanable funds, where the interests of savers and borrowers meet. In analyzing this market, Hayek used Wicksell's concept of a 'natural rate of interest', a rate that just equalizes savings and investment. The decision by households to save may also be viewed as a decision to forego present for future consumption. The funds saved are borrowed by firms for investment projects, that is, they are used for acquiring capital goods. The natural rate of interest coordinates the activities of these very different agents in a world in which production takes place through time. An example may help to make this clear.

Assume that there is an increase in a community's desire to save, that is, an increase in its preference for future over present goods. The natural rate of interest begins to fall, and firms discover that production processes that are more 'roundabout', that is, ones that take a longer

---

[31]Knut Wicksell, *Geldzins und Güterpreise: Eine Studie über die den Tauschwert des Geldes bestimmenden Ursachen* [1898], translated by R. F. Kahn as *Interest and Prices: A Study of the Causes Regulating the Value of Money* (London: Macmillan, 1936; reprinted, New York: Kelley, 1965); *Vorlesungen über Nationalökonomie* [1901, 1906], translated by E. Classen as *Lectures on Political Economy* (London: George Routledge & Sons, 1934, 1935; reprinted, Fairfield, N. J.: Kelley, 1977, 1978).

[32]Mises, *Theorie des Geldes und der Umlaufsmittel*, op. cit.

[33]The following summary synthesizes aspects of two of Hayek's early works on the cycle, *Geldtheorie und Konjunkturtheorie* (Vienna and Leipzig: Hölder-Pichler-Tempsky, 1929), translated by N. Kaldor and H. M. Croome as *Monetary Theory and the Trade Cycle* (London: Cape, 1933; reprinted, New York: Kelley, 1966), and *Prices and Production* (London: Routledge and Sons, 1931). Changes in this theory that may have taken place as a result of discussions with his critics in the 1930s are addressed in other volumes of *The Collected Works of F. A. Hayek*.

time to produce consumer goods, become profitable. A fundamental claim within the Austrian theory of capital (as developed by Eugen Böhm-Bawerk) is that more roundabout methods are also more productive ones. The movement to more roundabout methods allows firms to produce more goods in the future, thereby meeting the desires of consumers. The natural rate of interest, then, is itself a relative price. Its changes serve to coordinate a community's preferences concerning present and future consumption with the production processes that create the goods.

The theory also focuses on what is termed 'the structure of production'. 'Investment' does not simply mean the addition of more machines. Rather, the movement to more roundabout methods of production involves a change in the relative prices of a whole range of producer's goods, and these price changes bring about a change in the structure of the capital stock. In Austrian terminology, 'goods of a higher order', that is, capital goods that are further away (in time) from the production of first-order consumption goods, are added; the structure of production is lengthened. This change in the structure of capital would play a crucial role in the Austrian theory of the cycle.[34]

The price mechanism, then, coordinates economic activity. In a trade cycle, economic activity somehow becomes uncoordinated. In particular, in the crisis stage of the cycle an overproduction of capital goods exists. As such, any adequate theory of the cycle must explain how this situation of disequilibrium in this specific market arises. What keeps the interest rate from performing its coordinative function?

Once again Wicksell's framework proved helpful. Wicksell posited another interest rate, the 'market rate of interest'. The market rate is influenced by banks' lending activities and can differ from the natural rate: Specifically, it will fall below the natural rate whenever banks increase the amount of credit. Wicksell used the natural rate/market rate distinction to discuss movements in the general price level. The Austrian contribution was to posit the deviation of the market rate from the natural rate as the cause of the trade cycle.[35]

---

[34]In his original formulation, Hayek used Böhm-Bawerk's notion of an 'average period of production'. He replaced this with the 'structure of production' in *The Pure Theory of Capital* (London: Routledge and Kegan Paul, 1941; reprinted, Chicago: University of Chicago Press, 1975).

[35]Mises and Hayek provided different accounts of the origins of the cycle. Mises blamed the cycle on the actions of bankers, especially central bankers eager to finance government activities by printing money. For Hayek, the cycle was a virtually un- avoidable consequence of a credit economy. The expansion of credit could be due to a spontaneous action by bankers. But it also could be induced by an increase in the demand for loanable

A typical cycle unfolds as follows. Banks expand credit, lowering the market rate of interest to induce firms to borrow. Firms use their newly created purchasing power to begin lengthening the process of production, just as if there had been a fall in the natural rate. In a world in which all resources are fully utilized, this bids resources away from consumers. However, unlike the example in which the natural rate had fallen, consumers have not *voluntarily* reduced their real desired consumption. They are *forced* to consume less than they desire; Hayek accordingly attached the term 'forced savings' to this phenomenon. The partially unmet demand for current consumption goods begins to push up the prices of such goods relative to future goods, or, put another way, the market rate of interest begins to rise. This signals firms that their previous decisions to undertake more roundabout investment projects had been incorrect, that the demand for future goods had not truly risen. The more roundabout projects are no longer profitable and must be abandoned before they come to fruition. This initiates the crisis, or slump, phase of the cycle.

The only way to avoid the cycle is to 'neutralize' the effects of credit creation by keeping the market rate equal to the natural rate. Hayek put it succinctly: "Not a money which is *stable* in value but a *neutral* money must therefore form the starting point for the theoretical analysis of monetary influences on production...".[36] Alas, as a practical matter, keeping money neutral is easier said than done: No one knows what the natural rate is; only the market rate is observable.

Hayek was not optimistic about the prospects for effective counter-cyclical policy. The policy recommendation being considered most widely at the time (to watch the general price level, and to change the growth rate of the money supply in the opposite direction whenever the price level showed movement) would almost certainly exacerbate the cycle. Hayek believed that if the monetary authorities tried to keep the price level stable in an expanding economy (he associated falling prices with expansion), they would end up injecting too much credit, setting off a boom. Nor would other methods, like monitoring the amount of credit in the system (for example, by setting limits on bank reserves), be effective, since variability in the demand for credit would undermine any control that the monetary authorities might possess. Finally, Hayek's

---

funds by firms (that is, an increase in the velocity of circulation) caused by increased business optimism, or the discovery of some new product or process, or a change in the structure of production, or a change in the form of credit: any of these could render money 'non-neutral'. See Hayek, *Monetary Theory and the Trade Cycle*, op. cit., chapter 4; *Prices and Production*, op. cit., Lecture 4.

[36]Hayek, *Prices and Production*, op. cit., pp. 27–28.

theory implied that just prior to the onset of the crisis, consumer prices would begin to rise. If this rise were reflected in a rising aggregate price level, the monetary authorities might be induced to put on the brakes just as the economy was sliding into a recession, thereby making the cycle worse.

Once the crisis had started, Hayek felt that the best policy was simply to allow it to play itself out. Attempts to stimulate the economy through further injections of money would only keep the market rate artificially lowered that much longer, further distorting the structure of production, prolonging and deepening the crisis. Attempts to stimulate consumer demand would likewise be adding fuel to the fire, since excessive consumption demand was a characteristic of this stage of the cycle. Indeed, the slump stage of the cycle was the painful medicine by which equilibrium in the system was ultimately restored. As Ludwig Lachmann was later to observe, Hayek's early vision of how the cycle played out was preeminently a general equilibrium one:

> For Hayek Paretian general equilibrium was the pivot of economic theory, the centre of gravity towards which all major forces tended. For him the task of trade cycle theory was to show how it came about that these major forces were temporarily impeded and their effects delayed, and since the cycle was supposed to start with a boom and end with a depression, he saw in the depression the ultimate triumph of the equilibrating forces.[37]

Hayek spent the late 1920s working out the details of the theory, with the hope that his efforts might help to secure him a university professorship. To qualify for his *Habilitation*, he first had to write a book; *Geldtheorie und Konjunkturtheorie* was the result.[38] Hayek next underwent the *Habilitation* defense, a public presentation in which members of the faculty cross-examine the candidate on a work of his choice. The paper Hayek chose for this occasion was "Gibt es einen 'Widersinn des

---

[37]Ludwig Lachmann, "Austrian Economics under Fire: The Hayek-Sraffa Duel in Retrospect", in *Austrian Economics: History and Philosophical Background*, Wolfgang Grassl and Barry Smith, eds (London: Croom Helm, 1986), p. 227. See pp. 225–242 for additional discussion. It was not until the mid-1930s that Hayek began his retreat from the general equilibrium framework, a move that culminated in his developing a 'market process' view of the workings of the price system. For more on this see Bruce Caldwell, "Hayek's Transformation", *History of Political Economy*, vol. 20, Winter 1988, pp. 513–541.

[38]Translated as *Monetary Theory and the Trade Cycle*, op. cit.

Sparens'?", a translation of which is reprinted as chapter 2 in this volume. His presentation was well received, and Hayek became a *Privatdozent* in 1929.[39] For the next two years, in addition to his work at the business cycle institute (where he was joined by Oskar Morgenstern, who became his successor), Hayek taught classes at the University of Vienna. As he mentions in "The Economics of the 1930s as Seen from London", reprinted as chapter 1 of this volume, in his spare time Hayek produced a number of chapters on the monetary history of England for a massive text on money that he was writing. The book was never published; the editors abandoned it after the Nazis came to power.

The 'Paradox' of Saving

"The 'Paradox' of Saving" is a direct result of Hayek's American experiences. His recounting of the inventive promotional efforts of the now-forgotten Messrs Foster and Catchings makes for fascinating and entertaining reading. These two authors of numerous popular tracts were underconsumptionists: For them, the cause of the business cycle was excessive saving. The surfeit of savings flows into investment, which allows firms to increase their production of consumption goods. Alas, firms become too productive, so that the purchasing power in the hands of consumers is insufficient to buy up all of the new goods that have been produced. A glut of consumption goods appears on the market, and this constitutes the crisis stage of the cycle. Foster and Catchings's policy advice was straightforward: It is the obligation of the government to even out fluctuations in the demand for consumer goods. This requires that the government run deficits, which they recommended be financed by an expansion of the money supply, during times of crisis.

It is evident why Hayek would find such a theory and the attendant policy recommendations unsatisfactory. As he points out early in the article, underconsumptionist theories of the business cycle, though rejected by the majority of economists since the early 1800s, nonetheless have a way of periodically reemerging, especially in popular tracts by

---

[39]A *Privatdozent* merely had the right to teach at the university. To become a professor, one of the chairs (of which there were only three in economics at this time at the University of Vienna) had to be vacated, and one had to be chosen to fill it. For more on the intricacies and political intrigues of Austrian academic life, see F. A. Hayek, *Hayek on Hayek*, Stephen Kresge and Leif Wenar, eds (Chicago: University of Chicago Press and London: Routledge, 1994), pp. 51–56, p. 60; also Earlene Craver, "The Emigration of the Austrian Economists", *History of Political Economy*, vol. 18, Spring 1986, pp. 1–32.

non-economists. From a specifically Austrian perspective, Foster and Catchings's theoretical framework failed to grasp the role of interest rates in coordinating intertemporal consumption decisions.

Hayek felt confident that he had effectively countered Foster and Catchings's arguments. What he found more worrisome was the response of the rest of the economics profession to the policy conclusions that the Americans had proffered. Hayek was clearly exasperated by the outcome of the Prize Essay contest that the pair had set up, in which $5000 was awarded to the best criticism of their theory. Virtually none of the critics had challenged the proposition that an increase in the money supply proportional to the enlarged volume of production was an appropriate response to a slump. His own theory implied, of course, that an increase in the money supply once the slump had begun would only prolong and deepen the crisis.

Lionel Robbins and the LSE

Lionel Robbins was the newly appointed head of the Economics Department at the London School of Economics (LSE) as well as the youngest Professor of Economics in England. The LSE had been established in the 1890s by Fabian Socialists. Founders Sidney and Beatrice Webb were so convinced that the (socialist) truth would win out that they insisted that ideology should play no role in appointments at the School. An important motive in the founding of the LSE was to provide a counterweight to the theoretical approach being advanced by men like Alfred Marshall at Cambridge. It would be broadly correct to say that at the beginning of the century the historical approach was identified with London and the theoretical with Cambridge. By the 1920s, however, Marshallian economics and methods had emerged nearly uniformly victorious throughout Britain. A sensitivity to the importance of history (though not, as Hayek is quick to remind us in his portrait of Edwin Cannan that is an addendum to chapter 1 in this volume, an advocacy of the methods of historicism) remained strong at the LSE, embodied as it was in the persons of Cannan and Herbert Foxwell. In addition, the Director of the School, William Beveridge, felt an unremitting antipathy towards theory.

Lionel Robbins was intent on changing this. He wanted to establish the LSE as a center for theory. He did not want the institution to become a Cambridge on the Thames, however. Robbins deplored the insularity of English economics. At Oxford and Cambridge, this narrowness had its origins in the complacent belief that all one needed to know about economics could be found in Marshall's writings. To the extent that it existed in London, it followed (as Hayek tells us) from the preferences of Edwin Cannan. But Marshall had died in 1924, and Cannan had retired in 1926. From Robbins's perspective, the time was surely ripe for instituting at the LSE an approach to economics that was at once more theoretical and more cosmopolitan.

Robbins had yet another battle on his hands, this one with that most formidable of opponents, John Maynard Keynes. Keynes had invited Robbins in the late summer of 1930 to sit on a committee of the newly instituted Economic Advisory Council. The EAC was a large body; the smaller 'Committee of Economists' formed at Keynes's instigation was a select group, with Arthur Pigou, Josiah Stamp, and Hubert Henderson comprising the other members. The committee was to meet in private, and its final report was to be secret. Its brief was to come up with policies to combat the Depression, and Keynes hoped to use the committee to promote his own views. It was soon evident that Robbins disagreed with the rest of the committee both in his diagnosis of the origins of the downturn and in his recommendations for policy. He tried, unsuccessfully, to get the committee to hear evidence from others (Hayek among them) whose views were more in accord with his. After considerable effort, the committee was able to reach some common ground in its final report. But Robbins refused to go along with a proposed tariff on imports and requested permission to write a minority report on the issue. Keynes, furious, at first refused, claiming that a rule prohibited minorities of one from filing separate reports. When it was clear that Robbins would not be budged, and that Keynes's rule was, as Robbins later put it, "pure mythology", the elder economist finally relented. Keynes, however, reserved the last word to himself and read aloud to the committee his letter to the ministers 'explaining' the true reason for Robbins's dissent: "Robbins has a scruple of conscience about which he has worked himself up to a high degree of emotional feeling."[40]

The youthful Lionel Robbins was battling on a number of fronts and he was looking for allies. To counter the emphasis on history at the LSE, he sought first and foremost a qualified theorist. But he also wanted an economist who was conversant with other traditions, so that the LSE could become a leader in the internationalization of British

---

[40]Keynes's quote can be found in *Activities 1929–1931: Rethinking Employment and Unemployment Policies*, op. cit., p. 464. Robbins's typically mild account of the event is contained in his *Autobiography of an Economist* (London: Macmillan, 1971), pp. 150–156; cf. Susan Howson and Donald Winch, *The Economic Advisory Council 1930–1939: A Study in Economic Advice during Depression and Recovery* (Cambridge: Cambridge University Press, 1977), pp. 46–72.

economics. He finally needed someone who might serve as a counter-weight to J. M. Keynes. Friedrich Hayek certainly seemed to fit the bill. Though he could not get permission for Hayek to appear before the Committee of Economists, he was able as department head to invite him to give a series of lectures at the LSE. And that is exactly what Robbins did.

Hayek arrived in London in February 1931. His lectures, which would later appear in published form as *Prices and Production*, had been hurriedly prepared. His English was little less than awful. (He was later told that he was all but incomprehensible whenever he was reading, but became intelligible wher he paused to answer a question.) Despite all that, the lectures caused a huge stir; Hayek was offered first a one-year visiting professorship, and in the next year the Tooke Chair of Economic Science and Statistics.[41] During the same period he began preparing an assessment of Keynes's latest foray into economic theory, *A Treatise on Money*, the book that had provided the theoretical underpinnings for Keynes's policy proposals. As has long been the way among academic economists, the many differences between Hayek and Keynes would be fought out in that most indirect and rarefied of conflicts, a clash of theoretical models.

The Battle Is Joined

A Treatise on Money

Soon after completing the *Tract on Monetary Reform*, and probably beginning in July, 1924, Keynes began outlining what ultimately was to be his *A Treatise on Money*.[42] He worked on his 'egg' through the 1920s, receiving much feedback on early drafts of chapters from his old friend Dennis Robertson. The manuscript was finally finished in July, 1929, but a lengthy process of revision resulted in such extensive changes that the final version was split into two volumes and not released until October 31, 1930. One can see from his preface that Keynes was not particularly satisfied with the final result.

---

[41]Hayek's account of his trip to London may be found in *Hayek on Hayek*, op. cit., pp. 75–78.

[42]J. M. Keynes, *A Treatise on Money*, 2 vols [1930], reprinted as vols 5 and 6 (1971) of *The Collected Writings of John Maynard Keynes*, op. cit.

As I read through the page proofs of this book I am acutely conscious of its defects. It has occupied me for many years...during which my ideas have been developing and changing.... The ideas with which I have finished up are widely different from those with which I began. The result is, I am afraid, that there is a good deal in this book which represents the process of getting rid of the ideas which I used to have and of finding my way to those which I now have.[43]

The new ideas that Keynes was "finding his way" towards were, in the main, his views on policy. The problem with the *Treatise* was that Keynes's theoretical framework had not caught up with them.[44]

Keynes hoped that the *Treatise* would be the work to bring him recognition as an economic theorist equal to that he already enjoyed as an essayist, gadfly to policymakers, shaper of opinion, and prominent public figure. He also hoped to construct a theoretical edifice that reflected his policy views. Unfortunately the latter had evolved so quickly in the 1920s that he could not keep the two in tandem. Still, he was not altogether unsuccessful. Using the well-known "Fundamental Equations", Keynes argued that a failure of adjustment between savings and investment was the principal cause of problems for modern monetary economies. This at least had certain affinities with his policy view that Britain's problems in the 1920s resulted in insufficient domestic investment spending.

But Keynes was still partly stuck in a Marshallian world. His analysis implicitly assumed that total output was given, so that all adjustments would come through prices. This, of course, made it rather difficult to discuss the problem of unemployment that so vexed him. When the "Slump of 1930" was analyzed, he saw it as a special case in which high interest rates brought on by the return to gold and by problems associated with the payment of reparations generated the downturn.[45] Just as hard cases make for bad law, special cases do not make for good

---

[43]*Ibid.*, p. xvii.

[44]This was not a new problem for Keynes (though it was, perhaps, the first time that he had come to recognize that it was a problem). Along with brilliant discussions of the distributional effects of changes in the value of money, of forward markets for foreign exchange, and of alternative aims of policy, his earlier *Tract* had contained a straightforwardly Marshallian section on monetary theory, one that bore little resemblance to the subtle and complex reasoning that Keynes displayed elsewhere in the volume.

[45]The discussion occurs in a short section entitled "The Slump of 1930", *A Treatise on Money*, op. cit., vol. 6, pp. 338–347. As noted by Robert Dimand in *The Origins of the Keynesian Revolution: The Development of Keynes's Theory of Employment and Output* (Aldershot: Edward Elgar, 1988), pp. 30–35, Keynes discussed downwardly rigid nominal wages at two places in the *Treatise*, but he never linked this up to a theory of unemployment.

theory. It was not until *The General Theory* that output and employment effects, rather than price effects, became central concerns in Keynes's theoretical work. As he was to put it in the Preface, it was then that his long "struggle of escape from habitual modes of thought and expression" was finally complete.[46] Helping him to make his escape was a group of young economists at Cambridge who were known collectively as 'the Circus'.

The Cambridge Circus

A few weeks after the *Treatise* was published, a group of young academics began meeting in the rooms of Richard Kahn to discuss and criticize it. Members included Piero Sraffa, aged 32, whom Keynes had helped bring to Cambridge from Italy (Sraffa had translated the *Tract* into Italian) and whose 1926 article criticizing Marshall's theory of the firm sparked considerable debate among English economists in the late 1920s;[47] Joan Robinson, aged 27, who two years later would publish *The Economics of Imperfect Competition*;[48] her husband, Austin, aged 33, who became Keynes's assistant editor at the *Economic Journal* in 1934 and later acted as managing editor for Keynes's *Collected Writings*; and James Meade, aged 23, a visitor from Oxford whose distinguished career in international economics would earn him the Nobel Prize in 1977. The Circus met through May of 1931, gradually becoming more formal (meeting in a seminar room) and expanding to include a few of the best undergraduate students (by invitation, and only after surviving an interview by the screening committee of Austin Robinson, Kahn, and Sraffa). Keynes never attended the meetings. Instead, Kahn would report the results of the discussions to him, then return to the group with his replies. Though accounts differ as to the exact role the Circus played in the evolution of *The General Theory*, it is clear that its members were of great assistance in challenging Keynes to rethink his ideas, and in particular in getting him to see that the framework of the *Treatise* assumed a given level of output.[49] Later, some of their number

[46]J. M. Keynes, *The General Theory of Employment, Interest, and Money* [1936], reprinted as vol. 7 (1973) of *The Collected Writings of John Maynard Keynes*, op. cit., p. xxiii.

[47]Piero Sraffa, "The Law of Returns under Competitive Conditions", *Economic Journal*, vol. 36, December 1926, pp. 535–550.

[48]Joan Robinson, *The Economics of Imperfect Competition* (London: Macmillan, 1933; 2nd edition, London: Macmillan, 1969).

[49]There are no records of what went on in the meetings of the Circus. The account in Donald Moggridge, "The Cambridge Circus, 1930–1", in *The General Theory and After: Part I, Preparation*, ed. Donald Moggridge, vol. 13 (1973) of *The Collected Writings*, op. cit., pp.

would be instrumental in helping to demolish Keynes's critics and in spreading the Keynesian gospel in Britain. But we get ahead of our story.

Hayek gave his lectures on "Prices and Production" at the LSE in February of 1931. While he was in England, he agreed to give a talk to the economists at Cambridge. Keynes was not present, but members of the Circus were, including Joan Robinson. In her Richard T. Ely Lecture to the American Economics Association in 1971, entitled "The Second Crisis of Economic Theory", she described the session in this way:

> While the controversy about public works was developing, Professor Robbins sent to Vienna for a member of the Austrian school to provide a counter-attraction to Keynes. I very well remember Hayek's visit to Cambridge on his way to the London School. He expounded his theory and covered the blackboard with his triangles. The whole argument, as we could see later, consisted in confusing the current rate of investment with the total stock of capital goods, but we could not make it out at the time. The general tendency seemed to be to show that the slump was caused by inflation. R. F. Kahn, who was at that time involved in explaining that the multiplier guaranteed that savings equals investment, asked in a puzzled tone, "Is it your view that if I went out tomorrow and bought a new overcoat, that would increase unemployment?" "Yes", said Hayek. "But", pointing to his triangles on the board, "it would take a very long mathematical argument to explain why".
>
> This pitiful state of confusion was the first crisis of economic theory that I referred to.[50]

It is hard to imagine that Hayek was unable to explain the link between rising consumer prices and the slump, a link that was central

---

337–343, was based on an interview in 1971 of the five principals. Some question a lionizing of the Circus: For example, Don Patinkin, in "Keynes's Monetary Thought: A Study of Its Development", *History of Political Economy*, vol. 8, Spring 1976, p. 60, doubts James Meade's "cautiously confident" claim that when he returned to Oxford in the fall of 1931 he took back with him all of the essential ingredients of *The General Theory*.

[50]Joan Robinson, "The Second Crisis of Economic Theory", in *Contributions to Modern Economics* (New York: Academic Press, 1978), pp. 2–3. "His triangles" refers to the diagrams Hayek used to represent lengthening of the structure of production. Kahn is more generous in his reminiscences: "It is only fair to Hayek to mention that he had to condense the four lectures into one, and that they were written when he had a high temperature". See Richard F. Kahn, *The Making of Keynes's General Theory* (Cambridge: Cambridge University Press, 1984), p. 182.

to his theory.[51] Perhaps the illness that Kahn alludes to in his recollection of the day was to blame, or perhaps his command of English was still shaky and he didn't quite understand the question. He might even have sensed hostility coming from some of the audience, which might have affected his ability to think on his feet. But no matter what caused Hayek to respond in the way that Robinson reports, her mean-spirited comments, delivered nearly forty years after the event and at a time when the Keynesian paradigm was still dominant (though not, to be sure, Robinson's version of it—her label for a follower of the standard model was "bastard Keynesian"), bear the stamp of the nastiness that Hayek was to encounter in certain quarters of the English academic community.

Hayek's Review of the *Treatise*

The reader who has not made an extensive comparative study of Keynes's *A Treatise on Money* and Hayek's *Prices and Production* (and perhaps even some who have) may find that certain of the arguments in the exchange between them (reprinted as chapters 3 to 6 of this volume) are somewhat obscure. There are moments of tedium, as well, as each spends pages quibbling over the definitions of terms. If one gets beyond the definitional quagmire, however, it turns out that their models share many similarities. The essential theoretical difference between them is that Hayek integrates capital theory into his model, and Keynes does not.

Two features of Keynes's "Fundamental Equations" deserve emphasis. First, the natural rate of interest is that rate at which savings and investment are equal. This is the same in Hayek, though their definitions of savings and investment differ; hence the disputes over terminology. Second, 'windfall' entrepreneurial profits (losses) exist by definition whenever investment exceeds (is less than) savings. Thus for Keynes, in equilibrium, savings equals investment and windfall profits (in the aggregate) are zero. If the market rate of interest drops below the natural rate, spending by firms on new investment projects increases, investment spending exceeds savings, and windfall profits appear. Keynes

---

[51]A brief response to Kahn might have been: Your individual actions do not, of course, matter. However, if the government provides consumers with credit to expand their demand for raincoats and other consumer goods, firms will try to shorten the structure of production that much more quickly, causing unemployment in the capital goods industries to rise further. In addition, if consumption demand reaches an unsustainably high level, the structure of production will be shortened too much, ensuring additional readjustment problems in the future.

called this "profit inflation". Next, firms typically[52] begin to compete with each other to expand production. Because all resources are fully employed, this simply causes factor prices (wages) to be bid up, a phenomenon Keynes dubbed "income inflation". The final result is one that any Cambridge quantity theorist would predict: An increase in the money supply ultimately increases the price level proportionately. In this sense, the barebones model of the *Treatise* is simply Marshall with a Wicksellian twist, a twist that allowed Keynes to focus on the role of the interest rate in an economy with a developed banking system. We will see, however, that (just as in the *Tract*) Keynes's discussions in the *Treatise* of real-world complications often went far beyond his bare-bones model.

As the early part of his review makes clear, Hayek did not accept the set of definitions contained in Keynes's Fundamental Equations. But he did agree that a lowering of the market rate of interest below the natural rate causes entrepreneurs to increase investment spending, resulting in investment exceeding savings. It is at this crucial juncture, though, that their stories diverge. In contrast to Keynes's loose description of profit and income inflation, Hayek's model includes a detailed account of a specific sequence of changes in the prices of capital goods and consumption goods, a sequence that follows from the Austrian theory of capital. In addition, the capital theory that Hayek used and that was so noticeably absent in Keynes's was one that was familiar to Wicksell, whose first book had been an attempt to integrate the Austrian theory of capital and marginal productivity theory within a general equilibrium framework. Only after that was completed had he turned, in his second book, to a discussion of money.[53] From Hayek's perspective, Keynes had simply lifted the interest rate story out of its original context. Finally, by reintroducing the capital-theoretic structure, Hayek was able to construct a full-blown theory of the trade cycle. Keynes's *Treatise* was less successful in that it followed the more traditional

---

[52]Though not necessarily: If entrepreneurs choose to consume out of their profits, the "widow's cruse" phenomenon occurs. See Keynes, *A Treatise on Money*, vol. 5, op. cit., p. 125.

[53]Knut Wicksell, *Über Wert, Kapital und Rente*, translated by S. H. Frowein as *Value, Capital and Rent* [1893] (London: Allen & Unwin, 1954; reprinted, New York: Kelley, 1970); and *Interest and Prices*, op. cit. As Hayek put it (this volume, chapter 3, p. 130), "Mr. Keynes ignores completely the general theoretical basis of Wicksell's theory". Gunnar Myrdal offered a less generous critique, calling the *Treatise* an example of "the attractive Anglo-Saxon kind of unnecessary originality, which has its roots in certain systematic gaps in the knowledge of the German language on the part of the majority of English economists". Quoted in Patinkin, "Keynes's Monetary Thought: A Study of Its Development", op. cit., p. 49.

approach of explaining changes in the price level without systematically addressing the question of how output changes over the course of the cycle.

Hayek's attack on Foster and Catchings had also been from the perspective of the Wicksell-Mises theory of the cycle. But because his framework there was so different from that used by his opponents, readers unfamiliar with the Austrian approach would have had a difficult time following Hayek's argument. In contrast, Keynes had borrowed explicitly from Wicksell and, from an Austrian point of view, the borrowing was gratuitous. Hayek's job as critic was vastly simplified by Keynes. He might as well have painted a bull's eye on the cover of the *Treatise*.

Keynes Responds to Hayek

As one of his biographers attests, Keynes was not pleased with the review:

> Keynes was obviously very unhappy with the August part of the review, for his copy of that issue of *Economica* is among the most heavily annotated of the surviving copies of his journals, with no less than 34 pencilled marks or comments on the 26-page review. At the end of the review, Keynes summed up his reaction by writing: "Hayek has not read my book with that measure of 'good will' which an author is entitled to expect of a reader. Until he can do so, he will not see what I mean or know whether I am right. He evidently has a passion which leads him to pick on me, but I am left wondering what this passion is".[54]

Keynes's irritation is evident in his reply, published in November 1931 and reprinted as chapter 4 in this volume. That Keynes insisted on answering his critic before the second half of Hayek's review was even published suggests his anger, as does his strategy of using a reply to attack Hayek's own *Prices and Production*. And what an attack it was! Keynes characterized *Prices and Production* as follows:

> The book, as it stands, seems to me to be one of the most frightful muddles I have ever read, with scarcely a sound proposition in it

[54] *The General Theory and After: Part I, Preparation*, op. cit., p. 243. If one compares Keynes's reaction to Hayek's review with his response to Robbins's dissent from his policy prescription (this volume, p. 20), it would seem that Keynes was prone to interpret disagreement with his views as evidence of an overwrought state of mind.

beginning with page 45, and yet it remains a book of some interest, which is likely to leave its mark on the mind of the reader. It is an extraordinary example of how, starting with a mistake, a remorseless logician can end up in bedlam. Yet Dr. Hayek has seen a vision, and though when he woke up he has made nonsense of his story by giving the wrong names to the objects which occur in it, his Khubla Kahn is not without inspiration and must set the reader thinking with the germs of an idea in his head (this volume, p. 154).

This is wonderful phrase-turning, Keynes at his witty bitchy best. But for the preeminent English economist and editor of the prestigious *Economic Journal* to reply in such a manner to a junior scholar's lengthy critical review is, it must be said, pretty shabby. The reaction of Pigou is perhaps an appropriate rebuke:

> Are we, in our secret hearts, wholly satisfied with the manner, or manners, in which some of our controversies are carried on? A year or two ago, after the publication of an important book, there appeared an elaborate and careful critique of a number of particular passages in it. The author's answer was, not to rebut the criticisms, but to attack with violence another book, which the critic had himself written several years before! Body-line bowling! The method of the duello! That kind of thing is surely a mistake.[55]

Pigou was a bit shaky on his chronology, but his sentiments are clear enough. Whether one agreed with him or not, one thing was certain: A battle had begun.

If one pushes past the pyrotechnics and the definitional disputes, it seems that Keynes's substantive points were two. First, he conceded Hayek's claim that the *Treatise* lacked a capital-theoretic foundation. Since a number of Hayek's criticisms dealt with this deficiency, this appears at first to be a huge concession. Keynes softened the impact of his admission by adding that no complete theory of capital was yet available (Hayek would have agreed here). Keynes also appears to think that about all capital theory is good for is to explain the level of the natural rate of interest. This indicates that he had not grasped the crucial role given to capital in the Austrian theory of the cycle.

---

[55]A. C. Pigou, *Economics in Practice* (London: Macmillan, 1935), pp. 23–24. Jacob Viner thought that Keynes's treatment of Hayek was "very unmannerly", but that one should not have been surprised by it. Letter to Hayek, February 20, 1932, in the Jacob Viner papers in the Princeton University Library.

But little of that mattered. For Keynes's second claim was that Hayek had misunderstood in a fundamental way the thrust of the *Treatise*, and that many of Hayek's criticisms were therefore misdirected. What Hayek had missed, according to Keynes, was the claim that savings and investment could "get out of gear" within the framework of the *Treatise* for any of a number of reasons that were independent of changes in the amount of credit in the system. Keynes suggested that Hayek's misreading was due to his being trapped within an old framework, one in which only changes in credit could cause savings to differ from investment. Exposing Hayek's flawed framework was then Keynes's excuse for reviewing *Prices and Production*. How justified were Keynes's complaints?

Here, I think, the two principals mostly missed one another. Keynes was quite right to assert that the *Treatise* contains numerous discussions of why, in the real world, the bare-bones model might fail to function in the manner outlined above. He had argued in the book, for example, that savers and entrepreneurs are different people with different motivations, so that savings and investment can get out of gear on their own; that expectations play an important role, especially in financial markets; that indeed the old quantity theory relation between the money supply and the price level would hold only in theoretical equilibrium.[56]

But Keynes's claims notwithstanding, many sources of disturbance were possible within Hayek's model, too. One reason that Keynes may have missed this point is that he focused on *Prices and Production*, where the origins of the cycle take a back seat to the changes in the structure of production that constitute the cycle. In the fourth chapter of his earlier (and at that time available only in German) *Geldtheorie und Konjunkturtheorie*, Hayek described things other than the actions of banks that could cause, in Keynes's later terminology, the "marginal efficiency of capital" curve to shift.[57] But Keynes was right to say that for Hayek, the effects

---

[56]These discussions are scattered throughout the *Treatise*, op. cit.; see especially chapters 10–12.

[57]Hayek, *Geldtheorie und Konjunkturtheorie*, translated as *Monetary Theory and the Trade Cycle*, op. cit., pp. 142–152, 167–170. Hayek had sent Keynes a copy of the German version of *Monetary Theory* back in 1929, and Keynes's postcard acknowledging receipt may explain why he misunderstood Hayek: "Many thanks for sending me a copy of your book. I have been particularly interested in the last chapter. But I find your German dreadfully hard to make out!..." Postcard, Keynes to Hayek, March 26, 1929, in the Hayek collection, The Hoover Institution Archives, Stanford, Calif. Allin Cottrell points out the similarity of Hayek's discussion to Keynes's on the "marginal efficiency of capital" in his paper, "Hayek's Early Cycle Theory Re-examined", *Cambridge Journal of Economics*, vol. 18, April 1994, p. 199.

of the shift will necessarily be *transmitted* through the credit system: It cannot be otherwise in a monetary economy.

For his part, Hayek seems to have had the better part of the argument in showing that, though Keynes had asserted that savings and investment could get out of gear, he had not demonstrated how this could occur within the model described in the *Treatise*. This was the major thrust of the second part of Hayek's review, published in February 1932 and reprinted as chapter 6 of this volume.

Soon after the November exchange, Hayek and Keynes began a correspondence on the merits of their two frameworks.[58] Keynes's last letter in this exchange was dated March 29, after the second half of Hayek's review of the *Treatise*, as well as Sraffa's review of *Prices and Production*, had appeared. Keynes wrote in part:

> Having been much occupied in other directions, I have not yet studied your *Economica* article as closely as I shall. But, unless it be on one or two points which can perhaps be dealt with in isolation from the main issue, I doubt if I shall return to the charge in *Economica*. I am trying to re-shape and improve my central position, and that is probably a better way to spend one's time than in controversy.[59]

Keynes never did return to the charge, so Hayek probably felt that he had won the day. This letter is the source, too, for Hayek's later comment that since Keynes had "changed his mind" about the *Treatise*, and would probably do the same in regard to the arguments of *The General Theory*, there was little incentive to write a review of the latter book. Keynes had *not* changed his mind, of course, about the fact that intervention was necessary if capitalism was to survive. But it seems evident that by early 1932 he had given up the hope that his views could be expressed within the framework of the *Treatise*, and he was prepared to begin the hard work of constructing another one.

A final point about the battle. Hayek is sometimes interpreted as suggesting that 'neutral money' should somehow be used as a guide to policy, that the monetary authorities should try to keep the supply of money, in Keynes's phrase, "absolutely and forever unaltered".[60] But Hayek's point was actually a much more pessimistic one. The monetary authority is unable to control the supply of credit with sufficient

---

[58]The correspondence from this period is reprinted as an Appendix to chapter 5, this volume.

[59]See Appendix to chapter 5, this volume, letter no. 13, Keynes to Hayek, March 29, 1932.

[60]See chapter 4, this volume, p. 153.

precision to set the market rate equal to the natural rate, and even if it were, the natural rate is not itself an operational construct: It is in fact unknowable. Hayek's fundamental point is that the business cycle is an unfortunate but unavoidable concomitant of a credit economy. He hoped that the severity of its swings could be lessened somewhat, mostly through a better understanding of the phases of a typical cycle rather than through the use of policy. Attempts to eliminate it, and particularly those that he had seen discussed in the United States and England, were likely to only intensify its effects. As he later would put it, with characteristic modesty:

> [W]hat I had done had often seemed to me more to point out barriers to further advance on the path chosen by others than to supply new ideas which opened the path to further development.[61]

In early 1932, Hayek appeared to be the victor in the theoretical battle. His model, though unfamiliar to his English audience, at least seemed the more coherent. But was it the right model, did it really constitute a general theory of the cycle? If it did not, were Hayek's pessimistic policy views then mistaken, and Keynes, whose model was insufficiently worked out, really right after all? These were the questions that taxed economists in London and Cambridge in the spring of 1932. Disagreement over the matter would not last for long.

A Short Campaign

Explaining the Keynesian Ascendancy

Mark Blaug has suggested that "it is the amazing rapidity of the Keynesian ascendancy that poses the problem for any convincing account of the Keynesian revolution".[62] Blaug provides a multiplicity of reasons for why so many members of the economics profession so easily and quickly converted to the Keynesian creed. In reviewing the most important of these, it will be useful to compare the reasons for Keynes's success against those for Hayek's failure.

---

[61]F. A. Hayek, Foreword to Gerald O'Driscoll, *Economics as a Coordination Problem* (Kansas City, Kans.: Sheed, Andrews and McMeel, 1977), p. ix.

[62]Mark Blaug, "Second Thoughts on the Keynesian Revolution", in Mark Blaug, *Economic Theories, True or False* (Aldershot: Edward Elgar, 1990), p. 91.

The General Theory was, first and foremost, designed to explain episodes of severe and persistent unemployment, which the notion of an underemployment equilibrium does rather nicely.[63] It also aimed to provide (though indirectly; this was a theoretical work) the rationale for a policy response from the government. Hayek's model explained the cycle, which was one of its chief advantages over the model in the *Treatise*, but it argued against government intervention during the crisis stage. Given the human propensity to act in times of crisis, the Keynesian message was easily the more welcome one.[64]

The Second World War and the subsequent history of many of the Western powers seemed to many economists to provide confirmation of the Keynesian propositions.[65] Increased public expenditure during the war, the equivalent of expansionary fiscal policy, yielded no immediate dire consequences. Indeed, after a brief round of postwar inflation, a boom began that was sustained with only mild inflationary or recessionary interruptions until the 1970s. The postwar growth experience seemed the best evidence that, in Keynes's words, "The right remedy for the trade cycle is not to be found in abolishing booms and thus keeping us permanently in a quasi-slump; but in abolishing slumps and thus keeping us permanently in a quasi-boom".[66] By the mid-1960s, much of the American economic community felt that the business cycle could be (and perhaps had been) vanquished, that a permanent state of quasi-boom was indeed achievable. It was not until the 1970s that the costs of the policy began to become evident, and some of Hayek's more ominous prognostications started to materialize.

---

[63]In his earlier work, persistent unemployment was a disequilibrium phenomenon that was due to the existence of a 'special case'. In *The General Theory*, adjustments in income and employment bring the system back into equilibrium. But the equilibrium can be consistent with high levels of unemployment, so that the economy can get stuck (absent policy intervention) in an under-full-employment equilibrium.

[64]Blaug emphasized this particular point in correspondence with the editor, noting "the obvious unpopularity of a laissez-faire theory of the business cycle in a decade characterized by the worst, longest-lasting depression of all time and the rise of fascisms in response to it—even if Hayek had had a theoretically compelling theory, a theory with do-nothing implications was doomed in a decade like the 1930s". Letter, Blaug to Caldwell, August 7, 1993. I should note that Blaug does not in his letter endorse Hayek's cycle theory; for him it is not "compelling".

[65]Recent scholarship questions the article of faith that the Second World War was a confirming instance of successful demand management policy; see, for example, Robert Higgs, "Wartime Prosperity? A Reassessment of the US Economy in the 1940s", *Journal of Economic History*, March 1992, pp. 41–60.

[66]Keynes, *The General Theory*, op. cit., p. 322.

The formal characteristics of Keynes's model also gave him an advantage over Hayek. Keynes presented his ideas within what economists call a 'comparative static' framework, one that conveys a sense of both determinateness and rigorous simplicity. Hayek's model, though apparently leading to determinate conclusions, was, like most cycle theories of the time, a dynamic one. It was anything but simple, and the fact that few of his English readers were familiar with the capital theory that provided its foundation did not make matters easier. Keynes's model was easily translatable mathematically; those who tried to develop Hayek's framework met with failure.[67] In the decades to come, the ability to express one's ideas in terms of a mathematical model became the sine qua non of the 'serious' economic theorist. As the formalistic revolution progressed, models like Hayek's became curious antiquities.

Though its author was no fan of econometrics, *The General Theory* nonetheless provided categories that fit in well with empirical constructs being developed by national income accountants. Hayek's general worldview was antagonistic towards such aggregative statistical work; he was bypassed by the econometrics caravan, as well.

One must not overlook Keynes's style, which drew his readers in, alternately infuriating, befuddling, and intriguing them. His very obscureness left his audience with a host of unsolved puzzles, riddles that guaranteed that his followers would have much work to do. Paul Samuelson, who may have inadvertently been infected by Keynes's style, states the attraction:

---

[67]"Several of us made attempts at that translation; the journals of the 1930s are full of them. But what emerged, when we tried to put the Hayek theory into our own words, was not Hayek. There was some inner mystery to which we failed to penetrate". John Hicks, "The Hayek Story", op. cit., pp. 204–205. In contrast, Hicks was able to mathematize Keynes's framework almost immediately; see his "Mr. Keynes and the 'Classics': A Suggested Interpretation", *Econometrica*, vol. 5, April 1937, pp. 147–159. It was Paul Samuelson who, in the first and subsequent editions of *Economics* (New York: McGraw Hill, 1st edition, 1948) provided the famed C+I+G 'Keynesian Cross'. This was the simplification that made it possible for hordes of introductory economics students to imbibe the Keynesian spirits. Samuelson anticipated his own contribution in his 1946 obituary notice for Keynes "[P]erhaps most important from the long-run standpoint, the Keynesian analysis has begun to filter down into the elementary textbooks; and, as everybody knows, once an idea gets into these, however bad it may be, it becomes practically immortal". See his "The General Theory", reprinted in *The New Economics: Keynes's Influence on Theory and Public Policy*, ed. Seymour E. Harris (New York: Knopf, 1950), p. 147. Only recently have some principles of economics textbooks dropped the old C+I+G framework.

Herein lies the secret of *The General Theory*. It is a badly written book, poorly organized; any layman who, beguiled by the author's previous reputation, bought the book was cheated of his five shillings. It is not well suited for classroom use. It is arrogant, bad-tempered, polemical, and not overly generous in its acknowledgements. It abounds in mares' nests or confusions.... Flashes of insight and intuition intersperse tedious algebra. An awkward definition suddenly gives way to an unforgettable cadenza. When finally mastered, its analysis is found to be obvious and at the same time new. In short, it is a work of genius.[68]

Perhaps to his credit, Hayek was in these areas no match for Keynes.

Finally, there was the selling of *The General Theory*. Some of the promotional work was done by Keynes himself, who prior to publication gave talks and wrote popular articles which produced a general anticipation of his book. His lectures at Cambridge from 1932 to 1935 were in effect a public forum for working out his transition to *The General Theory*. When it finally was published, the book was offered at a low price. Led by R. B. Bryce, graduate students at Harvard arranged for boxes of the book to be sent to them immediately upon publication.[69]

These factors taken together do much to explain the rapid acceptance of the Keynesian paradigm by the larger profession. But our concern is with the more intimate conflict between Cambridge and London. In the end it came down to a battle for the minds of the rising generation of British-trained economists. The engagement was an intense one; Austin Robinson recalled that "discussion was conducted very much in the atmosphere of the revivalist meeting: Brother, are you saved?"[70] Keynes was assisted in his struggle by a number of others.

---

[68]*Ibid.*, pp. 148–149.

[69]On Keynes's lectures, see *Keynes's Lectures 1932–35: Notes of a Representative Student*, ed. Thomas K. Rymes (London: Macmillan, 1989). Donald Walker, "Why Keynes's *General Theory* Was a Success", *Economic Notes*, vol. 15, 1986, pp. 5–29, contains a discussion of Keynes's marketing activities.

[70]Austin Robinson, "John Maynard Keynes 1883–1946", *Economic Journal*, vol. 57, March 1947, p. 41. See also Gilles Dostaler, "The Debate between Hayek and Keynes", in *Themes in Keynesian Criticism and Supplementary Modern Topics*, ed. William J. Barber (Aldershot: Edward Elgar, 1991), pp. 90–93, for an account of the immediate aftermath of the exchange.

The Contributions of Joan Robinson and Brinley Thomas

Over the summer of 1931, after Hayek's talk at Cambridge but before the publication of either *Prices and Production* or of his review of the *Treatise*, Joan Robinson wrote a paper. A revised version was eventually published two years later, and in it she strikes the pose of "a muddle-headed reader of economics" trying to make sense of the *Treatise* in light of the debate between Keynes and Hayek.[71] Mrs. Robinson was thus involved from the very beginning in the contest between our two protagonists.

She was instrumental in getting students from the LSE together with members of the Circus. Meetings were held on weekends on 'neutral ground' midway between Cambridge and London. There were some beneficial results, among them the opening up of a dialogue and the founding of a new journal that was not to be tied to any particular academic institution, the *Review of Economic Studies*. But the meetings were also an effective vehicle for transmitting the latest turns in Keynes's thought. The Keynesians, of course, were at a decided advantage in these meetings. The argument was not between the Keynes of the *Treatise* versus the Hayek of *Prices and Production*; had this been the format, each side would have had an equal chance to prepare. Rather, it was Hayek's views versus a new framework, just then being developed and reported on by his disciples, a new theory that would repair all the deficiencies of the *Treatise*. It was at one of these weekend meetings that Abba Lerner saw the light and was turned from Hayekian into Keynesian.[72]

Mrs. Robinson's toils did not end with the publication of *The General Theory*. She did the yeoman's work of publishing a popularization of Keynesian ideas in 1937. But far more important, and notorious, was her eventual role as upholder and enforcer of doctrinal purity at Cambridge. Her harassment of the shy and reserved Dennis Robertson was viewed as outrageous even by some of those who sympathized in general with her theoretical outlook.[73]

[71]Joan Robinson, "A Parable on Savings and Investment", *Economica*, vol. 13, February 1933, pp. 75–84. Though she briefly criticized Hayek on forced savings, it appears that Robinson's main intent was to move Keynes away from the framework of the *Treatise*.

[72]The episode is recounted in Joan Robinson, "Reminiscences", in *Contributions to Modern Economics*, op. cit., p. xv.

[73]The story is told by Harry Johnson in "Cambridge in the 1950s", in Johnson and Johnson, eds, *The Shadow of Keynes: Understanding Keynes, Cambridge, and Keynesian Economics*, op. cit., pp. 127–150. The antagonism between Mrs. Robinson and Robertson apparently dated back to their earliest encounters. As even a sympathetic biographical account reveals,

The most important player outside of Cambridge was undoubtedly Brinley Thomas.[74] Thomas had spent a year in Sweden and another in Germany on a traveling fellowship and had returned to the LSE in 1935 to lecture on his experiences. The contrast he drew between the two countries was stark. Thomas reported that the Swedes agreed with Keynes on policy matters and that, furthermore, they were perfecting their own theoretical framework, one that fully justified interventionist measures. Deflationist policies in Germany, on the other hand, had abetted the emergence of Hitler and the National Socialists. Thomas's lectures and writings strongly influenced three other Hayekian sympathizers (Hicks, Nicholas Kaldor, and George Shackle) to convert to the Keynesian doctrine. Hicks's contribution of the IS-LM framework has already been mentioned. Kaldor, who had helped translate Hayek's *Monetary Theory and the Trade Cycle*, would later assist William Beveridge to provide the blueprint for a full employment policy for the British welfare state.[75] Shackle was so taken by the Keynesian vision that he tore up the thesis on capital theory that he had started under Hayek. Nearly thirty years later, he would write a history of the 1926–39 period in which Hayek's name would be mentioned but twice, and then only as the editor of a book in which an essay by Gunnar Myrdal appeared.[76] Ludwig Lachmann was later often to lament, "When I came up to the LSE in the early 1930s, everybody was a Hayekian; at the end of the decade there were only two of us: Hayek and myself".[77] Such was the completeness of the Keynesian victory in the intimate struggle between Cambridge and London.

civility is not a trait for which Joan Robinson is likely to be remembered. See Marjorie Turner, *Joan Robinson and the Americans* (Armonk, N. Y.: M. E. Sharpe, 1989).

[74]Thomas's role is recounted in Nadim Shehadi, "The LSE and the Stockholm School in the 1930s", in *The Stockholm School of Economics Revisited*, ed. Lars Jonung (Cambridge: Cambridge University Press, 1991), pp. 377–389.

[75]See Sir William Beveridge, *Full Employment in a Free Society* (London: G. Allen and Unwin, 1944; New York: Norton, 1945; 2nd edition, 1960). Hayek's review of Beveridge's book is reprinted in this volume, Addendum to chapter 10.

[76]See G. L. S. Shackle, *The Years of High Theory: Invention and Tradition in Economic Thought, 1926–1939* (Cambridge: Cambridge University Press, 1967). In a later article, Shackle offered an incisive, and broadly sympathetic, appraisal of Hayek's contribution; see his "F. A. Hayek, 1899– ", in D. P. O'Brien and John Presley, eds, *Pioneers of Modern Economics in Britain* (London: Macmillan, 1981), pp. 234–261.

[77]Lachmann's reminiscence is reported on p. 366 of Stephan Boehm's obituary notice, "L. M. Lachmann (1906–1990): A Personal Tribute", *Review of Political Economy*, vol. 3, July 1991, pp. 365–371.

Sraffa's Review of *Prices and Production*

If Joan Robinson and Brinley Thomas played key roles in convincing those in the Cambridge-London axis of the truth of Keynes's ideas, it was Piero Sraffa who took on the equally important task of discrediting the Hayekian framework. His means was the standard one among academics: a review of *Prices and Production*, which is reprinted as chapter 7 of this volume.

Even more than the exchange with Keynes that preceded it, the Hayek-Sraffa duel lacks clarity. After the review had appeared, Frank Knight wrote to Oskar Morgenstern, "I wish he [Hayek] or someone would try to tell me in a plain grammatical sentence what the controversy between Sraffa and Hayek is about. I haven't been able to find anyone on this side who has the least idea."[78] Still, if one forges ahead, it is possible to discern that Sraffa had three major complaints. Let us take them up in turn.

The first was that in his book Hayek, from Sraffa's perspective, refused to address the role of money. That is, of course, a serious deficiency in a treatise whose presumptive goal is to elucidate the nature of a monetary economy. Hayek's concentration on what would occur in a moneyless world, and his definition of the natural rate as the interest rate that would prevail if money were 'neutral', seemed perverse to Sraffa.

If one gets beyond Sraffa's sarcastic tone, one can have some sympathy with his complaint. *Prices and Production* is not an easy book to read. Hayek's treatment of difficult topics is terse, particularly in the two theoretical chapters. Furthermore, though the first chapter is a history of monetary theories, money fades into the background in later chapters, where changes in the structure of production take centre stage.[79]

For Hayek's approach in *Prices and Production* to be comprehensible, one must first have read his *Monetary Theory and the Trade Cycle*. There he painstakingly built up the role of money in a market system and justified the conceit of starting with a moneyless world. It also must be noted that *Monetary Theory* is by far the better-written book. Unfortunately, it

---

[78]The letter is cited in Michael Lawlor and Bobbie Horn, "Notes on the Hayek-Sraffa Exchange", *Review of Political Economy*, vol. 4, 1992, p. 318.

[79]Sraffa's own treatise, *Production of Commodities by Means of Commodities: Prelude to a Critique of Economic Theory* (Cambridge: Cambridge University Press, 1960), a paradigmatic example of concisely obscure academic writing, is apt to produce in the reader of today a reaction not unlike that caused by reading *Prices and Production* without benefit of Hayek's earlier work.

had yet to be translated when Sraffa was writing his review. In his reply, Hayek quite appropriately urged his critic to consult the forthcoming translation.

This does not mean, of course, that Sraffa would have been satisfied with what Hayek had to say in *Monetary Theory*. For what was really at issue between them here is the self-adjusting nature of the market system. Hayek assumed that the adjustment mechanism, formally described in what he called "equilibrium theory", works faultlessly in a world in which money is absent. This is precisely why he started his analysis with such a world, only later to introduce money as the disturbing factor. Sraffa questioned the initial and crucial premise of a self-adjusting system. This is the bedrock-level conflict that underlies their arcane dispute about how best to model a monetary economy.

The next problem concerned Hayek's analysis of forced savings. Recall that in the Austrian theory of the cycle the lengthening of the structure of production, begun under a regime of forced savings, never gets completed. It is always the case that rising consumer prices signal firms that their earlier decision to employ more roundabout methods was in error. Firms abandon their incomplete capital projects and thereby precipitate the crisis. But isn't it possible that the transition to more capital-intensive production methods could be completed in time? Might not the consumer goods produced by using more roundabout methods come onto line just as consumer demand begins to rise? In short, why must the traverse to a new structure of production always be interrupted before completion?[80]

Hayek admitted in his reply that "it is upon the truth of this point that my theory stands or falls".[81] And, sadly for Hayek, his insistence that the traverse could never be completed strikes many current commentators as being the chief deficiency of his theory of the cycle. The general consensus is that, while the scenario painted by Hayek is a possible one, he neither demonstrated its necessity nor gave adequate attention to the

---

[80]In his review, Sraffa raised a number of different issues that connect, in one way or another, with this central point. The articles by Lachmann, "Austrian Economics under Fire: The Hayek-Sraffa Duel in Retrospect", op. cit.; Lawlor and Horn, "Notes on the Hayek-Sraffa Exchange", op. cit.; and Cottrell, "Hayek's Early Cycle Theory Re-examined", op. cit., provide more extensive treatment of the intricacies of Sraffa's attack and of Hayek's response.

[81]See chapter 8, p. 212, this volume.

lags implicit in the process of adjustment that he portrayed.[82] Hayek's theory fits some, but not all, trade cycles: It is not, as Hayek purported it to be, a general theory of the cycle.

The third area of contention involves the concept of the natural rate of interest. Sraffa argued that in the sort of moneyless world that Hayek was fond of positing, "there might be at any one moment as many 'natural' rates of interest as there are commodities, though they would not be 'equilibrium' rates".[83] Hayek conceded that there might be as many natural interest rates as there are commodities, but insisted that all would be equilibrium rates.[84] Ludwig Lachmann later remarked sagely that this exchange demonstrates that Hayek and Sraffa were operating with two very different definitions of equilibrium.[85] In any event, Hayek's acknowledgement undermines the notion of a single natural rate that would prevail in a moneyless world. And as Sraffa noted in his rejoinder, the way was not open for Hayek to invoke some average of these natural rates (that is, one that might hold for a "composite commodity"), since Hayek had so frequently and "emphat- ically repudiated the use of averages".[86]

We remember that Hayek spoke in early 1931 to an audience that included members of the Circus. It would have been evident to them as they were working through their critique of Keynes's *Treatise* that Hayek, like Keynes, was making use of a Wicksellian framework. It is interesting to conjecture whether this knowledge provided additional impetus to the members of the Circus to reach the conclusion that the theoretical framework of the *Treatise* was flawed and required rejection.

In any case, Sraffa's criticisms were adopted by Keynes in *The General Theory*. He cited Sraffa's review at the beginning of chapter 17 on "The Essential Properties of Interest and Money". Later in the chapter he commented on his use of the natural rate of interest in the *Treatise* as

---

[82]This is the judgement rendered by, for example, Hicks, "The Hayek Story", op. cit.; Cottrell, "Hayek's Early Cycle Theory Re-examined", op. cit.; and David Laidler, "Hayek on Neutral Money and the Cycle", in *The Economics of F. A. Hayek*, Marina Colonna, Harald Hagemann, and Omar Hamouda, eds (Aldershot: Edward Elgar, forthcoming).

[83]See this volume, chapter 7, p. 205.

[84]See this volume, chapter 8, pp. 218–219.

[85]Lachmann, "Austrian Economics under Fire: The Hayek-Sraffa Duel in Retrospect", op. cit., p. 237. Terming Hayek's admission "a fatal concession", Lachmann went on to "close this particular breach of the Austrian rampart" by positing an overall equilibrium of interest rates of a type not envisaged by either of the antagonists, one similar to that which might be obtained by "vigilant and efficient arbitrage" in international currency markets. See *ibid.*, p. 238.

[86]Chapter 9, p. 225, this volume. Sraffa would revisit the notion of a "composite commodity" in his *Production of Commodities*, op. cit.

follows: "I am now no longer of the opinion that the concept of a 'natural' rate of interest, which previously seemed to me a most promising idea, has anything very useful or significant to contribute to our analysis".[87] Lest anyone doubt his opinion of those still foolish enough to use such a construct, and especially of those who might link it to such concepts as 'forced savings' or 'neutral money', Keynes offered the following obloquy:

> But at this point we are in deep water. "The wild duck has dived down to the bottom—as deep as she can get—and bitten fast hold of the weed and tangle and all the rubbish that is down there, and it would need an extraordinarily clever dog to dive after and fish her up again".[88]

The Riddle of the Review

A riddle remains: Why did Hayek fail to write a review of *The General Theory?* Keynes had sent him an advance copy. In his letter of thanks, Hayek mentioned that he was puzzled by some parts, and found other parts troubling, and concluded that "if my present doubts remain I shall probably ask for your hospitality for some notes on particular points in the E. J. [*Economic Journal*]".[89] One suspects that his doubts were not dispelled by further study. So why did he never produce a review?

Hayek suggested some answers in three of the retrospective pieces included in this volume.[90] He returned to the question often, probably because, as he put it, "I have to the present day not quite got over a feeling that I had then shirked what should have been a plain duty".[91] What reasons did Hayek offer to explain his uncharacteristic shirking?

The first invokes Hayek's experience with his review of Keynes's *Treatise*. Having spent a good deal of time preparing his critique, and having felt that he had demolished Keynes's position in his review,

---

[87]Keynes, *The General Theory*, op. cit., p. 243. The citation of Sraffa appears on p. 223.

[88]*Ibid.*, p. 183.

[89]Letter, Hayek to Keynes, February 2, 1936, reprinted in *The General Theory and After: A Supplement*, ed. Donald Moggridge, vol. 29 (1979) of *The Collected Writings of J. M. Keynes*, op. cit., p. 208.

[90]See "The Economics of the 1930s as Seen from London", pp. 59–61, this volume; "Personal Recollections of Keynes and the Keynesian Revolution", pp. 240–241, this volume; "The Keynes Centenary: The Austrian Critique", pp. 251–252, this volume.

[91]"The Economics of the 1930s as Seen from London", p. 60, this volume.

Hayek was quite disappointed to receive a letter from Keynes saying that he had changed his mind and was working out a new model. Hayek wrote no review of *The General Theory* then because he assumed that by the time he had completed the task, Keynes would have changed his mind again.

On the face of it, this makes some sense. Keynes was famous, and not just among economists, for changing his mind. Indeed, mutability was part and parcel of his public persona: He was dubbed "the boneless man" in the press for his vacillation on free trade; despite his earnest (though unsuccessful) efforts on behalf of Lloyd George in the 1929 General Election, Keynes four years later released a scathing portrait of the "goat-footed bard" at Versailles in his *Essays in Biography*; and one must not forget the Thomas Jones barb about five economists with six conflicting opinions. For many observers, Keynes was more Mercury than Cassandra.[92]

But if Keynes's inconstancy in regard to theory were Hayek's sole reason for holding back criticism, then he was guilty of a serious misjudgement. Keynes manifestly had not changed his mind about the necessity of saving capitalism from itself. And given that Keynes called his book, in his own modest way, *The General Theory*, his intent should have been clear enough. Keynes's theoretical promiscuity is not, by itself, sufficient to account for Hayek's diffidence. If anything, it could well have provided just the ammunition that was needed for an effective counterattack.

In "The Economics of the 1930s as Seen from London", Hayek linked the 'Keynes-would-change-his-mind' argument to another: his own "tiredness from controversy".[93] This clearly constitutes a separate reason. To be sure, Hayek had good reason to be tired by 1936: He had been the centre of other controversies, fighting with Frank Knight over capital theory and with market socialists over planning; he had been unable to

---

[92]See footnote 20, this chapter, on Jones, and Johnson and Johnson, *The Shadow of Keynes*, op. cit., p. 17 on the boneless man. Keynes had originally sketched his impressions of "the Welsh witch" Lloyd George in *The Economic Consequences of the Peace*, op. cit., but he ended up excising the most offensive sections from the text. These were later reprinted in his *Essays in Biography* [1933], reprinted as vol. 10 (1972) of *The Collected Writings of J. M. Keynes*, op. cit. As always, Keynes was the most lyrical of butchers: "Lloyd George is rooted in nothing; he is void and without content; he lives and feeds on his immediate surroundings; he is an instrument and a player at the same time which plays on the company and is played on by them too; he is a prism, as I have heard him described, which collects light and distorts it and is most brilliant if the light comes from many quarters at once; a vampire and a medium in one" (*Ibid.*, p. 24).

[93]This volume, p. 60.

forestall the defection of his own students to Keynes's camp; and the brutality of his previous exchanges with Keynes and Sraffa had doubtless left him both mentally fatigued and wary. But why did Hayek confuse his own weariness with Keynes's variability?

Hayek may have conflated the two reasons because of the dual message that Keynes had delivered in his letter announcing that he was changing his mind. Recall again the last sentence of the letter: "I am trying to re-shape and improve my central position, and *that is probably a better way to spend one's time than in controversy*" (emphasis added).[94] In 1936 Hayek, too, was re-shaping and improving his own model. He may have anticipated that once he was finished, members of the profession would again have their choice between two theories, and that this was a more appropriate, perhaps a more fruitful, and certainly (given his past experience), a less emotionally taxing way to proceed against his old nemesis.

Things did not work out that way, of course. By the time that Hayek published his next major theoretical work, *The Pure Theory of Capital*, the world was at war. Few in the profession even noticed the book. Furthermore, it was clear to Hayek that even after a prodigious effort he had not gotten very far. True enough, he had been able to clear away Böhm-Bawerk's "average period of production" and replace it with the far more complex notion of a structure of production, thereby securing the capital-theoretic foundation of Austrian theory. But he had made no further progress towards building on this new foundation a fully dynamic theory of the cycle. Hayek never returned to this task, hoping that it would be completed by others. It remains unfinished.

The third reason offered by Hayek is a straightforward methodological one. Both "The Economics of the 1930s as Seen from London" and "Personal Recollections of Keynes and the Keynesian Revolution" were written in the 1960s. In them, Hayek recounted that after the release of *The General Theory* he had a feeling, vague but enduring, that in order to do a full critique of Keynes he would need to do more than to criticize his model. Hayek disagreed with Keynes on both theory and policy. But it was Keynes's methodological approach, specifically his use of aggregates, that Hayek came to view in retrospect as being his opponent's most dangerous contribution.

Now, it is easy to understand that Hayek might put things in this way in essays written in the 1960s. Macroeconomic modelling was then at its zenith, as was hubris about the economics profession's ability to control

---

[94]This volume, Appendix to chapter 5, letter no. 13, Keynes to Hayek, March 29, 1932.

the business cycle by applying fiscal 'fine-tuning'. What doesn't ring quite true in Hayek's claim is that he was only vaguely becoming aware of this difference over methodology in the 1930s. As we saw in our discussion of Hayek's earlier work on the United States economy, opposition to the use of statistical aggregates had long been a methodological principle among Austrians. Aggregates mask the movement of relative prices, and relative price movements are the central foci of Austrian theory.

I would like to suggest that there may indeed have been another methodological argument that Hayek was just becoming aware of in the mid-1930s. As I have argued elsewhere,[95] it was during this time that Hayek began to lose faith in the 'equilibrium theory' portrayal of the market mechanism. The equilibrium theory of Hayek's day was static, timeless, and assumed that all decision-makers have full and correct information. In the real world, forward-looking agents make decisions in real time, based on dispersed and subjectively-held (hence fallible) information. In the real world, the ultimate question is: How do the actions of such agents ever get coordinated? Equilibrium theory, with its focus on end-states in which coordination is already achieved, assumes the most important question away. Hayek eventually abandoned the equilibrium theory characterization of markets and moved to a 'market process' understanding of social coordination, one in which a pivotal informational role is assigned to freely adjusting relative prices.

If a movement away from an equilibrium story and towards a market process story characterizes the actual change in Hayek's thinking that began in the 1930s, why did he not put it in this way in his reminiscences? It was not that the new orientation undermined his policy views. The market process story, with its emphases on the dispersion and subjective aspects of human knowledge and on the essential complexity of social phenomena, supports the contention that policy-makers will seldom, if ever, have sufficient knowledge to intervene effectively in the economy. Furthermore, many interventions (in particular, those associated with central planning) have the demonstrably negative effect of impeding relative prices from performing their coordinative function. The market process story leads at a minimum to policy scepticism; and in many cases policy pessimism seems fully warranted.

The market process story does not fit in well, however, with the theory of the business cycle that Hayek had articulated in the early 1930s. In a market process world, it is possible to predict broad patterns of outcomes, it is possible to make what Hayek later would call 'pattern

---

[95]Caldwell, "Hayek's Transformation", op. cit.

predictions'. One can, for example, predict that price ceilings will result in shortages, queues, black markets, deterioration in product quality, and the like. But unless one resorts to an equilibrium theory world, it is not possible accurately to predict a precise sequence of changes in relative prices of the sort found on the pages of *Prices and Production*.[96]

There is a final reason, albeit one that is not emphasized by Hayek, that may have been a factor in his decision not to write a review of *The General Theory*. In 1931, Keynes could legitimately have been viewed as 'the enemy' by Hayek and his friends at the LSE. As the decade unfolded, however, the situation gradually altered. The rise of fascism brought about changes in the climate of opinion among the intelligentsia in Britain and in the other surviving Western democracies. Even those who might appear only to be seeking a 'middle way' still favoured substantial amounts of state planning.[97] Hayek's debates with the market socialists, as well as the rise in influence of even more radical groups, made it clear that his opponents were not monolithic. Though Hayek clearly had his differences with Keynes, the latter had not, at least, wholly forsaken his Liberal origins.[98] Anything that might weaken his influence could potentially strengthen the hand of the planners or other more radical groups. Given the climate, Hayek decided to mute his

[96]Hayek seems to recognize this in his discussion of *The Pure Theory of Capital* in *Hayek on Hayek*, op. cit. He notes that after he jettisoned Böhm-Bawerk's average period of production, "the thing becomes so damned complicated it's almost impossible to follow it". He goes on to say that: "Like so many things, I am afraid, which I have attempted in economics, this capital-theory work shows more a barrier to how far we can get in efficient explanation than sets forth precise explanations. All these things I've stressed—the complexity of the phenomena in general, the unknown character of the data, and so on—really much more points out limits to our possible knowledge than our contributions that make specific predictions possible". *Ibid.*, pp. 159-160.

[97]The title of Arthur Marwick's study of the period in Britain captures the mood nicely: "Middle Opinion in the Thirties: Planning, Progress and Political 'Agreement'", *English Historical Review*, April 1964, pp. 285–298. Radical thought was not limited to England. Describing the University of Chicago during the mid-1930s, Milton Friedman recalls that: "[C]lose to a majority of the social scientists and the students in the social sciences were either members of the Communist Party or very close to it....It was an environment that was strongly prosocialist. It was strongly in favour of government going all the way to take over the whole economy." In Edmund Kitch, ed., "The Fire of Truth: A Remembrance of Law and Economics at Chicago, 1932–1970", *Journal of Law and Economics*, vol. 26, April 1983, pp. 178–179.

[98]Indeed, recent scholarship suggests that, as the 1930s progressed, Keynes may have begun to lose some of his enthusiasm for activist fiscal policy. See Bradley Bateman, "In the Realm of Concept and Circumstance", *History of Political Economy*, vol. 26, Spring 1994, pp. 99–116.

criticisms of Keynes.

In any event, relations between Keynes and Hayek appear to have been quite good during the war. When London evacuated, Keynes arranged to get Hayek rooms at Cambridge. Keynes spent his weekends there, and they often met on social occasions. Apparently economics was rarely discussed.

Keynes's 1940 pamphlet, "How to Pay for the War", was also clearly important in mending any broken fences.[99] The wartime economy had brought some economic benefits: There was full employment, and hence an increase in incomes. But the war also brought with it reduced production of consumer goods. With increased purchasing power chasing a reduced number of goods, the question arose: How should existing goods be allocated? Keynes's plan called for a tax increase, the encouragement of savings, and (its most novel idea) a deferred payment scheme that would delay the receipt of a percentage of all incomes until after the war.

Keynes's plan was significant because it established his opposition to the two other likely alternatives, both of which Hayek had also rejected. One of these was to simply permit inflation to take its course, that is, to allow the prices of consumer goods to rise. The other was the standard combination of price-fixing with rationing. (Keynes's plan allowed this only for certain household staples.) "How to Pay for the War" revealed to Hayek that Keynes was no inflationist, and further that he appeared to recognize the allocative and coordinative role of relative prices.

Keynes's reaction to *The Road to Serfdom*, published in 1944, must also be mentioned. Keynes read the book on one of his crossings to America, and later sent Hayek a letter expressing qualified agreement with many of the themes of the book. In his opening paragraph, Keynes bordered on the effusive:

> The voyage has given me the chance to read your book properly. In my opinion it is a grand book. We all have the greatest reason to be grateful to you for saying so well what needs so much to be said. You will not expect me to accept quite all the economic dicta in it. But morally and philosophically I find myself in agreement with virtually the

---

[99]Keynes, "How to Pay for the War", reprinted in *Essays in Persuasion*, op. cit., pp. 367–439. The pamphlet first appeared as two long articles published in *The Times* in November, 1939.

whole of it; and not only in agreement with it, but in a deeply moved agreement.[100]

This made a dramatic contrast to the reception offered by the academic community, particularly in the United States, where Hayek's views were excoriated.

No, the problem was not with Keynes. By war's end, the real danger was his followers, those who sought to use his name to pursue their own agendas. This explains the content of the last conversation between Keynes and Hayek. By 1946, Hayek was trying hard to get Keynes to speak out against people like Joan Robinson and Richard Kahn. His death a few months later led to Keynes's canonization. His Cambridge followers moved quickly to claim his mantle. Theirs was the most extreme version of 'Keynesian' thought, its influence restricted mostly to England. A milder version, propagated in the United States by men like Alvin Hansen and Paul Samuelson, became for nearly thirty years the dominant paradigm in economics.

Hayek's stay in England ended sadly. Politically, all that he had fought against was coming to pass. Economics at Cambridge was slowly but surely being taken over by the young Keynesians. In 1946, his close friend Robbins would deliver the Marshall lectures there and repudiate his own earlier beliefs on the cycle.[101] Though there were also personal reasons involved in his decision to move, Hayek four years later took a position on the Committee for Social Thought at the University of Chicago. Though he would always consider England as his cultural home, the place where he felt the most comfortable, Hayek would never spend any significant time there again.

"Which Was Right, Keynes or Hayek?"

We have avoided the key question until now: Which was right, Keynes or Hayek? It is a question on which honest disagreement exists, and one that may be posed on a number of different levels.

Regarding their respective theories, my own opinion, as is perhaps evident in the preceding text, is that neither was right. Both purported to be supplying a general theory of the cycle, and in this neither was successful. Both were able to provide theories that had specific applica-

---

[100]Letter, Keynes to Hayek, June 28, 1944, reprinted in *Activities 1940–1946: Shaping the Post-War World: Employment and Commodities*, ed. Donald Moggridge, vol. 27 (1980) of *The Collected Writings of J. M. Keynes*, op. cit., p. 385.

[101]Lionel Robbins, *The Economic Problem in Peace and War* (London: Macmillan, 1947), pp. 67–68.

tions to particular times and places, which is no small feat. Their sin, if there was one, was to generalize on the basis of limited experience. This is a temptation that social scientists, and perhaps economists in particular, have repeatedly found it near impossible to resist.

To judge who was right on matters of policy is even more complicated, since the economic profession's experience in this area is both country-specific and still relatively limited. With this caveat in mind, one might cautiously argue that both Keynes and Hayek provided some wisdom regarding policy. Keynes was right to argue against the return to gold in the environment of the early 1920s. He was also among many at the time to recognize that worker resistance to reductions in nominal wages in countries with strong labour movements make persistent high unemployment in such regimes more likely. Recent experience in the European Community suggests that structural unemployment of this sort is intransigent in the face of policy countermeasures.[102] Hayek appears to have been right in arguing that, though the severity of cyclical swings can be moderated by policy, sustained efforts to maintain full employment will eventually cause inflation to worsen. The economic history of the United States since the end of the Second World War seems to support his prediction. The swings of the business cycle appear to have been less severe than in earlier times,[103] but this has been accompanied by higher average levels of inflation, with the stagflation of the 1970s being the clearest confirming instance of his general policy pessimism.

Hayek and Keynes differed sharply on what they thought could be done in the world. There were numerous dimensions to their disagreement. Keynes was a progressive, an optimist, and not least of all, an aesthete. He despised the Victorian taste for narrow limits on proper behaviour. In the frightening new world that was emerging after the Great War, he feared that a blind adherence to outmoded tradition would only serve to hasten the victory of totalitarian regimes. These he detested, partly for their crass emphasis on the material world, but also on aesthetic grounds. There could be little room in such a world for the individual variation that made life rich, vibrant, worth living. His confidence in the new and in the powers of humankind to shape its environment show that he shared in the progressive illusions of his

---

[102]See Charles Bean, "European Unemployment: A Survey", *Journal of Economic Literature*, vol. 32, June 1994, pp. 573–619.

[103]Some recent research disputes even this modest claim about the comparative volatility of the cycle. See Christina Romer, "Is the Stabilization of the Postwar Economy a Figment of the Data?", *American Economic Review*, vol. 76, June 1986, pp. 314–344.

times. In this respect, Keynes, unique in many of his views, was very much a representative character of his day.

In contrast, Hayek's worldview was dark, sobering, sober. His regard for savings bordered on the puritanical. A profound epistemological pessimism led him to a kind of stoicism regarding policy: Because our knowledge is dispersed, particular, and limited, our ability to enact effective public policy is severely circumscribed. In Hayek's opinion, understanding the extent of our own limitations was often the best way to avoid error, and avoiding error was often the loftiest goal to which it was reasonable to aspire. None of this accommodated the progressive and scientist presumptions of his day, in England or elsewhere. Hayek never quite fit; he was viewed as a curious kind of conservative, sincere and honest but a bit quaint. Three generations of policy experience later, it might now be the optimism of the progressives that seems quaint. Would it not be a sweet irony if, in the end, Hayek turned out to be the real Cassandra?

John Maynard Keynes and Friedrich Hayek differed profoundly in their responses to the interwar world that they inhabited. Both observed a world gone mad. Keynes saw salvation in a thorough revision of the liberal order. Hayek saw it in the rediscovery of one. Their debate over this question continues to this day; it is perhaps the most important issue that democratic regimes, old or new, must address.

Bruce Caldwell

PART I

HAYEK COMES TO THE LONDON SCHOOL OF ECONOMICS AND POLITICAL SCIENCE

ONE

THE ECONOMICS OF THE 1930s
AS SEEN FROM LONDON[1]

When I look back to the early 1930s, they appear to me much the most exciting period in the development of economic theory during this century. This is probably a highly subjective impression, determined both by my age at that time and the particular circumstances in which I was placed. Yet even when I try hard to look at the period as objectively as I can, the years between about 1931, when I went to London, and say 1936 or 1937, seem to me to mark a high point and the end of one period in the history of economic theory and the beginning of a new and very different one. And I will add at once that I am not at all sure that the change in approach which took place at the end of that period was all a gain and that we may not some day have to take up where we left off then.[2]

Perhaps I can anticipate my main point by saying that just as it seemed that we were succeeding in establishing a unified tradition in economic theory and abolishing all separate 'schools', a new rift appeared which divided the economic theorists in different lines. I want to speak here first about the process of consolidation of which, I believe, the London School of Economics was the centre just at the time when I joined it. The strongest impression one would gain was that all the different traditions which till then had prevailed at the different centres were at last fusing into a common, internationally accepted body of

---

[1][This chapter, which has not been previously published, is one of five lectures delivered by Hayek at the University of Chicago in October 1963, under the sponsorship of the Charles O. Walgreen Foundation. It should be noted that Hayek had intended to revise the lecture before publication but was unable to do so. It is reproduced here in its original form. Another of the lectures, "The Economics of the 1920s as Seen from Vienna", is published in F. A. Hayek, *The Fortunes of Liberalism*, op. cit. —Ed.]

[2][The reference is to the shift to macroeconomics inspired by the publication of Keynes's *The General Theory of Employment, Interest and Money* [1936], reprinted as volume 7 (1973) in *The Collected Writings of John Maynard Keynes* (London: Macmillan, 1971–1989). —Ed.]

economic theory. It is true that the Italian economist Maffeo Pantaleoni[3] had claimed a good many years earlier that there were only two schools of economists, good economists and bad economists. But that was more a pious wish than a fact. The tendency towards integration which had been noticeable before the first Great War had been halted and partly reversed by that war and its aftermath. Though during the 1920s I believe in all the important centres, London, Harvard, Cambridge, Vienna, and Stockholm, and a few Italian, French, and German universities, eager young men were trying hard to find what of the work of other schools they could usefully incorporate into their local tradition, it was still a situation in which the frameworks into which these improvements were placed were determined by the different works of the great founders of the respective traditions, Marshall, Walras, and Pareto, or Menger—with perhaps Wicksell in Sweden and Taussig at Harvard already trying to provide a synthesis.[4]

[3][Maffeo Pantaleoni (1857–1924) taught at the University of Rome and served briefly in the Italian Parliament. His textbook *Principii di Economia Pura* [1889], translated as *Pure Economics* (London: Macmillan, 1898; reprinted, New York: Kelley and Millman, 1957) helped introduce the Austrian School's marginalism to Italian- and English-speaking audiences. —Ed.]

[4][Alfred Marshall (1842–1924), Professor of Political Economy at Cambridge from 1884 through 1908, was the dominant figure in British economics between J. S. Mill and Keynes. His *Principles of Economics: An Introductory Volume* (London: Macmillan, 1890; 8th edition, 1920; reprinted, Philadelphia: Porcupine, 1990) was the leading English-language economics textbook. It was Marshall's ideas that required Keynes to engage in the "long struggle of escape" mentioned in the Preface to his *General Theory*, op. cit., p. xxiii. Cf. also J. M. Keynes, "Alfred Marshall, 1842–1924", in A. C. Pigou, ed., *Memorials of Alfred Marshall* (London: Macmillan, 1925; reprinted, New York: Kelley, 1966).

Léon Walras (1834–1910), French economist whose *Eléments d'Economie Pure* [1874–77], translated as *Elements of Pure Economics* (Homewood, Ill.: Irwin, 1954), introduced the general equilibrium approach and established him as one of the co-founders (with W. S. Jevons and Carl Menger) of the Marginalist Revolution. The Italian economist Vilfredo Pareto (1848–1923) succeeded to Walras's chair at the University of Lausanne, Switzerland, in 1893. Pareto expanded on Walras's approach in his *Cours d'Economie Politique* [1896–97], translated as *Manual of Political Economy* (New York: Kelley, 1971), but later in his life turned away from economics and towards sociology.

Carl Menger (1840–1921), Austrian economist, author of *Grundsätze der Volkswirtschaftslehre* [1871], translated as *Principles of Economics* (New York: New York University Press, 1981), and founder of the Austrian School of Economics of which Hayek was a third-generation member. Cf. Hayek's article "Carl Menger 1840–1921" and the Addendum, "The Place of Menger's *Grundsätze* in the History of Economic Thought", reprinted as chapter 2 of *The Fortunes of Liberalism*, op. cit.

Knut Wicksell (1851–1926), Swedish economist who attempted to synthesize Eugen Böhm-Bawerk's theory of capital and the marginal productivity theory of distribution with the general equilibrium framework of the Lausanne School of Walras and Pareto. His distinction between the real and natural rates of interest in his *Geldzins und Güterpreise*,

The London School of Economics had then just gone through its first change of the faculty. Most of the men who had formed its first faculty on its foundation thirty-five years earlier had recently either died or retired and been replaced by a much younger group. Some of the older men like Graham Wallas,[5] and more rarely since he lived at Oxford, Edwin Cannan,[6] still appeared in the Common Room, and that famous book collector, Foxwell,[7] was at least still active from his Cambridge retreat. Above all, the two founders of the school, Sidney and Beatrice Webb,[8] were still very much in evidence. A recent publication of the documents concerning the foundation of the School by its present [1963] director[9] has made it clear to what extent indeed it had been the personal creation of Sidney Webb. Though Beatrice was in many ways the more colourful personality and we know so much more about her than about him, I for my part have no doubt that he was the solid mind of the famous combination, a master of marshalling facts, of organization and of tactics. He did profoundly believe that an impartial study of social phenomena would inevitably lead to a rational reorganization of society on socialist lines and that therefore any contribution to the better understanding of the life of society was also a step towards socialism. He did believe that the main need was a greater knowledge of facts and he was not really interested in theory.

---

translated as *Interest and Prices*, op. cit., influenced the monetary frameworks of both Hayek and Keynes. See this volume, chapter 3, n. 10.

Frank Taussig (1859–1940) was called "the American Marshall" by Joseph Schumpeter in his obituary article with A. H. Cole and E. S. Mason, "Frank William Taussig, 1859–1940", *Quarterly Journal of Economics*, vol. 55, May 1941, p. 363. Taussig's *Principles of Economics* (New York: Macmillan, 1911; 4th edition, 1939) was the leading US textbook on the subject until after the Second World War. —Ed.]

[5][Graham Wallas (1852–1932), close friend of Sidney Webb and an early member of the Fabian Society, taught political science at the LSE from the time of its founding until his retirement in 1923. —Ed.]

[6][Edwin Cannan (1861–1935), British economist whose 1904 edition of Adam Smith's *Wealth of Nations* (London: Methuen, 1904; reprinted, Chicago: University of Chicago Press, 1976) is still in use. See Hayek's essay on Cannan in this volume, Addendum to chapter 1. —Ed.]

[7][Herbert Foxwell (1849–1936), British economic historian and Professor of Political Economy at the University of London. There was a bit of a flap when Marshall's favourite student, the youthful A. C. Pigou, was picked instead of Foxwell to succeed to Marshall's chair in 1908. —Ed.]

[8][In addition to their work at the London School of Economics, Sidney Webb (1859–1947) and Beatrice Webb (1858–1943) are remembered as the creators of Fabian Socialism. —Ed.]

[9][Sir Sydney Caine, *The History of the London School of Economics and Political Science* (London: G. Bell & Sons for the London School of Economics and Political Science, 1963). —Ed.]

But in creating the School he simply went out to get the best men in their field who were available so long as they had shown some realistic sense, irrespective of political opinion. And one curious result of this was that, so far as economics was concerned (as distinguished from politics, sociology, and similar subjects) the London School of Economics had become one of the very few centres of teaching in which the tradition of classical liberalism was carried on. This was almost entirely due to one man, who was at the same time one of the greatest students of classical economic theory and one of the shrewdest interpreters of the facts of current economic life, who in his sound, hard common sense had few peers, Edwin Cannan.

At the time Cannan and his generation departed from the school and had to be replaced, the guiding figure was however no longer Sidney Webb but the fourth of the succeeding directors he had chosen for it, Sir William (later Lord) Beveridge.[10] Since his works also have left their mark on the economic thinking of our time, I must say some words about him. What is significant in the present connection is mainly that his great gifts did not include an understanding of economics. He possessed an exceptional power of lucid and persuasive exposition and when writing from the briefs of one of the able young men he knew so well to choose, he would be extraordinarily effective.[11] He would have made a great barrister or a great journalist (the two professions in which he had started) and his gift in delineating great plans for development have greatly assisted the school with the big foundations. But his temperament was not that of a scientist, and quick as he was to grasp a particular point when explained to him, he had really little conception what economic theory was about. I do not think that he ever saw that the inflation about which he complained so much during his last years was an inevitable consequence of a policy of full employment as he had defined it, i.e., a policy aiming at a state in which there were more jobs offered than demanded.

Still, it was under his directorship that the London School of Economics became in the 1930s perhaps the most lively centre of

[10][William Beveridge (1879–1963) was director of the London School of Economics from 1919 to 1937. Though a critic of Keynes in the 1930s, he outdistanced his former adversary in terms of uninhibited enthusiasm for state intervention by the 1940s. Indeed, the underlying principles for the post-war British welfare state are fully mapped out in his *Social Insurance and Allied Services: The Beveridge Report in Brief* (London: HMSO, 1942). —Ed.]

[11][Hayek is referring here to Beveridge's *Full Employment in a Free Society: A Report* (New York: W. W. Norton, 1945). Hayek's review of the book is included as an Addendum to chapter 10, this volume. —Ed.]

economic discussion. On Cannan's retirement in 1926, his chair had for one year been filled by Allyn A. Young,[12] a subtle thinker of whom great things were expected but who left little published work when he died suddenly soon after his return to the United States. Some years earlier the second chair, in money and banking, had already been filled, after Foxwell's retirement, by T. E. Gregory,[13] who combined with a rare knowledge of monetary and banking history and organization great familiarity with the continental literature in the field. He had then recently struggled with Keynes on the Macmillan Committee and I believe the most valuable descriptive and historical parts of the report of that committee are mainly due to him, though he did not prevail over Keynes in the policy recommendations.[14] Like Cannan he was a convinced liberal. Indeed, the only socialist among the economists at the London School of Economics at that time had been Hugh Dalton,[15] mainly known for his work on public finance, who during the 1920s had been one of the most influential figures but who left academic work for politics just about the time I went to London.

The new generation which took over around 1930 were mostly former students of the School and pupils of Edwin Cannan. The first of them to be appointed to a professorship who after the departure of Allyn Young decisively shaped the development of economics was Lionel Robbins.[16] I shall next time have to refer to those decisive contributions

[12][Allyn Young (1876–1929), American economist who accepted a three-year term in 1926 as head of the Economics Department at the LSE. He was unhappy in the post and had decided to return to the United States. He died in March 1929, in London, a victim of an influenza epidemic. —Ed.]

[13][T. E. Gregory (1890–1970), Cassel Professor of Economics at the LSE from 1927 to 1937, served on the Macmillan Committee (1929–31) and was a supporter of England's return to the gold standard. —Ed.]

[14][Hayek refers to the Committee on Finance and Industry, chaired by Lord Macmillan, which met from November 1929 through May 1931. Keynes was both a member of the committee and offered evidence before it. Though in its final report the committee judged maintenance of the exchange rate as the principal policy goal, its Addendum 1, signed by Keynes and some other leading members, also called for import restrictions and a public works program. —Ed.]

[15][Hugh Dalton (1887–1962), economist and Labour politician, had studied under Keynes and Pigou and became a Reader in economics at the LSE from 1923 to 1936. Dalton was among those who argued against Hayek and Robbins that income redistribution increased economic welfare. —Ed.]

[16][Lionel Robbins (1898–1984) was picked at the age of thirty to succeed Young as Head of the Economics Department at the LSE, a position he held until 1960. Robbins was largely responsible for bringing Hayek to the LSE. Their famous seminar in the 1930s is described later in this chapter. See also Lionel Robbins, *Autobiography of an Economist* (London: Macmillan, 1971). —Ed.]

to the development of economics which will never find an appropriate place in the histories of the science. I believe Robbins's efforts for the consolidation and integration of economics in these years—and what I said about his in the beginning was largely his work—belongs to this class. His catholic approach and extensive knowledge of the classic and contemporary literature, English and foreign, had few equals. But his influence operated not mainly through his published work, not even his deservedly successful book on the *Nature and Significance of Economic Science*,[17] a book whose profound influence on economic thinking in the English-speaking world I did not foresee, as to me it seemed largely a brilliant exposition of ideas which were largely familiar to the Austrian tradition. What I have in mind are his activities as teacher and particularly in the thankless task of editor. It is due to him that Wicksteed, then almost forgotten, became again available, that Wicksell and Mises were translated and that the work of such forgotten geniuses as Mountiford Longfield and Samuel Bailey (among many others) were made readily accessible and that, last but not least, the first six chapters of *Risk, Uncertainty and Profit* became the standard introduction to the current state of economic theory for the serious student.[18]

[17][Lionel Robbins, *An Essay on the Nature and Significance of Economic Science* [1932], revised edition (London: Macmillan, 1935). —Ed.]

[18][Mountiford Longfield (1802–1884) was an Irish jurist and a founder of the Dublin Statistical Society. Samuel Bailey (1791–1870) was an English merchant and banker. On Longfield and Bailey see E. R. A. Seligman, "On Some Neglected British Economists", *Economic Journal*, vol. 13, 1903, pp. 335–363, 511–535. The American economist Frank Knight (1885–1962) laid out the conditions for perfect competition and distinguished between risk and uncertainty in his book *Risk, Uncertainty and Profit* (Boston: Houghton Mifflin, 1921; reprinted, Chicago: University of Chicago Press, 1971). He also clashed with Hayek on capital theory in the 1930s.

The LSE Series of Reprints of Scarce Tracts in Economics and Political Science, supervised (one might as easily say 'inspired') by Robbins, included Philip Wicksteed's *Co-ordination of the Laws of Distribution* [1894], reprinted as number 12 of the series, 1932; Wicksell's *Über Wert, Kapital und Rente* [1893], number 15, 1933; Longfield's *Lectures on Political Economy* [1834], number 8, 1931; Bailey's *A Critical Dissertation on the Nature, Measures and Causes of Value* [1825], number 7, 1931; and Knight's *Risk, Uncertainty and Profit* [1921], number 16, 1933. Robbins also wrote introductions for the second edition of Wicksteed's *Common Sense of Political Economy* (London: Routledge and Kegan Paul, 1933); Wicksell's *Lectures on Political Economy* (London: Routledge & Sons, 1934, 1935; reprinted, Fairfield, N. J.: Kelley, 1977, 1978); and the first English edition of Ludwig von Mises's *Theory of Money and Credit* (London: Jonathan Cape, 1934; reprinted, Indianapolis: Liberty*Classics*, 1981), and he arranged for Jacques Kahane to translate Mises's *Socialism* (London: Jonathan Cape, 1936; reprinted, Indianapolis: Liberty*Classics*, 1981). —Ed.]

Whatever may have been the state of affairs in the 1920s, there developed in the 1930s a strong contrast between the somewhat insular, purely Marshallian tradition of Cambridge and Oxford and the truly international synthesis of London. It is true that before the war Pigou had once reviewed one of the early books of Wicksell, and Keynes, Mises's *Theory of Money*.[19] But what Keynes once said of himself, that in German he could understand only what he knew already, seems to have been true of both men.[20] And though, of course, in Edgeworth[21] Oxford had had one of the most erudite of economists, his influence on students was small, and after his retirement and death the teaching at Oxford seems to have become as exclusively Marshallian as at Cambridge. In a literal sense Edwin Cannan, of course, also had been somewhat insular—when in his brilliant *Review of Economic Theory*,[22] the essence of the lectures he had so long given, he avails himself, as he explains, of the privilege of a reviewer to pick out what he likes, this meant in practice that he confined himself almost exclusively to English economics. But it was nevertheless a very broad base and did not have the result that only what had entered into one bible of economics was regarded as important and the reading of any other and particularly older books considered unnecessary.

The Cannan tradition, with its hard, sound common sense, its strong

---

[19][J. M. Keynes, "Review of Ludwig von Mises's *Theorie des Geldes und der Umlaufsmittel*", *Economic Journal*, vol. 24, September 1914, pp. 417–419; A. C. Pigou, "Review of Knut Wicksell's *Vorlesungen über Nationalökonomie*", *Economic Journal*, vol. 23, December 1913, pp. 605–606. Keynes's review was politely dismissive of Mises's efforts. Another book was reviewed along with that of Mises (the book was by a German economist, the now-forgotten Friedrich Bendixen), and the last two sentences of the review capture well both Keynes's assessment and tone: "Dr. von Bendixen is without the cultivated subtlety of Dr. von Mises, but his practical wisdom is of a high order. Hamburg's mind is not so clever as Vienna's, but more comes of it" (p. 419). Pigou was only slightly less penurious regarding Wicksell: "The somewhat laborious character of the exposition, coupled with the general familiarity of the ground covered, makes it unlikely that this new textbook will find many English readers—unless, an English as well as a German translation is produced" (pp. 605–606). —Ed.]

[20][Keynes's remark that "in German I can only clearly understand what I know already!" appears in his *A Treatise on Money*, vol. 5, op. cit., p. 178, n. 2. —Ed.]

[21][Francis Ysidro Edgeworth (1845–1926), Drummond Professor of Political Economy at Oxford from 1891 to 1922, was editor of the *Economic Journal* from 1890 to 1911 and co-editor with Keynes from 1919 until his death. Author of *Mathematical Psychics* (London: Kegan Paul, 1881; reprinted, New York: Kelley, 1967), he pioneered the use of mathematics and statistical inference in economics. —Ed.]

[22][Edwin Cannan, *A Review of Economic Theory* (London: King and Son, 1929; 2nd edition, 1930; reprinted, New York: Kelley, 1965). —Ed.]

interest in the institutional setting of economic life, and slight contempt for all over-refinement of economic theory—a tradition whose value as a guide in all practical problems of economic policy I have come to esteem more and more highly as I grow older, was continued at the London School of Economics mainly by Arnold Plant and Frederic Benham, both of whom had joined the staff of the school shortly before me.[23] But I myself was at first drawn mainly into the more purely theoretical discussions of which the Robbins seminar, in the conduct of which I soon joined, was the centre. Already Robbins had brought the staff of the School some exceptionally gifted young men, above all John R. Hicks and R. G. D. Allen, and raised a first crop of brilliant theorists among his own students, of whom Abba Lerner and Nicholas Kaldor are now the best known, though there were then two or three others nearly as promising.[24] And there was a continuous flow of foreign, chiefly American, visitors and students, who greatly enriched the discussion.

That seminar was a fairly big group, some thirty or forty students and often half a dozen members of the staff participating. But it still preserved an intimate character through the informal development of a sort of front bench of the older members and more active participants in the discussion, while the newer members would at first mainly listen and gradually, on the strength of the contributions, advance to the front row—or rather to that circle of students and faculty among whom the conversation mainly took place.

The topics were, during the early 1930s, mainly problems of standard neoclassical or microeconomic theory, determined largely by current publications and aiming at the synthesis of the various still-prevailing schools. Though my own preoccupation was mainly with the problems

[23][Arnold Plant (1909–1978) and Frederic Benham (1902–1962) were Professors of Commerce at the LSE. —Ed.]

[24][Sir John Hicks (1904–1989) was Drummond Professor from 1952 to 1965 and shared the 1972 Nobel prize in economics with Kenneth Arrow. Hicks is widely credited with introducing two tools of intermediate economic analysis, the indifference curve and IS-LM frameworks. British economist R. G. D. Allen (1906–1983) taught at the LSE and made important contributions to mathematical economics, statistics, and econometrics. Romanian-born Abba Lerner (1905–1982) studied at the LSE before going to the United States to teach. He is regarded, along with Oskar Lange, as a founder of the theory of market socialism. Nicholas Kaldor (1908–1986), later Lord Kaldor of Newnham, taught at the LSE and Cambridge. He started out as a follower of Hayek and translated, with H. M. Croome, Hayek's *Monetary Theory of the Trade Cycle*, op. cit. By the end of the 1930s he was a committed Keynesian and ultimately became one of the leaders of the Post-Keynesian School of Economics. —Ed.]

of money and capital, my liveliest recollections are of the discussions connected with the work of John Hicks which resulted in the Hicks-Allen article on "A Reconsideration of the Theory of Value" and later *Value and Capital*.[25] Hicks had come from Oxford to London as a good Marshallian, and I still remember clearly an early discussion when, curiously, I, the Austrian, tried to persuade Hicks of the merits of the indifference-curve approach of which he was so soon to become the acknowledged master. For some time, however, if I remember rightly, the theory of production concerned us even more than the theory of utility and the elaboration of all the attributes of the production function was long a favourite topic of the seminar. I have ever since retained a conviction that for teaching purposes it is really more expedient to begin not with utility but with the conditions of production, and especially to introduce indifference curves only after the student has become thoroughly familiar with the more tangible technique of isoquants.

There were, of course, also the first rumblings of the imperfect competition debate. Clapham's attack on the "empty boxes" of economic theory was in fresh memory, Sraffa had already raised the main problem, and even before Chamberlain and Joan Robinson burst upon us Harrod had made us familiar with the marginal-revenue curve.[26] I will admit, however, that this was an excitement which I never quite shared. I had

[25] [John R. Hicks and R. G. D. Allen, "A Reconsideration of the Theory of Value", *Economica*, N.S. vol. 1, 1934, pp. 52–76 and 196–219. John R. Hicks, *Value and Capital* (Oxford: Clarendon Press, 1939; 2nd edition, 1946). —Ed.]

[26] [John Clapham (1873–1946), Professor of Economic History at Cambridge from 1928 to 1946, was author of "Of Empty Economic Boxes", *Economic Journal*, vol. 32, September 1922, pp. 305–314. The Italian economist Piero Sraffa (1898–1983) was a member of the Cambridge Circus and a Fellow of Trinity College, 1927–83. Sraffa had translated Keynes's *A Tract on Monetary Reform* into Italian and came to Cambridge on Keynes's invitation. His paper "The Laws of Returns under Competitive Conditions", *Economic Journal*, vol. 36, 1926, pp. 535–550, criticized Marshall's theory of the firm and paved the way for the theory of imperfect competition. The Oxford economist Roy Harrod (1900–1978) studied economics for two terms in 1922–23 under Keynes at Cambridge. He took over editorship of the *Economic Journal* from Keynes in 1945 and served as co-editor with Austin Robinson until 1966. He is remembered for developing a Keynesian macroeconomic model of economic growth; see his *Towards a Dynamic Economics* (London: Macmillan, 1948). Hayek here refers to his "Notes on Supply", *Economic Journal*, vol. 40, June 1930, pp. 232–241. Edward H. Chamberlain (1899–1967), Professor at Harvard University 1927–67, based his *The Theory of Monopolistic Competition* (Cambridge, Mass.: Harvard University Press, 1933) on his 1927 dissertation written under Allyn Young. Joan Robinson (1903–1983) was a member of the Cambridge Circus and taught at Cambridge from 1931 to 1971. She was later to disavow the method of comparative statics used in her book *The Economics of Imperfect Competition* (London: Macmillan, 1933; 2nd edition, 1969). —Ed.]

never been able to swallow the assumption of a horizontal demand curve and Wieser[27] had already given us in his lectures a fairly detailed analysis of what he called monopoloid market positions, i.e., the forms intermediate between full competition and monopoly. The whole discussion seemed to me to arise so much out of the peculiar assumptions of the Marshallian system, his concept of "the industry" and the whole partial equilibrium approach, that I did not find it very profitable.

I did, however, at once get involved into a discussion with Keynes. I had, during the last couple of years at Vienna, been working on a large textbook on money, or rather on a somewhat over-dimensioned historical introduction to such a textbook—a book that never got finished because, just when I meant to resume work on it after the interruption caused by my move to London, the German publisher asked to be relieved from the contract because of Hitler's advent to power.[28] It was mainly as a result of this work that I was able to write in a few weeks—I am normally a very slow worker—the little book on *Prices and Production*[29] when I was asked to give some lectures at the London School of Economics early in 1931 and to undertake at this visit to review the newly published *Treatise on Money* for *Economica*.

Keynes, I should say, was then something of a hero to us Central Europeans. His *Economic Consequences of the Peace* had made him even more famous on the continent than in England—though Mises had shown us from the beginning that Keynes was supporting a good cause by some very bad economic argument (on international trade theory). We all read eagerly his famous contributions to the *Manchester Guardian Reconstruction Supplement* and my admiration for him was only enhanced by the fact that he anticipated in the *Tract on Monetary Reform* my first little discovery.[30] But when I first met him, at an international confer-

[27][Friedrich von Wieser (1851–1926), who with Eugen Böhm-Bawerk (1851–1914) comprised the two most prominent members of the second generation of Austrian economists. Böhm-Bawerk died before Hayek began his studies, but Wieser was his teacher at the University of Vienna. See the translation of Hayek's obituary article on Wieser in F. A. Hayek, *The Fortunes of Liberalism*, op. cit., chapter 3. —Ed.]

[28][Much of this unfinished book has now been published in English as chapters 9–12 of *The Trend of Economic Thinking*, W. W. Bartley III and Stephen Kresge, eds, being vol. 3 of *The Collected Works of F. A. Hayek*, op. cit. See note 1, p. 127 of that work for the details of Hayek's project. —Ed.]

[29][F. A. Hayek, *Prices and Production*, op. cit. —Ed.]

[30][His pieces in the *Manchester Guardian* supplements provided much of the material for Keynes's *A Tract on Monetary Reform* [1923], vol. 4 (1971) of *The Collected Writings of John Maynard Keynes*, op. cit. The discovery to which Hayek refers is the recognition that, under a system of fixed exchange rates, policy-makers must choose between stabilizing the domestic price level and the rate of exchange. —Ed.]

ence which the London and Cambridge Economic Service had called in 1929, we at once had our first theoretical clash—on some issue of the effectiveness of changes in the rate of interest. Though in such debates Keynes would at first try ruthlessly to steam-roller an objection in a manner somewhat intimidating to a younger man, if one stood up to him on such occasions he would develop a most friendly interest even if he strongly disagreed with one's views. Our personal relations in fact always remained most cordial and I owe it to his kindness that I finally spent the war years as a member of the High Table of his College at Cambridge and came to know him fairly well. During the 1920s, however, the main occasions for discussion were the meetings of the editorial board of the London and Cambridge Economic Service, on which he, with Gerald Shove and Austin Robinson,[31] represented Cambridge and where we would, four times a year, have long discussions of the current economic situation which, of course, usually turned upon questions of monetary policy.

I put then a lot of hard work into a detailed analysis of the theoretical structure of volume 1 of the *Treatise,* and Keynes replied to the first part of my review article with what was more an attack on my *Prices and Production* than a defence of his own position.[32] But, although I still believe that I succeeded in demolishing his main theoretical structure, I feel now that I did not do justice to the unsystematic but highly suggestive discussion of volume 2 from which much later development sprung and which deserves to be better known than it is now. It provided in particular the suggestion for John Hicks's article on "A Suggestion for Simplifying the Theory of Money",[33] which still seems to me, more than *The General Theory*, the most valuable result of the monetary discussions of the period.

---

[31] [Cambridge economist Gerald Shove (1888–1947) contributed to the internal-external economies debate of the late 1920s. It is Shove who supposedly said of Keynes that "Maynard had never spent the twenty minutes necessary to understand the theory of value", reported in Joan Robinson, *Economic Philosophy* (Chicago: Aldine, 1962), p. 79. Austin Robinson (1897–1993), Cambridge economist, member of Keynes's Circus and husband of Joan Robinson, served as co-editor of the *Economic Journal* and as Managing Editor of the Royal Economic Society's *The Collected Writings of John Maynard Keynes*. The London and Cambridge Economic Service provided a survey of current business conditions. —Ed.]

[32] [Hayek's review and Keynes's reply constitute chapters 3 and 4 of this volume. —Ed.]

[33] [John R. Hicks, "A Suggestion for Simplifying the Theory of Money", *Economica*, N.S. vol. 2, 1935, pp. 1–19. —Ed.]

To me the somewhat disappointing upshot of all the pains I had taken with the *Treatise* was that not long after I had published the second part of my review article it became known that Keynes had himself fundamentally altered his theoretical framework and was preparing a new and very different version. I must confess that it was partly due to this experience that when *The General Theory* appeared I did not return to the attack—out of a feeling that before one could complete a systematic examination, Keynes would probably again have changed his views. I have to the present day not quite got over a feeling that I had then shirked what should have been a plain duty. But there was also another reason than mere tiredness of controversy which made me hesitate. I did feel from the beginning, though I did not see it then as clearly as I do now, that the difference did no longer concern particular points of analysis but rather the whole method of approach—that there had been a gradual change in Keynes's whole view of the proper scope and method of theoretical analysis which went far beyond the particular issues with which he was concerned. As I saw it, an examination of the validity of *The General Theory* would have made it necessary to take issue with the whole macrodynamic approach, the treatment of the economic process in terms of aggregates and statistical totals, a theory which was concerned only with price levels and total income streams and in effect took the whole structure of relative prices for granted and provided no tools to explain changes in relative prices or their effects.[34]

The more I think about it, the more I become convinced that the crucial change of the middle 1930s was not the success of the particular theory contentions expounded in *The General Theory*. The success of this work was merely symptomatic of, or perhaps helped decisively, the displacement of what is called microeconomics by macroeconomics. It was a development for which the Marshallian tradition was more disposed than the Austrian or the Lausanne or the Jevonian or the American tradition. It is certainly more than a coincidence that *The General Theory* appeared only three years after the foundation of the Econometric Society—even Keynes had no particular sympathy with the members of that group. It would be an interesting problem to trace the intellectual development by which, for example, one of the founders of this society, Joseph Schumpeter, who in 1908 had still explicitly argued (as I still believe to be true) that magnitudes like the national income and similar aggregates had no place in the theoretical account of the

---

[34][For additional reasons why Hayek failed to review *The General Theory*, op. cit., see this volume, Introduction and part 3, *Essays on Keynes.* —Ed.]

economic process, twenty-five years later became one of the outstanding advocates of what in his youth he had regarded as a futile effort.[35]

To me it seems as if this whole effort were due to a mistaken effort to make the statistically observable magnitude the main object of theoretical explanation. But the fact that we can statistically ascertain certain magnitudes does not make them causally significant, and there seems to me no justification whatever in the widely held conviction that there must be discoverable regularities in the relation between those magnitudes on which we have statistical information. Economists seem to have come to believe that since statistics represent the only quantitative data which they can obtain, it is these statistical data which are the real facts with which they deal and that their theories must be given such a form that they explain what is statistically ascertainable. There are of course a few fields, such as the problems of the relation between the quantity of money and the price level, where we can obtain useful approximations to such simple relations—though I am still not quite persuaded that the price level is a very useful concept. But when it comes to the mechanism of change, the chain of cause and effect which we have to trace in order to be able to understand the general character of the changes to be expected, I do not see that the objectively measurable aggregates are of much help. That the concept of investment, for example, in the sense in which it is relevant to an understanding of fluctuations in production and employment, may not be an objectively ascertainable magnitude, that is, one discernible by external criteria, but something whose essential characteristic is the effect on future output expected by those who make the decision, seems to me to be fairly clear, and to concentrate on some magnitude so defined that it can be statistically measured may well make it theoretically wholly uninteresting.

But I must not allow myself to be drawn again into methodological discussion, although to me one of the main results of most of the discussions of the 1930s was to create an interest and an awareness of the methodological problems of our science which I had not had before. And it was of course not only the Keynes discussion, though much the most lively, which tended in this direction or which was then a subject of general interest. It is perhaps the most interesting aspect of the

---

[35] [Joseph Schumpeter (1883–1950), Austrian economist and author of *Das Wesen und der Hauptinhalt der theoretischen Nationalökonomie* (Leipzig: Duncker & Humblot, 1908). See F. A. Hayek, *The Fortunes of Liberalism*, op. cit., chapter 5, for Hayek's views on Schumpeter. —Ed.]

period in how many different aspects of economic theory the majority of the theoretically interested still could take an active interest and feel that they were still understanding what went on in the different fields. The foundations of the theory of welfare economics were in the latter half of the 1930s one other such subject. There went of course through the greater part of the period that running controversy on the theory of capital in which I was somewhat involved. But some of the most interesting suggestions came to me from being rather unintentionally drawn into the discussion of economic calculation under socialism—at first through a purely editorial effort of making available to the English reader the important contributions to this problem which had taken place on the continent.[36]

It was somehow in thinking through anew these problems which had much occupied us in Vienna ten or fifteen years earlier that I had suddenly the one enlightening idea which made me see the whole character of economic theory in what to me was an entirely new light, and which I tried to convey in my presidential address to the London Economic Club on "Economics and Knowledge".[37]

I do not want to become too autobiographical and explain in detail how one who then still felt that he was probably for the rest of his life committed to work in pure theory was gradually and insensibly more and more drawn into problems of the philosophy of science, of social philosophy, and the history of ideas. Another more or less accidental factor which contributed arose out of the circumstances of the time. I found myself differing very strongly in the interpretation of the political events in Germany from the view then generally current in England and particularly held by the majority of my socialistically inclined colleagues in the other departments of the London School of Economics. They all tended to interpret the National Socialist regime of Hitler as a sort of capitalist reaction to the socialist tendencies of the immediate post-war period, while I saw it rather as the victory of a sort of lower-middle-class socialism, certainly thoroughly anti-capitalistic and anti-liberal but taking over all the methods of socialism. It was in the end one of the memoranda which we occasionally did to prevent Sir William Beveridge

---

[36][Hayek refers to *Collectivist Economic Planning* (London: Routledge & Sons, 1935; reprinted, Clifton, N. J.: Kelley, 1975), which he edited and to which he contributed two essays, "The Nature and History of the Problem" and "The Present State of the Debate". —Ed.]

[37][Published in *Economica*, N.S. vol. 4, February 1937, pp. 33–54. For an explication of the significance of this paper within Hayek's larger research program, see Bruce Caldwell, "Hayek's Transformation", op. cit. —Ed.]

from committing himself publicly to a thesis which we thought wrong that I first sketched the thesis. It caused so much surprise and disbelief that I developed it further in an article published in an English monthly and then, at the suggestion of Harry Gideonse in Chicago, into a pamphlet[38] which he published in that series of Public Policy Pamphlets in which had appeared Henry Simon's *Positive Program for Laissez Faire*[39] and a number of other studies in which the post-war neo-liberalism was first outlined. How that little essay gradually grew, after I had prematurely rushed *The Pure Theory of Capital* into print in the feeling that the war would soon make any such publications impossible, into *The Road to Serfdom*, belongs already to the next decade.[40] I do not propose, however, to continue this account into a discussion of the economics of the 1940s as seen from Cambridge (where I spent at least the first half of that decade) or a discussion of the economics of the 1950s as seen from Chicago, or the economics of the 1960s as seen from Freiburg. That I might do if you ask me again in twenty years' time, though I am not sure that I was still enough of an economist during that period to qualify.[41]

[38] [F. A. Hayek, "Freedom and the Economic System", *Contemporary Review*, April 1938, enlarged as *Freedom and the Economic System* (Chicago: University of Chicago Press, 1939), Public Policy Pamphlet no. 29 in the series edited by Harry D. Gideonse. —Ed.]

[39] [Henry C. Simons (1899–1946), Professor of Economics at the University of Chicago from 1927 to 1946, argued that the proper role of government is to provide a framework in which competition can work and in which monetary disturbances are minimized. See his *Positive Program for Laissez Faire: Some Proposals for a Liberal Economic Policy* (Chicago: University of Chicago Press, 1934), Public Policy Pamphlet no. 15 in the series edited by Harry D. Gideonse. —Ed.]

[40] [F. A. Hayek, *The Pure Theory of Capital*, op. cit.; *The Road to Serfdom* (London: Routledge and Kegan Paul; Chicago: University of Chicago Press, 1944; reprinted, 1976). —Ed.]

[41] [During the 1950s and 1960s, Hayek's publications were mostly in the fields of public policy, political science, philosophy, psychology, and the history of ideas. —Ed.]

Addendum: Edwin Cannan

I[42]

With the quite sudden demise on April 8 of this year[43] of Edwin Cannan, Professor Emeritus of London University, one of the most original and most distinguished representatives of the nearly decimated great generation of economists has vanished from the scene. Cannan's rank and importance were probably never sufficiently appreciated outside his own country—or at least the English-speaking areas—as can be readily explained.[44] He was so deeply rooted in every respect in the British tradition and was at the same time so remote from all fashionable trend prevailing in his discipline during his lifetime that far more than a superficial acquaintance with a few of his works is needed to do justice to his achievements. Anyone for whom scholarly distinction lies in strikingly original formulations, abstract conceptual refinements, or speculations about the methodological basis of our field will never be able to understand why Edwin Cannan is honoured as one of the truly great and especially one of the most independent thinkers of his generation.

The fact that the 'historical school' has had such an untoward influence on the development of economic theory has unfortunately led to underestimating the importance of historical perspective and historical training for economists. Edwin Cannan was one of the few who were fortunate enough to move from history to economics without falling prey to historicism or turning their back on theory. It is true that he initially was under the decisive influence of Adolf Held's *Zwei Bücher zur sozialen Geschichte Englands*,[45] an influence that is manifest in his first great work, *History of the Theories of Production and Distribution in English Political Economy from 1776 to 1848*.[46] But he never committed the sort of distortions and blunders that led Held to explain Ricardo's theory of ground-rent as "simply dictated by moneyed capitalists' hate against landowners". Cannan

---

[42] [Translated from Hayek's obituary article, "Edwin Cannan", in *Zeitschrift für Nationalökonomie*, vol. 6, no. 2, Vienna, 1935, pp. 246–250. The translation is by Dr. Grete Heinz. —Ed.]

[43] [1935. —Ed.]

[44] [On Cannan, see also Hugh Dalton, "Professor Cannan's General Contribution", in *London Essays in Economics: In Honour of Edwin Cannan*, T. E. Gregory and Hugh Dalton, eds (London: Routledge, 1927; reprinted, Freeport, N. Y.: Books for Libraries Press, 1967), pp. 3–27; A. L. Bowley, "Obituary: Edwin Cannan", *Economic Journal*, vol. 45, June 1935, pp. 385–392; and C. R. Fay, "Edwin Cannan: The Tribute of a Friend", *Economic Record*, vol. 11, June 1937, pp. 1–21. —Ed.]

[45] [Adolf Held, *Zwei Bücher zur sozialen Geschichte Englands* [1881] (reprinted, New York: B. Franklin, 1970). A 'socialist of the chair', the youthful Held was Professor of Political Science at the University of Bonn and then briefly at the University of Berlin prior to his death in an accident. Gustav Schmoller succeeded to his chair at Berlin. —Ed.]

[46] [Edwin Cannan, *A History of the Theories of Production and Distribution in English Political Economy from 1776 to 1848* [1893], 3rd edition (London: P. S. King, 1917; reprinted, New York: Kelley, 1967). —Ed.]

64

limited himself to adopting the legitimate conclusion that classical economics could be rightly understood only if its approach to problems and its formulations were interpreted in the light of contemporary conditions rather than as infallible revelations, as had become fashionable among their orthodox disciples. Cannan's interpretation may be challenged today with respect to specific points. As was to be expected in a pioneering effort of this kind, he may well at times have gone too far in linking economic doctrines with specific historical circumstances or special interests and may consequently have failed to do justice to the theoretical validity of certain propositions. On the whole, however, this first critical history of the classical construct is even now, forty years later, by far the best analysis available and undoubtedly remains the greatest work on the history of economic doctrine to be found in English economic literature.

Although this is the work on which Cannan's international reputation rests, it is by no means his first work. Five years earlier he had published his short and extremely popular *Elementary Political Economy*.[47] As Cannan himself later reported (in the autobiographical sketch contained in the introduction to *Economic Outlook*[48]), the small book originated from his previous investigation of problems of socialism and was actually a revised version of part of a prize-winning study devoted to these problems. This short work already demonstrates many of the special characteristics of Cannan's subsequent works: a simple presentation that never loses touch with concrete reality, avoidance of all unclear or ambiguous concepts (the term 'capital' is not even mentioned in it) and above all a refreshing measure of sound common sense.

In the fall of 1895, Cannan began to give lectures at the newly founded London School of Economics and Political Science, which at that time was a completely independent institution leading to neither examinations nor degrees. The first series of lectures held there on "The History of Local Rates in England" appeared in book form the following year.[49] Cannan served as university professor from 1907—when the London School of Economics was attached to the University of London—until his reaching emeritus status in 1926. He exerted his strongest influence as a professor at this institution. Although his teaching activity was limited—he always lived in Oxford and came to London only a few days a week—and he was not gifted as a lecturer, his activity there has had a very strong impact and will continue to endure through the activity of his students who are now on its faculty.[50]

[47] [Edwin Cannan, *Elementary Political Economy* (London: Oxford University Press, 1888). —Ed.]

[48] [Edwin Cannan, *The Economic Outlook* (London: T. Fisher Unwin, 1912). —Ed.]

[49] [Edwin Cannan, *History of Local Rates in England: Five Lectures* (London and New York: Longmans, 1896). A second, enlarged edition was published as *History of Local Rates in England in Relation to the Proper Distribution of the Burden of Taxation* (London: P. S. King, 1912). —Ed.]

[50] [This essay was published in 1935. Among the many students of Cannan who later became prominent were Lionel Robbins (1898–1984) and W. H. Hutt (1899–1988). See Lionel Robbins, "A Student's Recollections of Edwin Cannan", *Economic Journal*, vol. 45,

Cannan's magisterial lecture on economic theory was basically a masterly review of its historical development, as published later in a book that we will discuss below. In the first years of his professorial activity, he still concentrated on the history of economic doctrine. The editing of Adam Smith's *Lectures on Justice, Police, Revenue, and Arms* (1896) and the critical edition of *Wealth of Nations*, prepared with unrivalled knowledge of the subject and the most painstaking care, date from this period.[51] In later years, Cannan's interest was devoted primarily to current economic questions, with which he dealt in superbly clear and generally short essays. Cannan's special talent for applying the wealth of knowledge accumulated in economic literature to current economic problems without a pretentious scholarly apparatus and in terms accessible to a wide audience are exemplified best in the two collections of these essays, which he published over the years, *The Economic Outlook*[52] and particularly *An Economist's Protest*.[53] Cannan's willingness to speak for economic good sense before a wide public was especially beneficial during the war. The shorter writings dating from this time and published in the second of the above-mentioned books are very characteristic for Cannan.

One product of Cannan's pedagogic activity was his extremely successful short textbook *Wealth*,[54] which was intended to replace his *Elementary Political Economy*. This work is not only one of the best introductions to the subject with which I am familiar but has a singular charm even for the expert in its unconventional yet not eccentric presentation. Its complement, *Money*, is a very notable contribution to monetary theory despite its popular style and has a close relationship to the views expounded by Mises on basic theoretical questions.[55] In the same year Cannan published *Paper Pound 1797–1821*, a new edition of the "Bullion Report" of 1810, with an excellent introduction intended as a contribution to the battle against inflation.[56] After Cannan's retirement there followed his

---

June 1935, pp. 393–398. —Ed.]

[51][Adam Smith, *Lectures on Justice, Police, Revenue, and Arms, delivered at the University of Edinburgh, reported by a Student*, edited, with an Introduction and Notes, by Edwin Cannan (Oxford: Clarendon, 1896); Adam Smith, *An Inquiry into the Nature and Causes of the Wealth of Nations*, edited, with an Introduction, Notes, Marginal Summary, and an Enlarged Index, by Edwin Cannan (London: Methuen, 1904; reprinted, Chicago: University of Chicago Press, 1976). —Ed.]

[52][Op. cit. —Ed.]

[53][Edwin Cannan, *An Economist's Protest* (London: P. S. King, 1927; New York: Adelphi, 1928). See Hayek's review of this work, now translated and published as part 2 of this essay. —Ed.]

[54][Edwin Cannan, *Wealth: A Brief Explanation of the Causes of Economic Welfare* (London: P. S. King, 1914). —Ed.]

[55][Edwin Cannan, *Money: Its Connection with Rising and Falling Prices* [1918], 7th edition (London: P. S. King, 1932). The views of Ludwig von Mises on monetary theory may be found in his *Theory of Money and Credit*, op. cit. —Ed.]

[56][*The Paper Pound of 1797–1821. The Bullion Report*. Edited with an introduction by Edwin Cannan. [1919] 2nd edition (London: P. S. King, 1925; reprinted, New York: Kelley, 1969). In 1797, the Bank of England had suspended payments in cash for sterling. In

great work, *Review of Economic Theory*,[57] which basically follows the order of his lectures for advanced students on the development of modern theory from its beginnings. I would like to reiterate here a few sentences that I used in a review of Cannan's book in trying to spell out the distinctive features of his approach. "The tools that Cannan uses, or, more accurately, that he assembles to fit his needs, in order to come to grips with the great problems addressed by economics, are almost exclusively 'made in England'. It is due only partially to linguistic obstacles that—as far as I can see—no author except a few of the older French writers is quoted from the original unless his works at least also appeared in English. Names like Gossen, Walras, and Pareto are completely absent in this *Review of Economic Theory*.[58] But even authors whose works appeared in English originally or who were translated into English and are generally recognized as contributors to the development of economic thought such as A. A. Cournot, F. Wieser, and J. B. Clark, are not represented.[59] In scanning the evolution of economic thought to discover the solutions offered by modern theory, Cannan limits himself almost exclusively to English contributions and even there disregards many of the most modern refinements. What is strange and thought-provoking about this procedure is the fact that it produces no shortcomings of any kind and that it does not make Cannan's work seem unduly conservative or even obsolete. The final conclusions that he reaches, on the contrary, are so distinctive—without ever becoming eccentric—and seem to flow so naturally and inevitably from the development presented in the book that one is almost tempted to believe that vast amounts of refinements applauded by the experts in the discipline were merely superfluous mental gymnastics. Cannan himself would probably be the last to make this claim. But he has a way of sifting through the conceptual confusion offered by the history of economics and

---

1810, after Ricardo suggested that the rise in the value of gold indicated an overissue of banknotes, the House of Commons appointed a committee to investigate. The authors of the landmark report, Henry Thornton, Francis Horner, and William Huskisson, found that the overissue of banknotes was, in fact, responsible for the rise in the value of bullion and recommended a resumption of convertibility. See Hayek's discussion of these matters in F. A. Hayek, *The Trend of Economic Thinking*, op. cit., chapters 9–14. —Ed.]

[57][Edwin Cannan, *A Review of Economic Theory*, op. cit. —Ed.]

[58][On Hermann Heinrich Gossen (1810–1858), see the translation of Hayek's introduction to the third German edition of his *Entwicklung der Gesetze des menschlichen Verkehrs und der daraus fliessenden Regeln für menschliches Handeln* (Berlin: R. L. Prager, 1927), pp. ix–xxiii, found in F. A. Hayek, *The Trend of Economic Thinking*, pp. 352–371. For more on Walras and Pareto, see this volume, chapter 1, n. 4. —Ed.]

[59][Antoine Augustin Cournot (1801–1876), French economist, was the author of *Recherches sur les Principes Mathématiques de la Théorie des Richesses* (Paris: Hachette, 1838), translated as *Researches into the Mathematical Principles of the Theory of Wealth* (New York: Macmillan, 1927; reprinted, New York: Kelley, 1971). John Bates Clark (1847–1938) taught economics at Columbia University from 1895 to 1923. His works include *The Distribution of Wealth* (New York: Macmillan, 1899; reprinted, New York: Kelley, 1965), in which he developed a marginal productivity analysis of distribution. See this volume, chapter 1, note 25 for more on Wieser. —Ed.]

coming up with solutions that seem to be derived solely from sound common sense. What matters to him are neither theories nor systems but only more or less successful answers to the problems presented directly by reality, an approach that may incline students to be unduly contemptuous of any other sort of theory. It is this refusal to be burdened down by conventional methodological and systematic considerations, coupled in Cannan's case with a fanatical conceptual clarity, that marks this work as thoroughly British, aside from the facts already mentioned earlier. It is totally different from anything published in the scholarly literature of other countries and particularly Germany."[60]

Cannan's literary activity continued unabated even after the publication of this second magnum opus. Two small volumes, *Modern Currency and the Regulation of Its Value* and *Economic Scares*, were published in 1931 and 1933 respectively.[61] In his last three years Cannan still gave three brilliant lectures at the annual meetings of the Royal Economic Society, to which he was elected president for the second time, demonstrating his indestructible mental vigour.[62] The title of the second of these lectures, "The Need for Simpler Economics", epitomizes one of the guidelines of Cannan's lifelong scholarly endeavours. He was primarily interested in the effectiveness and applicability of economics in the furtherance of human welfare, and for this the most urgent task was to make it comprehensible. No contemporary economist devoted himself more singlemindedly and more successfully to this objective. In the light of this objective, he considered no problem as solved unless the solution had penetrated general consciousness. He never felt it to be below his dignity to clarify elementary verities over and over again and in new forms. There may be differences of opinion about Cannan's standing as a great theorist in the ordinary sense of the word. Quite possibly no definite contribution to our theoretical knowledge will be connected with his name and future generations will remember him above all as a historian of economic theory. But he had gifts that are rarer than that of advancing theory in some specific domain: He was better able to assimilate the outcome of the mental efforts of previous generations than almost any other economist and applied the theoretical apparatus most successfully to shed light on the economic problems of our time. If we had more economists of Cannan's sort, economics would enjoy far greater respect and influence than is the case today. With his passing, not only have economists lost one of their most venerable and

---

[60]F. A. Hayek, "Review of Edwin Cannan: *A Review of Economic Theory*", *Archiv für Sozialwissenschaften*, vol. 63, 1930, pp. 199–203.

[61][Edwin Cannan, *Modern Currency and the Regulation of Its Value* (London: P. S. King, 1931); *Economic Scares* (London: P. S. King, 1933). —Ed.]

[62][Cannan addressed the forty-second annual meeting of the Royal Economic Society as President-Elect on May 26, 1932; the address, "The Demand for Labour", appears in *Economic Journal*, vol. 42, September 1932, pp. 357–370. His address to the forty-third annual meeting, as President, on "The Need for Simpler Economics", appears in *Economic Journal*, vol. 43, September 1933, pp. 367–378. On April 20, 1934, he addressed the annual meeting of the society, again as President, on "The Future of Gold in Relation to Demand", which appears in *Economic Journal*, vol. 44, June 1934, pp. 177–187. —Ed.]

delightful teachers, but the world has been deprived of one of the most forceful and successful combatants against economic obfuscations.

II[63]

The economist Edwin Cannan at the London School of Economics, mainly known to German readers only through his *History of the Theories of Production and Distribution*,[64] a book that appeared many years ago, has—in the present collection of some eighty smaller essays, memoranda, and letters from the years 1914 to 1926—produced an uncommonly stimulating book. The effect created by these writings, every one of them reprinted completely unchanged, is of an economist's marginal glosses on the economic policy of that period. They show as do few other documents how far economic policy in all countries departed from what economic reason would have called for. They also show what an endlessly fertile field of activity would lie open to men as knowledgeable as they are courageous, were it not that they still remain, amidst the multitude of economists, rare and solitary birds whose cries fade away everywhere unheard. Seldom, however, have clear-sighted economists been more condemned to ineffectualness than in that calamitous decade in which the writings of Cannan that are collected here originate.

Still, the authority accorded these economists in England was higher than, for instance, in Germany or Austria. And to this circumstance may well be due the fact that in England, to the very end, there were a few like J. S. Nicholson[65] and Cannan himself who did not permit themselves to become discouraged and who exploited every opportunity to point out again and again, in public and to those in positions of authority, the absurdity of the economic policy being pursued. To be sure, they also had an easier time of it not only because the censorship was evidently less strict, but above all because in England far more attention was paid to economic problems during the war, and incomparably more material produced by inquiries and official investigations was available than on the continent. Yet Cannan, too, is able to tell of rejections and the unfriendly reception of articles in the explanatory remarks with which he precedes each piece. Even mockery and pointed attacks do not seem to have been lacking.

The present collection is made so especially appealing by the fact that in the efforts it assembles to help economic reason to victory, Cannan shows himself to be not only both a rare master of his discipline and of linguistic expression, but at the same time an uncommonly vigorous and amiable personality. Moreover, the changing form of exposition—papers for scientific journals and

---

[63][This section was first published by Hayek as a review of Edwin Cannan, *An Economist's Protest*, op. cit., in *Zeitschrift für Nationalökonomie*, vol. 1, no. 3, November 15, 1929, pp. 467–470. Translation by Ralph Raico. —Ed.]

[64][Op. cit. —Ed.]

[65][Joseph Shield Nicholson (1850–1927) held the Chair of Political Economy at the University of Edinburgh from 1880–1925. Among his books are *War Finance* (London: P. S. King, 1917) and *Inflation* (London: P. S. King, 1919). —Ed.]

private letters, popular presentations and memoranda to official authorities and a vast number of detailed book reviews, as well as the variegated succession of the different subjects following from the chronological arrangement—make for quite diversified reading. This is not altered by the fact that, as Cannan himself notes in the Foreword,[66] underlying all of the different writings are two basic ideas: the fight against economic nationalism and the fight against all those pernicious expedients, particularly in the area of monetary policy, which, in spite of all the warnings of science, statesmen again and again resort to in every predicament, and more than ever in a great crisis such as war. These basic ideas, and even more so certain details of his theoretical standpoint, especially in the area of monetary theory, as well as certain details of population theory, establish a kinship with the similar crusade which Ludwig von Mises led in the German-speaking world. To be sure, it must be added at once that Cannan by no means develops economic liberalism to its ultimate consequences with the same ruthless consistency as Mises.[67]

Already the first two essays, dating from the prewar months of 1914, deal with problems that acquired yet far greater significance on account of the war and the circumstances of the years that followed. Indeed, the first, on the international economic solidarity of the labour force, even examines the effects that a large war indemnity would necessarily exert on the situation of the working classes of the countries involved; while the second, in the course of reviewing the report of an investigating commission, lays bare all the weaknesses inherent in the usual position of 'social interventionists'[68] towards the 'housing problem'. The first wartime article, taking the slogan "Business as usual", already strikes a note that recurs over and over in Cannan's writings of the war years and continues to play a large role in the later discussions of monetary policy: The emphatic advice on the unavoidability of curtailing all other consumption if the means to wage war are to be found.

The particular measures and catchwords of economic policy in the following years gave Cannan rich opportunity to return critically again and again to his position in this matter and to oppose price controls and the rest of the allocational regulations and various measures in financial policy. Side by side to this runs a fervent effort at enlightenment, directed as much against the widespread explanation of the war as due to petty commercial jealousies as against the lunacy being propagated at the time of an economic war as an unrestricted continuation of military warfare. In Cannan's hands, the free trade arguments acquire fresh force as he throws into relief the exclusively military significance of the economic autarchy at which every protectionist system aims. In the essays from 1925 and 1926, Cannan touches further on various problems in

---

[66] *An Economist's Protest*, op. cit., p. v.

[67] [Hayek may have in mind Ludwig von Mises, *Liberalismus* [1927], translated by Ralph Raico as *The Free and Prosperous Commonwealth* (Princeton, N. J.: D. Van Nostrand, 1962). A third edition was issued under the new title *Liberalism: In the Classical Tradition* (Irvington-on-Hudson, N. Y.: Foundation for Economic Education, 1985). —Ed.]

[68] [*Sozialpolitiker.* —Tr.]

population theory which, as is well known, gained from him important suggestions that were later developed further by his student Lionel Robbins.[69] Various crackpot reform programmes, which prove that even in England and America a familiarity with the basic concepts of theoretical economics cannot always be presumed even among professors of this science, also provide Cannan with an opportunity to take up the basic problems of our science once more and draw from him for once the despairing groan: "Have Jevons and the Austrians written in vain?"[70]

In 1917, Cannan opened the "Campaign against Inflation", which was to claim most of his effort for the next three years. As he recalls, until then only J. S. Nicholson had, already in the first year of the war, expressed concern about the matter. Cannan, who unreservedly acknowledges the noted monetary theorist of the British Treasury as "one of the ablest and most learned of our monetary experts"[71], says of himself, with excessive modesty, "I am not a monetary expert"[72]. Yet during the war and postwar years, he not only demonstrated a greater understanding of England's situation in regard to monetary policy than probably any other English economist, but also contributed more to spreading this understanding. Apart from his excellent little book *Money, Its Connection with Rising and Falling Prices (1918)*[73] and his new edition of the *Bullion Report*[74] (*The Paper Pound of 1797 to 1821*), which he furnished with a highly instructive introduction, Cannan then attempted in every possible way to call attention to the fact and the dangers of accelerating inflation. We might single out merely his amusing attempt to bring charges against the Chancellor of the Exchequer for profiteering on the grounds that he was selling for a pound a commodity whose production cost him less than a penny, namely the one-pound note itself—thus making a profit of at least 23,900 per cent.[75] His most scientifically valuable arguments concern the relation of loans and taxation and his repeated advocacy of a restriction on the quantity of money, as against the demand of Keynes and Hawtrey[76] for a restriction on the volume of credit. This of course is closely connected with another of Cannan's doctrines, one for which he will

---

[69] [See, for example, Lionel Robbins, "The Optimum Theory of Population", in *London Essays in Economics: In Honour of Edwin Cannan*, op. cit., pp. 103–134. See this chapter, note 15, for more on Robbins. —Ed.]

[70] *An Economist's Protest*, op. cit., p. 39.

[71] *Ibid.*, p. 205.

[72] *Ibid.*, p. 109.

[73] [Op. cit. —Ed.]

[74] [Op. cit. —Ed.]

[75] *Ibid.*, p. 196.

[76] [Ralph George Hawtrey (1879-1975) received little formal training in economics, picking it up instead while serving with the Treasury: He is the "noted monetary theorist of the British Treasury" alluded to in note 70 of this chapter. Among his works is *Currency and Credit* [1919], 4th edition (London: Longmans, 1950) and *Trade Depression and the Way Out* (London: Longmans, 1933). See this volume, chapter 4, note 23 for more on Hawtrey. Hawtrey and Keynes, respectively, called for focusing on credit rather than on the quantity of money in *Currency and Credit*, op. cit., p. 52, and in *A Tract on Monetary Reform*, op. cit., p. 146. —Ed.]

hardly find many supporters among theoreticians and on which he is quite definitely wrong, his denial of the possibility that banks "create" credit. Cannan's bitter struggle against this latter theory is all the less comprehensible, since it goes without saying that he must concede the essential facts of the matter and is only taking issue with their interpretation or, actually, merely with the term applied to them. However, even this position of the distinguished scholar—albeit in itself hardly understandable—may have done some good against certain exaggerated views current even in England on the possibilities that were open to the banks.

From 1921 on, deflation naturally becomes the main theme of the essays. Here Cannan shows himself to be a convinced supporter of deflationary policy, which is surely, if I am not mistaken, what chiefly earned him Keynes's reproach that he is "unsympathetic with nearly everything worth reading" that has been written on monetary theory during the last ten years.[77] Cannan took this reproach as the occasion for a highly instructive essay on "Recent Improvements in Monetary Theory". There is in addition a series of essays from recent years on the reparations problem and, particularly, on the doctrine of the balance of trade as the measure of a people's ability to pay, an idea that, as he himself says, affects him as a red flag does a bull.[78] Postwar protectionism also offered him renewed occasion to emphasize with great severity the position that he had already taken during the war against propaganda for economic warfare. Of the purely theoretical papers from this period we may point out his very detailed review of Henderson's *Supply and Demand*.[79] Especially recommended for German readers is the article on "Knapp's Bubble", a review of the English translation of G. F. Knapp's *Staatliche Theorie des Geldes*.[80] This book was issued in 1924 by the Royal Economic Society, as Cannan tells us, from the notion, among other reasons, that the best way to destroy the influence of a bad German book is to translate it into good English. The volume closes with a stimulating memorial lecture which Cannan gave in 1926 on the occasion of the one-hundred-and-fiftieth anniversary of *The Wealth of Nations*.

This sizable yet never wearying volume will draw from most readers the lament: If only we had had in recent years many more economists as able and

---

[77][Keynes's reproach may be found in "A Comment on Professor Cannan's Article", *Economic Journal*, vol. 34, March 1924, p. 68. —Ed.]

[78]*An Economist's Protest*, op. cit., p. 351.

[79][Hubert D. Henderson (1890–1952) lectured on economics at Cambridge, served as editor from 1923 to 1930 of the weekly *Nation and Athenaeum*, and later taught at Oxford, where he was Drummond Professor of Political Economy from 1945 to 1951. His introductory textbook *Supply and Demand* (New York: Harcourt Brace, 1922; revised ed., New York and London: Pitman, 1948) carried an introduction by Keynes and was very popular in England in the interwar period. —Ed.].

[80][Georg F. Knapp (1842–1926), German professor and co-founder of the *Verein für Sozialpolitik*, author of *Staatliche Theorie des Geldes* [1905], 4th edition (Munich and Leipzig: Duncker and Humblot, 1923), translated as *The State Theory of Money* (London: Macmillan, 1924). —Ed.]

willing to protest as was Cannan! If however the past is no longer to be changed, nor have the last two decades added any particular credit to the influence of economists, nonetheless just such a book as this can contribute much to showing new generations of learned economists what they are capable of accomplishing for the common good. It would be excellently suited for use as a textbook or reader for the economist who wants to learn how to make the results of his science generally useful.

TWO

THE "PARADOX" OF SAVING[1]

I

The assertion that saving renders the purchasing power of the consumer insufficient to take up the volume of current production, although made more often by members of the lay public than by professional economists, is almost as old as the science of political economy itself. The question of the utility of 'unproductive' expenditure was first raised by the Mercantilists, who were thinking chiefly of luxury expenditure.[2] The idea recurs in those writings of Lauderdale

---

[1]The following article is a translation of an essay by Dr. Hayek, which has already appeared in the *Zeitschrift für Nationalökonomie*, vol. 1, no. 3, under the title, "Gibt es einen 'Widersinn des Sparens?'" In view of the great contemporary interest in the subject it deals with and its high degree of relevance to current discussions of monetary theory here and in America, it has been thought desirable to render it available for English-speaking readers. [Published as "The 'Paradox' of Saving", *Economica*, vol. 11, May 1931, pp. 125–169. —Ed.]

The translation is the work of Mr. Nicholas Kaldor and Dr. Georg Tugendhat. Certain minor alterations have been made in the text and a few passages incidental to the main discussion have been omitted and some further explanations added by the author. [For more on Kaldor, see this volume, chapter 1, note 23. —Ed.]

[2][The English Mercantilists were merchants and businessmen who wrote scores of pamphlets and monographs on economic policy during the seventeenth and eighteenth centuries. Mercantilists viewed bullion as wealth, and a favourable balance of trade (attained through the use of various governmental restraints) as the chief means for securing the surplus. It was against the "Commercial or Mercantile System" of Europe that Book 4 of Adam Smith's *The Wealth of Nations*, op. cit., was directed. Their doctrines long considered fallacious, certain of the Mercantilist beliefs were rehabilitated by Keynes in his "Notes on Mercantilism", chapter 23 of *The General Theory of Employment, Interest and Money*, op. cit., pp. 333–371.

Hayek refers here to those Mercantilists who argued that certain 'unproductive expenditures' (for example, spending on luxury goods, expenditures which, as their name suggests, were considered morally repugnant) might serve the positive purpose of taking an excess of goods off the market, thereby avoiding a 'general glut' or economic downturn. Though this was not a central concern of the Mercantilists, it can be found in the writings of Mandeville, among others. See Donald Walker, "Keynes as an Historian of Economic Thought: The Perspectives of the *General Theory*", *Research in the History of Economic*

and Malthus which gave rise to the celebrated *Théorie des Débouches* of James Mill and J. B. Say, and, in spite of many attempts to refute it, permeates the main doctrines of socialist economics right up to Tugan-Baranovsky, Thorstein Veblen, and J. A. Hobson.[3] But while in this way the idea has found a greater popularity in quasi-scientific and propagandist literature than perhaps any other economic doctrine hitherto, fortunately it has not succeeded as yet in depriving saving of its general respectability, and we have yet to learn that any of the numerous monetary measures intended to counteract its supposedly harmful effects have been put into practice. On the contrary, we have recently witnessed the edifying spectacle of a 'World Savings Day', on which central bank governors and ministers of finance vied with each other in attempting to disseminate the virtue of saving as widely as possible throughout their respective nations. And even though there are those who demand an increase in the currency on the grounds that there is an increased tendency to save, it is hard to believe that the presidents of central banks at any rate will prove very ready listeners.

This state of affairs, however, may yet be endangered by a new theory of underconsumption now current in the United States and in England. Its authors are people who spare neither money nor time in the

---

Thought and Methodology, vol. 4, 1986, pp. 18–19. —Ed.]

[3][James Maitland, eighth earl of Lauderdale (1759–1839), author of *An Inquiry into the Nature and Origin of Public Wealth* [1804] (New York: Kelley, 1962), and Thomas Robert Malthus (1766–1834), author of *Principles of Political Economy* [1820], 2nd edition (London: Pickering, 1836; reprinted, New York: Kelley, 1964), both raised in their works 'over-savings' or 'under-consumptionist' theses that posited excessive savings as a principal cause of downturns in the trade cycle. James Mill (1773–1836) in his *Commerce Defended* (London: C. & R. Baldwin, 1808; reprinted, New York: Kelley, 1965) and Jean Baptiste Say (1776–1832), who in his "Théorie des Débouches" [Theory of Markets], contained in his book *Traité d'Economie Politique* [1803], translated as *A Treatise on Political Economy* (Philadelphia: Claxton, Remsen & Haffelfinger; reprinted, New York: Kelley, 1971), denied the possibility of a general overproduction of goods. Their counterargument has ever since been known as 'Say's Law'. Hayek also mentions Mikhail Tugan-Baranovsky (1865–1919), a Russian economist who in his master's thesis on industrial crises in Britain criticized Say's Law and offered a new underconsumptionist model; Thorstein Veblen (1857–1929), American institutionalist, iconoclast, and author of *The Theory of the Leisure Class* (New York: Macmillan, 1899; New York: Viking, 1967) and *The Theory of the Business Enterprise* (New York: Scribner's, 1904; reprinted, New York: Kelley, 1965), whose elaborate, rich and rambling discourses on all aspects of society make impossible any brief characterization of his work (for example, though Veblen was a lifelong proponent of free trade, Hobson considered him a socialist); and John A. Hobson (1858–1940), who advanced his own over-savings thesis in his book with A. F. Mummery, *The Physiology of Industry: Being an Exposure of Certain Fallacies in Existing Theories of Economics* [1889] (New York: Kelley and Millman, 1956). Both Malthus and Hobson are praised by Keynes in his "Notes on Mercantilism", op. cit., pp. 362–370. —Ed.]

propagation of their ideas. Their doctrine is no less fallacious than all the previous theories of underconsumption, but it is not impossible that with able exposition and extensive financial backing it may exert a certain influence on policy in Anglo-Saxon countries. For this reason it seems worthwhile subjecting this theory to detailed and exhaustive criticism.

II

The teachings of Messrs Foster and Catchings,[4] with which I am primarily concerned in this study, attained their widest circulation in the United States where they have achieved considerable repute not only among members of the public, but also among professional economists. To understand this success it is necessary to know something of the background of the theory and the very able means by which it has been and still is being propagated. Quite apart from its analytical significance, for European observers at any rate the story has a certain spectacular interest. I propose, therefore, to deal with it at some length.

Let us start with the two authors. The history of their joint careers provides certain points which give a clue to the origin of their teaching. Waddill Catchings was born in the South; he had a successful career as a lawyer and banker, finally reaching a high position in the iron and steel industry. In 1920 he, and a number of fellow students from Harvard, decided to commemorate a deceased friend. For this purpose they founded the "Pollak Foundation for Economic Research". They appointed as director another Harvard friend, William Trufant Foster, a pedagogue, at one time a college president. The Foundation had an annual income of $25,000 and it soon began to be responsible for the publication of important books on economic subjects, some of them by well-known economists, such as Irving Fisher's *Making of Index-Numbers*,[5] others by members of the Foundation, such as H. B. Hasting's *Costs and*

---

[4][Waddill Catchings (1879–1967) was the founder and William Trufant Foster (1879–1950) the director of the Pollak Foundation for Economic Research, an organization which published a number of monographs on economic issues during the 1920s. —Ed.]

[5]Irving Fisher, *The Making of Index Numbers* (Boston: Houghton Mifflin, 1922; reprint of 3rd revised edition, New York: Kelley, 1967). [The American economist Irving Fisher (1867–1947) also made contributions in monetary theory and in the theory of interest and was a founding member and first president of the Econometric Society. —Ed.]

Profits,[6] and, above all, *Money* by Messrs Foster and Catchings themselves.[7] In this latter work, although it is primarily a very able and instructive exposition of the theory of money, the authors laid the basis of their theory of trade depression later to be fully expounded in their work on *Profits*.[8] In *Money*, they emphasise especially those parts dealing with the circulation of money and the effects on markets of changes in the rate of flow. After describing how circulation starts from the market for consumption goods, from which it passes into the market for production goods, and finally returns to its original source, they discuss the conditions under which this process creates a steady demand for the goods offered for sale, and the factors which influence the circulation of money either by accelerating or retarding it. While, in a barter economy, supply and demand are necessarily identical, the appearance of money is shown to be capable of disturbing this equilibrium, since it is only possible to maintain production at the existing level if the producers spend money at the same rate as that at which they receive it. Thus the circulation of money between the various stages of the economic process becomes the central problem of all investigation, not only of changes in the value of money, but also of the influences affecting cyclical fluctuations.

Indeed they even go so far as to lay it down that: "Money spent in the consumption of commodities is the force that moves all the wheels of industry. When this force remains in the right relation to the volume of commodities offered for sale, business proceeds steadily. When money is spent faster than the commodities reach the retail markets, business booms forward. When commodities continue to reach the retail markets faster than money is spent, business slackens. To move commodities year after year without disturbing business, enough money must be spent by consumers, and no more than enough, to match all the commodities, dollar for dollar."[9]

It is this theory which forms the basis of the trade cycle theory, which is set forth in great detail in *Profits*, published three years later. In this voluminous work, with which we shall be concerned in the next sections,

[6]Hudson Bridge Hastings, *Costs and Profits*, Publications of the Pollak Foundation for Economic Research, No. 3 (Boston: Houghton Mifflin, 1923). [Hastings was a Professor-Elect of Administrative Engineering at Yale when he published this book. —Ed.]

[7]W. T. Foster and W. Catchings, *Money*, Publications of the Pollak Foundation for Economic Research, No. 2 [1923], 3rd edition (Boston and New York: Houghton Mifflin, 1928).

[8]W. T. Foster and W. Catchings, *Profits*, Publications of the Pollak Foundation, No. 8 (Boston and New York: Houghton Mifflin, 1925).

[9]*Money*, op. cit., p. 277.

Messrs Foster and Catchings give the most elaborate and careful exposition of their theory. But, despite the clear and entertaining exposition, it failed to secure for the theory the wide circulation desired by its authors. They proceeded, therefore, to restate the main principles in popular language, first in their *Business without a Buyer*,[10] and later in abridged form in an essay in the *Atlantic Monthly*, which was distributed freely as a reprint in hundreds of thousands of copies.[11] Most effective, however, in advertising their ideas was the peculiar competition held in connection with the publication of *Profits*. By offering a prize of $5,000 for the best adverse criticism of the theory contained in this work, the promoters invited the whole world to refute them. But before dealing with the results of this competition it is necessary to consider the general principles of their work.

III

The theory of crises advanced by Messrs Foster and Catchings in *Profits* is preceded by a detailed explanation of the organization of the present economic structure. This justification of the existing "Money and Profit System", as it is called by the authors, fills about one-half of the volume of four hundred pages. For our purpose, it is sufficient to mention that in this part the function of entrepreneur's profit as a factor determining the direction and extent of production is investigated; but it is worth remarking even at this juncture that the authors succeed in completing this investigation without at any point making clear the real function of capital as a factor of production. Our main concern in this article, however, is confined to the fifth and last part of *Profits* which deals with "Money and Profits in Relation to Consumption", and which, according to the authors themselves, represents a

[10]W. T. Foster and W. Catchings, *Business without a Buyer*, Publications of the Pollak Foundation for Economic Research, no. 10 [1923], 2nd revised edition (Boston and New York: Houghton Mifflin, 1928).

[11]W. T. Foster and W. Catchings, *The Dilemma of Thrift* (Newton, Mass.: Pollak Foundation, 1926). Reprinted from *The Atlantic Monthly* (vol. 137, no. 4, April 1926, pp. 533–543), together with another article published in the *Century* magazine, July 1928 ["Progress and Plenty: A Way Out of the Dilemma of Thrift", *Century Magazine*, vol. 116, no. 3, July 1928, pp. 257–268. —Ed.]. Copies of the pamphlet were supplied by the Pollak Foundation free on request. A German translation also appeared in the *Finanzpolitischer Korrespondenz*, copies of which could also be obtained free on request.

more or less independent object for critical study.[12] It will be necessary in this connection also to refer in some detail to the short essay entitled "The Dilemma of Thrift".

The main thesis of the book is stated as follows: "The one thing that is needed above all others to sustain a forward movement of business is enough money in the hands of consumers".[13] Now in the present state of affairs a situation arises from time to time when the buying power in the hands of the consumers is insufficient to purchase the whole industrial output at prices which cover costs. The consequent diminution in sales in the market for consumption goods results in unemployment of factories and plants, that is to say, in crises and trade depressions. The question is: Where does the deficit in the consumers' income originate? The earlier exposition in *Money* and *Profits* affords no explanation of this phenomenon, since it does not take into account the three principal factors upon which the velocity of circulation, and therefore the "annual production-consumption equation" depend: i.e., the influence of saving, of profits, and of changes in the volume of currency. The most important of these factors is saving, both individual and corporate. To elucidate this point the authors proceed to examine a series of numerical examples and, in the course of this examination, they introduce a number of fictitious assumptions, which, as we shall see later, have an important bearing upon their conclusions. They assume, namely, that by a process of vertical and horizontal integration, the whole industry of the isolated country considered has been united into one single enterprise, payments from which in the form of wages, dividends, and salaries form the only source of the community's income. (There are no taxes or government expenditure of any kind.) It is assumed further that the price level, the volume of currency, and the velocity of circulation remain constant, and that wages are received and spent during the same economic period in which the goods are manufactured, while these goods are only sold in the following period, and the profits earned on them are also distributed and spent by the recipients during this same period.[14]

With the aid of numerical examples of this sort, the authors demonstrate that, under these conditions, there can be no difficulty in selling the goods manufactured, either in the case of a constant volume of production or of a rising volume per wage-unit, so long as "industry

[12]*Pollak Prize Essays: Criticisms of "Profits"*, W. T. Foster and W. Catchings, eds (Newton, Mass.: Pollak Foundation, 1927).

[13]*Ibid.*, p. 11.

[14]*Profits*, op. cit., p. 268.

continues to return to consumers in some way all the money that it took from consumers in the sales price of its product, and as long as consumers spend all that they receive".[15] But as soon as the company retains part of the profits in the business, not for the purpose of carrying larger stocks, financing the sale of an increased product, or in *unsuccessful* attempts to improve equipment—for these things are comparatively harmless—but in order to improve "capital facilities", which puts it in the position to increase the volume of production, this happy state of affairs changes. As soon as the increased volume of products reaches the market, it is inevitable that the means of payment in the hands of the consumer should prove insufficient to take up the product at remunerative prices. So long as the process of investment is going on no difficulty arises, since the rise in the total wage bill resulting from the increased number of workmen necessary to carry out the extension equals the loss in the shareholders' income resulting from the reduction in dividends, and thus the relation between the volume of production and the money spent on it remains unaltered. The crisis sets in with the appearance on the market of the surplus output. The money in the hands of the consumer does not increase any further (the sums necessary for the extension of production having already been spent by the wage-earners in the previous period to take up the smaller volume) and, since it is assumed that there is no fall in prices, a proportion of the enlarged product must therefore remain unsold.

In *The Dilemma of Thrift*, Messrs Foster and Catchings provide the following description of the events leading up to this crisis: "Suppose, however, it [the corporation] uses the remaining one million dollars of profits to build additional cars, in such a way that all this money goes directly or indirectly to consumers. The company has now disbursed exactly enough money to cover the full sales-price of the cars it has already marketed; but where are the consumers to obtain enough money to buy the additional cars? The corporation has given them nothing with which to buy these cars".[16] The new cars, therefore, must remain unsold, "unless the deficiency [in consumers' income] is made up from outside sources".[17]

According to Messrs Foster and Catchings the significant difference between the money spent upon consumption goods and money invested

---

[15]*Ibid.*, p. 273.

[16]*Dilemma of Thrift*, op. cit., p. 15.

[17]*Profits*, op. cit., p. 281, where the following remark is appended to that qualification: "We here make that qualification, once and for all, with respect to every case in this and the following chapters", which later gave the authors' critics an opportunity to accuse them (*Prize Essays*, op. cit., p. 12) of a misunderstanding of the main point of their argument.

rests upon the fact that money of the former kind is "used *first* to take away consumers' goods, whereas in many cases money invested is used *first* to produce more consumers' goods".[18] "Money that is once used to bring about the production of goods is again used to bring about the production of goods, before it is used to bring about the consumption of goods. In other words, it is used twice in succession to create supply; whereas if the $100,000 in question, instead of having been *invested* in the production of additional goods, had been paid out as dividends and *spent* by the recipients, the $100,000 would have been used alternately to bring goods to the markets and to take goods off the markets".[19] Statements of this sort, which are repeatedly used by the authors, have led even so acute a thinker as Mr. D. H. Robertson to remark that he could not attach any sense to them whatever.[20] It therefore seems worthwhile attempting to restate this part of the theory in more familiar language. Granting the initial presuppositions of the authors it is, I think, unassailable. So long as the total disbursements during the course of production are spent on consumption goods, the expenses of production are necessarily equal to the proceeds of the sale of the goods purchased. If, however, certain amounts, such as interest earned on capital, or profit, which could be spent on consumption goods without reducing the existing capital stock, are applied to purchasing additional means of production, the sum total spent on production rises without being accompanied by an equivalent increase in the sums available to buy the final product. It is in this 'short-circuit' in the circulation of money, as Mr. P. W. Martin,[21] whose ideas are closely related to those of Messrs Foster and Catchings, describes it, that we find the alleged cause of the deficiency in the buying power of the consumer.

Now since the results of corporate saving and of individual saving must be alike, since individuals as well as corporations must save if they are to progress, but since, if this theory is correct, they cannot save at present without frustrating to a certain extent the social purpose

[18]*Profits*, op. cit., p. 284.

[19]*Profits*, op. cit., p. 279.

[20]D. H. Robertson, "The Monetary Doctrines of Messrs Foster and Catchings", *Quarterly Journal of Economics*, vol. 43, May 1929, pp. 473–499. [Dennis Robertson (1890–1963) was a British economist who worked closely with Keynes (both wrote books on monetary theory in the 1920s), but split with his friend over *The General Theory* in the 1930s. —Ed.]

[21]P. W. Martin, *The Flaw in the Price System* (London: P. S. King, 1924); *The Limited Market* (London: Allen and Unwin, 1926), and *Unemployment and Purchasing Power* (London: P. S. King, 1929). [Percival W. Martin (1893–1972) was a British civil servant and author of four books and several articles on macroeconomic theory and policy. —Ed.]

of saving, the "dilemma of thrift" is unescapable. "From the stand-point of society, therefore, it is impossible to save intelligently without first solving the problem of adequate consumer income. As it is today, certain individuals can save at the expense of other corpora-tions; and, from the standpoint of the individual and of the corpora-tion, these savings are real. But society as a whole cannot save any-thing worth saving at the expense of consumers as a whole, for the capacity of consumers to benefit by what is saved is the sole test of its worth".[22]

After the main thesis of the theory has thus been expounded the authors drop a number of artificial assumptions, and attempt to bring the theory nearer to reality. The first assumption to be abandoned is that of a stable price-level (this assumption, by the way, was never consistent with their other assumptions). They then examine the effects of falling prices, which alone make it possible to sell the whole of the enlarged product. But falling prices, they argue, make it impossible for industry to maintain production at the new level. The fall of prices causes profits to disappear, and with profits every incentive to the continuation of production.[23] Moreover, it is argued, it is a matter of experience that falling prices render an extension of production impossible. "If there is any fact concerning which our statistical evidence fully supports our reasoning, it is the fact that falling prices put a damper on productive activity".[24] Only on paper is it possible, in spite of falling prices, to carry out productive extensions by means of falling costs, because only on paper can you regulate the diminution of cost so that even the enlarged product can be sold with sufficient profits. In the existing economic system, with the many independent units composing it, such a development is not to be expected. On the contrary, we should rather expect price movements in the wrong direction. A fall in the price of consumption goods, therefore, must always bring about a diminution of production.[25]

Having thus attempted to show that a general fall in prices can never bring about a solution of the problem, the authors next proceed to consider *changes in the volume of money*. After all that has been said, it is argued, it should be clear that even changes in the volume of money can only solve the problem in so far as they influence the "production-

[22] *Profits*, op. cit., p. 294.
[23] *Ibid.*, p. 299.
[24] *Ibid.*, p. 302.
[25] *Ibid.*, pp. 302–313.

consumption equation". "It is not sufficient for this purpose that the total volume of money be increased. The money must go into circulation in such a way that the flow of new money into the hands of the consumers is equal in value, at the current retail price-level, to the flow of new goods into consumers' markets. The question is not, then, whether currency or bank-credit, or both, should be increased year after year, but in what way the new money should be introduced into the circuit flow".[26]

Now unhappily, under the existing system of money and credit, additional money gets into circulation, not on the side of the consumers but on the side of the producers, and thus only aggravates the evil of the discrepancy between producers' disbursements and consumers' money expenditure. Moreover, this system of increasing the money supply through productive credits has the further effect that additions to the money supply take place when they are least necessary. The extension of production which they finance is a response to a lively demand. But when a falling off of consumers' demand is noticeable then credit is restricted and the trouble is aggravated. Thus the modern claim to restrict credit at the first sign of increasing warehouse stocks, and vice versa, is thoroughly pernicious. "In this way...every advance towards higher standards of living would promptly be checked; for whenever it appeared that consumer income was too small, it would be made smaller still through wage reductions, and underproduction would follow promptly".[27] Nevertheless, it would be easy to arrange an increase in consumers' credits, and it is only in this way that the deficiency in the purchasing power of the consumer, and thus the cause of the depression, can be removed. "Theoretically, then, it is always possible to add to the money circulation in such a way as to benefit the community. ... In any conceivable situation...an all-wise despot could make a net gain to the community by increasing the volume of money in circulation. ... If any safe and practicable means could be devised, in connection with increased public works and decreased taxes, or in any other connection, of issuing just enough money to consumers to provide for individual savings and to enable them to buy an enlarged output, and business men were confident that issues to consumers would continue at this rate and at no other rate, there would be no drop in the price-level and no reason for curtailing production, but, on the contrary, the most powerful incentive for increasing production".[28]

[26]*Ibid.*, p. 307.
[27]*Ibid.*, p. 324.
[28]*Ibid.*, pp. 330–331.

In *Profits*, the authors do not go further than to hint at these proposals. After a necessarily unsuccessful attempt at statistical verification—a quite unnecessary deference to prevalent fashions—they conclude that, under the present order of things, every attempt at increasing production must be checked by the fact that the demand of the consumer cannot keep pace with the supply. To remove the causes of this underconsumption is one of the most promising and urgent problems for the present generation. "Indeed, it is doubtful whether any other way of helping humanity holds out such large immediate possibilities".[29]

But before such reforms can be achieved professional economists will have to admit the inadequacy of their present theories. "If the main contentions of *Money* and *Profits* are sound, much of our traditional economic teaching is unsound, and overlooks some of the fundamentals which must be better understood before it will be possible to solve the economic problem".[30] Conversion of professional economists was therefore the main purpose of the campaign which was launched by the famous prize competition.

IV

The result of this competition for the best adverse criticism of their theory was the most remarkable success achieved by Messrs Foster and Catchings. The three members of the jury, Professor Wesley C. Mitchell, the well-known business-cycle theorist; the late Allyn A. Young, a most distinguished theoretical economist; and Mr. Owen D. Young, the President of the General Electric Company, of "Young Plan" fame, had no less than four hundred and thirty-five essays to examine.[31] In the

---

[29] *Ibid.*, p. 417.

[30] *Ibid.*, p. 416.

[31] [Wesley Clair Mitchell (1874–1948), American economist, author of *Business Cycles: The Problem and Its Setting* (New York: NBER, 1927). A pioneer in the collection and analysis of empirical data, Mitchell served as the director of the National Bureau of Economic Research from 1920 to 1945. He was also a doctrinal historian, and Hayek attended his lectures when he visited the United States in the early 1920s. A student preserved and had published Mitchell's *Lecture Notes on Types of Economic Theory* (New York: Kelley, 1949). See Hayek's obituary notice on Mitchell in F. A. Hayek, *The Fortunes of Liberalism*, op. cit., pp. 40–42. Allyn Young (1876–1929) was an American economist who published little but whose influence in his time was great: for example, he was thesis advisor to both Frank Knight and Edward Chamberlin. Just prior to his death he served briefly as department head at the London School of Economics; see this volume, chapter 1, note 11, for more on this. Owen D. Young (1874–1962) was Chairman of the Board of the General Electric

introduction to the little volume in which the prize essay and others were published,[32] Messrs Foster and Catchings relate, with some pride, that at least fifty universities, forty-two American states, and twenty-five foreign countries were represented. Among the authors were at least forty authors of books on economics, fifty professors of political economy, sixty accounting experts, bankers, editors, statisticians, directors of large companies etc.—among them "some of the ablest men in the Federal Reserve System", a functionary of the American Economic Association, a former President of that Society, and "several of the most highly-reputed economists in the British Empire".

But despite this highly respectable mass-attack of adverse criticism, Messrs Foster and Catchings remained convinced that their theory still held its own. Moreover, they were able to quote the opinion of one of the umpires,[33] that notwithstanding all that had been said against it, the substance of the theory remained untouched. This sounds extraordinary. But what is more extraordinary is that a candid perusal of the various criticisms which have been published forces one to admit that it is true. So far the main theory, and what in my opinion is the fundamental misconception of Messrs Foster and Catchings, has remained unanswered. The meritorious and readable works which were published in the *Prize Essays*, equally with criticism published elsewhere,[34] direct their criticism only against details. They accept the main thesis of Messrs Foster and Catchings. Only the two essays of Novogilov and Adams,

---

Company. He chaired the committee that in 1930 set up the Bank for International Settlements; the 'Young Plan' refers to his proposal for such an institution. —Ed.]

[32]*Pollak Prize Essays: Criticisms of "Profits"*, op. cit. Includes essays by R. W. Souter, Frederick Law Olmsted, C. F. Bickerdike, Victor Valentinovitch Novogilov. See also the introduction to *Business without a Buyer*, op. cit.

[33]*Prize Essays*, op. cit., p. 6. See also the introduction to *Business without a Buyer*, op. cit.

[34]To be mentioned especially are: A. B. Adams, *Profits, Progress and Prosperity* (New York: McGraw Hill, 1927); A. H. Hansen, *Business Cycle Theory, Its Development and Present Status* (Boston: Ginn, 1927) (a prize essay published separately); H. Neisser, "Theorie des wirtschaftlichen Gleichgewichtes", *Kölner sozialpolitische Vierteljahrschrift*, vol. 6, 1927, especially pp. 124–135; D. H. Robertson, "The Monetary Doctrines of Messrs Foster and Catchings", op. cit. [Arthur B. Adams (1887–1959), was a Professor of Economics and Dean of the Business School at the University of Oklahoma; Alvin Hansen (1887–1975), was initially critical of Keynesian analysis but soon became the leading American expositor of his ideas through his *A Guide to Keynes* (New York: McGraw-Hill, 1953); Hans Neisser (1895–1975), a German-born monetary economist who left Germany in 1933 to teach in the United States, wrote, with his student Franco Modigliani, *National Income and International Trade* (Urbana: University of Illinois Press, 1953); for more on Robertson see this chapter, note 21 above. —Ed.]

which we shall have occasion to mention later on, touch upon the critical points, and even here they do not make their respective objections the basic part of their criticism or develop them into an independent refutation.

In the case of Novogilov's work, it is possible that this is an injustice. In the *Prize Essays* it was published only in abridged form and just that part dealing with the influence of varying quantities of product at the various stages of production on the level of profits was entirely left out.[35] It is to be hoped that one day it will be published in its entirety. Mr. A. B. Adams's essay, on the other hand, whose criticism on many points coincides with that developed in this essay, and which in an incidental remark foreshadows one of its main theses,[36] suffers from the fact that the author himself does not realize the full importance of his objections, and therefore only criticizes the application of Messrs Foster and Catchings's theory to the case of investment in fixed capital, while admitting its correctness in the case of investment in circulating capital. But even Mr. Adams seems insufficiently to appreciate the function of capital and the conditions determining its utilization—a deficiency which is common both to the authors of the theory and to all their critics.

As for the rest, they all endeavour to prove that the existing currency organization suffices to increase the supply of money in the course of an extension of production so as to avoid a fall in the price-level. Some of them also point out that the extension of production can also bring about a diminution in costs per unit, so that falling prices need not always put a damper on production. But the alleged necessity to ease the sale of the enlarged product by an increase in the money supply is, in general, allowed to pass unquestioned. In doing this, however, the critics place themselves in a difficult position. For the contention of Messrs Foster and Catchings that productive credits aggravate still more the deficiency in the purchasing power of the consumer is clearly a corollary of the fundamental concept on which the claim for increasing the volume of money by productive extensions is based. To meet this difficulty the critics resort to various expedients. Some make very ingenious investigations into the order of succession of various money movements. Some attempt to refute the rather shaky assumptions in regard to the formation of profits in the course of productive extensions. Correct as these objections may be, they miss the point. The main thesis remains untouched.

[35]Cf. *Prize Essays*, pp. 118–124.
[36]See this volume, p. 110.

V

It is clear that this is the opinion of Messrs Foster and Catchings, for in their *Business without a Buyer*, published after the close of the prize competition, they do not make any significant alterations in the exposition of their theory. Fortified by the result of the competition, they then proceeded to develop the practical consequences of their theory. In *The Road to Plenty*,[37] which embodies the results of these further reflections, they make no attempt to appeal to economists. Despite the extremely favourable reception of their former books, it appears they are far from satisfied with professional economists. Both in the introduction to the *Prize Essays* and in *Business without a Buyer* they dwelt with some sprightliness on the lack of enlightenment in such circles. Now they turn to the general public and cast their theory in the form of a novel. The book records a conversation in the smoking compartment of a train where the complaints of a warm-hearted friend of humanity cause a genial businessman to explain the causes of crises and unemployment according to the theory of the authors, and then to defend the latter against the objections of a solicitor and a professor of economics (who, of course, comes out worst). Finally, all those present (including a member of the House of Representatives) are roused to a great pitch of enthusiasm about the concrete proposals based upon it.

These proposals are formulated still more clearly in a further essay, "Progress and Plenty",[38] and before proceeding to examine the theory it is worthwhile setting them forth explicitly. The first demand of the authors, and the condition for the execution of their further proposals, is an extension of business statistics in the direction of a more exact knowledge of the sales of consumption goods—in the first place, a complete and reliable index of retail prices; secondly, statistics of all factors influencing these prices (i.e., all possible economic data). These should be collected by public authorities and published promptly, in

---

[37]W. T. Foster and W. Catchings, *The Road to Plenty*, Publications of Pollak Foundation, No. 11 (Boston and New York: Houghton Mifflin, 1928; second edition, revised, 1928). A popular edition of *The Road to Plenty* was published in 50,000 copies and sold (120 pp., in full cloth binding) for 15 cents! [It is interesting to speculate whether this title influenced Hayek's choice of title for his book *The Road to Serfdom*, op. cit. —Ed.]

[38]"Progress and Plenty", op. cit. The second edition of *The Road to Plenty*, which I received after writing this article, takes over almost word for word the statements quoted here from *Progress and Plenty*.

order to give information and orientation to the business world. On the basis of such statistics, all public works and all financial operations of the government should be directed in such a way as to even out fluctuations in the demand for consumption goods. In "Progress and Plenty",[39] Messrs Foster and Catchings recommend the delegation of the business of collecting data, and their application to the distribution of public works to a separate body, the "Federal Budget Board". Just as the Federal Reserve Board directs a system for the financing of production, the Federal Budget Board should direct the financing of consumption and prevent disturbances of the economic system arising from consumption lagging behind production.

So far, apart from the demand for a new Board, the proposal contains nothing beyond the much-discussed plan for distributing public works in time in such a way as to concentrate all those capable of being postponed to times of depression. But Messrs Foster and Catchings are not satisfied with this. They realise that such a plan would have undesirable effects if the necessary sums were collected and locked up in the public Treasury in times of prosperity and spent in case of need. On the other hand, to raise the money by taxation at the time when it is needed for public works would be still less likely to achieve the desired end. Only an increase in the volume of money for the purpose of consumption can solve the problem: "Progress requires a constant flow of new money to consumers. If, therefore, business indexes show the need for a reinforced consumer demand which cannot be met without additional Government expenditure, the Board should bring about such expenditure, not only out of funds previously accumulated for that purpose, but at times out of loans which involve an expansion of bank credit. *This feature of the plan is essential*.[40] It follows that the government should borrow and spend the money whenever the indexes show that the needed flow of money will not come from other sources."[41]

As might be expected, the authors protest[42] that all this is not to be regarded as inflationary. Before its publication they had promised that it should contain "nothing dangerous or even distasteful", and that it

---

[39]Op. cit., p. 16 of the independent reprint, p. 37 of the reprint together with *The Dilemma of Thrift*. See also *The Road to Plenty*, op. cit., 2nd edition, p. 188.

[40]My italics.

[41]"Progress and Plenty", op. cit., p. 22 (p. 42 in the reprint together with *The Dilemma of Thrift*), and almost in the same words in *The Road to Plenty*, 2nd edition, p. 193.

[42]*The Road to Plenty*, op. cit., 2nd edition, p. 209.

would not involve "unlimited issues of fiat money".[43] We shall deal critically with these proposals in the last section of this article. At present, it need only be remarked that even critics who sympathise with Messrs Foster and Catchings's theory have been unable to conceal their scruples on this point. Mr. D. H. Robertson[44] remarks very correctly that he has no doubts that "they were born with a double dose of the inflation bacillus in their composition; and though they have done their best to exorcise it with prayer and fasting, so that they are able to look down with detached pity on more gravely affected sufferers, such as Major Douglas,[45] yet at critical moments the bacillus is always apt to take charge of the argument". It is, therefore, all the more astounding that they are able to quote in the advertisements to *The Road to Plenty* (it is true without mentioning the source) the opinion of no less an authority than the late Professor A. A. Young, that "on economic grounds, the plan for prosperity" proposed in *The Road to Plenty* "is soundly conceived", and that (according to the same source) Mr. W. M. Persons[46] should have thought the plan "practicable and important".

In wider circles, the proposals of Messrs Foster and Catchings seem to have had an extraordinary effect. President Hoover's pledge to carry out, within practical limits, such a regulation of public works as would alleviate unemployment has been a powerful lever to their argument. In a recent pamphlet[47] they announce that Senator Wagner from New York has already brought a bill before Congress for creating a "Federal

[43] *Prize Essays*, op. cit., p. 5.

[44] *Ibid.*, p. 498.

[45] [British engineer and airman Major Clifford Hugh Douglas (1879–1952) was the founder of the Social Credit movement. His underconsumptionist doctrines were expressed in the "A + B Theorem" and, to the chagrin of most economists, these ideas gained some measure of popular following in the 1920s. Even Keynes could muster only the weakest of praise for Douglas's work in his "Notes on Mercantilism", *The General Theory of Employment, Interest and Money*, op. cit.: "Yet he [Major Douglas] has scarcely established an equal claim to rank—a private, perhaps, but not a major in the brave army of heretics—with Mandeville, Malthus, Gesell and Hobson." (p. 371). —Ed.]

[46] [American economist Warren Milton Persons (1878–1937) wrote on the construction of index numbers and on the forecasting of business and financial conditions. —Ed.]

[47] W. T. Foster and W. Catchings, *Better Jobs and More of Them. The Government's Part in Preventing Unemployment*, reprinted from the *Century Magazine*, vol. 118, no. 3, July 1929, pp. 277–284. [Senator Robert F. Wagner (1877–1953) of New York was unsuccessful in creating an unemployment stabilization board. He introduced a number of pieces of New Deal legislation, including the Wagner Act (1935), which provided legal status to unions and set up the National Labor Relations Board for the adjudication of disputes. —Ed.]

Unemployment Stabilization Board", with very similar functions to their "Federal Budget Board". But in America it takes some time for any bill to become law; and up to the present I have not heard of the success of Senator Wagner's proposals. So far it has not been proposed that this Board should finance public works with additional bank money, and even Messrs Foster and Catchings have guarded themselves from demanding the execution of this part of their proposals—even in connection with the Hoover Plans. Instead they have concentrated on a criticism of the policy of the Federal Reserve board in raising its discount rate at a time of falling prices and falling employment.[48] It is pressure of this sort which constitutes a danger both in America and elsewhere if such theories gain further popularity. At this point, therefore, we may pass to a criticism of their validity.

VI

It is constantly assumed by Messrs Foster and Catchings that the investment of savings for the extension of production necessarily increases the total costs of production by the full amount of the invested savings. This follows clearly from their continual emphasis on the 'fact' that the value of the increased product is raised by the amount invested, and that therefore it can only be sold profitably for a proportionately higher sum. It is implied by the examples, in which it is always assumed that the increase in the current outlay in wages, etc., exactly corresponds with the sums invested. Now there is a certain initial obscurity in this assumption, since it is obvious that the costs of the product produced during an economic period cannot rise by the whole of the newly invested sum if this is invested in durable instruments, but only in proportion to the depreciation of the new durable capital goods; a fact which is not made clear in their exposition. My main objection, however, is not concerned with this circumstance—which it is impossible to believe that the authors could entirely overlook—but rather with their assumption that generally, over *any* length of time, the costs of production can increase by the whole of the newly invested amount. This view, which is based on a complete misunderstanding of the function of capital as a 'carrying' agent, assumes that the increased volume of production brought about by the new investments must be undertaken with the same methods as the smaller volume produced before the new movement took place. Such an assumption may be true

[48]*Ibid.*, p. 17.

for a single enterprise, but never for the industry as a whole. For in industry as a whole every increase in the available supply of capital always necessitates a *change* in the methods of production in the sense of a transition to more capitalistic, more 'roundabout', processes.

For in order that there may be an increase in the volume of production without a change in the methods of production, not only the available supply of capital, but also the supply of all other factors of production, must be increased in similar proportion. In regard to land, at any rate, this is practically impossible. It is just as inadmissible to assume that the complementary factors which are necessary for the extension of production are previously unemployed, and find employment only with the appearance of the new savings.[49]

A correct view of the reactions on production as a whole of the investment of new savings must be envisaged in this way: At first the new savings will serve the purpose of *transferring a portion of the original means of production previously employed in producing consumers' goods to the production of new producers' goods.* The supply of consumers' goods must therefore temporarily fall off as an immediate consequence of the investment of new savings (a circumstance constantly overlooked by Messrs Foster and Catchings).[50] No unfavourable effects on the sales of consumption goods follow from this, for the demand for consumption goods and the amount of original means of production employed in producing them decrease in similar proportions. And indeed even Messrs Foster and Catchings do not make any such assertion. Their difficulties begin only at the moment when the increased volume of consumption goods, brought about by the new investment, comes on to the market.

Now this increase in the volume of consumption goods can only be effected through an increase in the volume of capital employed in

---

[49]Messrs Foster and Catchings seem to avail themselves of the assumption of an "industrial reserve army"—a notion much favoured in trade cycle theory—from which the labour power necessary for a proportional extension of production can always be obtained at will. Quite apart from the incompatibility of this assumption with the known facts, it is theoretically inadmissible as a starting point for a theory which attempts, like Messrs Foster and Catchings, to show the causes of crises, and thus of unemployment, on the basis of the modern 'equilibrium theory' of price determination. Only on the basis of an economic theory which, like the Marxian, tried to explain the existence of permanent unemployment of considerable proportions independently of crises would such an assumption be theoretically permissible.

[50]Novogilov, who—as far as I can see—is the only critic who emphasizes this circumstance (op. cit., p. 120), puts a favourable interpretation on the exposition in *Profits*, namely that the authors assume that "the population as a whole must increase its expenditure of labour, but consume not more than in the first years" (p. 108). But how should savings occasion an increased expenditure of labour?

production. Such capital, once it has been brought into existence, does not maintain itself automatically. This increase makes it necessary that, henceforward, a greater proportion of the existing means of production should be permanently devoted to the production of capital goods, and a smaller part to finishing consumption goods; and this shift in the immediate utilization of means of production must, under the conditions prevailing in the modern economic system, conform with a change in the relative amount of money expended in the various stages of production. But this question of the relation between the sums of money expended in any period on consumption goods on the one hand and on production goods on the other brings us to the fundamental flaw in Messrs Foster and Catchings's theory.

VII

Messrs Foster and Catchings base the whole of their exposition on an hypothesis of what may be called single-stage production, in which, in a state of equilibrium, the money received in every period from the sale of consumption goods must equal the amount of money expended on all kinds of production goods in the same period.[51] Hence they are incapable of conceiving an extension of production save, so to speak, in the 'width'—an extension involving the expenditure of the new savings side by side with the sums which were already being spent on the ultimate factors of production, this is to say, the recipients of net income. It is easy to see how they arrive at this position. They assume a single enterprise in which all goods are produced from beginning to end (there will be much to say about this later), and because of this they entirely overlook the phenomenon of changes to more or less capitalistic methods of production.

---

[51]This conception, which is completely erroneous at any rate so far as it applies to a modern economic system, is very often met in economic literature, and may be traced back as far as Adam Smith, who wrote: "The value of the goods circulated between the different dealers never can exceed the value of those circulated between dealers and consumers; whatever is bought by the dealer being ultimately destined to be sold to the consumer" (Smith, *An Inquiry into the Nature and Causes of the Wealth of Nations*, ed. Edwin Cannan (London: Methuen, 1904), vol. 1, p. 305). [See Smith, op. cit., p. 342. —Ed.] It is interesting to note that this statement of Smith is quoted by T. H. Tooke in support of the doctrines of the banking school. Cf. *An Inquiry into the Currency Principle* (London: Longman, 1844), p. 11. [Thomas Tooke (1774–1858) was a leading member of the Banking School. His book was reprinted in the LSE Series of Reprints of Scarce Works on Political Economy, no. 15, 1959. Hayek's chair in Economic Science and Statistics at the LSE was named after Tooke. —Ed.]

Let us for the time being avoid this assumption, and, instead, consider an economy in which the different stages and branches of production are divided into different independent enterprises. We can return later to the special case of single-enterprise production considered by Messrs Foster and Catchings. But we will adhere throughout to another assumption which they make: the assumption that the amount of money in circulation remains unchanged. It is especially important to do this because most of the criticisms of the theory which have been made up to the present have sought the solution of the alleged dilemma chiefly in a proportional adjustment of the supply of money to the enlarged volume of production.[52] To me, at any rate, the fundamental error of the theory seems to arise rather in the presentation of the origin of the dilemma, the supply of money remaining unchanged. I shall return to the question of the effects of a change in the supply of money in the last section, in which I deal with Messrs Foster and Catchings's proposals for positive reform.

What happens, then, under the conditions assumed, when somebody saves a part of his income hitherto devoted to consumption, or when a company does not distribute its profits, and the sums thus saved are reinvested in production? At first, clearly the demand which is directed to means of production increases, and that directed to consumption goods correspondingly decreases. Does that mean that the expenditure on production will now be greater than is justified by the sums of money which will be available for the purchase of consumption goods?

That this need not be the case is surely clear from the most superficial consideration of the modern capitalistic economy. For, at every moment of time, raw materials, semifinished products, and other means of production are coming into the market, the value of which is several times greater than the value of the consumption goods which are simultaneously offered in the market for consumption goods.[53] It follows

---

[52]Cf. the criticism of Olmsted (op. cit., p. 68), where it is expressly stated: "This brings us back to the 'Dilemma', and also brings us back to *the obvious and only escape from the Dilemma*; namely, the progressive increase, in relation to the price level of goods, of the scale of money compensation to individuals for their productive effort if that productive effort is progressively increasing in efficiency". (Italics mine.)

[53]M. W. Holtrop computes on the basis of statistical data taken from publications of I. Fisher and the National Bureau of Economic Research that in the United States in the year 1912 the sum of all money payments was more than twelve times larger than the sum of all money incomes (M. W. Holtrop, *De omloopsnelheid van het geld* (Amsterdam: H. J. Paris, 1928), p. 181). Cf. also his further exposition which gives interesting figures in regard to the variations of this proportion in the course of the trade cycle. [Dutch banker Marius Wilhelm Holtrop (1902–1988) went on to serve as a Governor of the International Monetary Fund (1952–1967) and as President and Chairman of the Board of the Bank for

that the sum spent on the purchase of means of production of all kinds at any period is several times greater than the sum spent on the purchase of consumption goods at the same time. The fact that the total costs of production are, nevertheless, not greater than the value of the consumption goods produced is explained by the circumstance that every good on its way from raw material to finished product is exchanged against money as many times, on the average, as the amount of money expended on the purchase of means of production at every period exceeds the amount spent on consumption goods. And it is just a lengthening of this average process of production (which, on our assumption, shows itself in an increase of the number of independent stages of production) which makes it possible, when new savings are available, to produce a greater amount of consumption goods from the same amount of original means of production.

The proposition that savings can only bring about an increase in the volume of production by enabling a greater and more productive 'roundaboutness' in the methods of production has been demonstrated so fully by the classical analysis of Böhm-Bawerk that it does not require further examination. It is necessary here only to go further into certain monetary aspects of the phenomenon.

The questions which interest us are as follows: How does the increase in the money-stream *available for productive purposes* following the investment of new savings distribute the additional demand for means of production through the economic system, and under what conditions is this distribution effected in such a way as to achieve the purpose of saving with the smallest possible disturbance. After what has been said already in this connection it will be of fundamental importance to distinguish between changes in the demand for original means of production, i.e., labour and land, and changes in the demand for means of production which are themselves products (intermediate products or capital goods) such as semifinished goods, machinery, implements etc. On the other hand it is not important for our present purpose to distinguish between durable and non-durable means of production because it is irrelevant, for instance, that a loom has only to be renewed after eight periods of time, since, in a continuous process of production, this amounts to the same thing as if every eighth loom is to be renewed in every period.

For the sake of simplicity, we may assume that the path from the original means of production to the final product is of equal length for

International Settlements (1958–1967). —Ed.]

all parts of the total money-stream, although, in fact, this differs according to the moment when the particular original means of production are employed in the different stages of production; so that the assumed uniform length of the roundabout ways of production only corresponds to the *average* length of the various processes which lead to the production of a consumption good. The only case in real life strictly corresponding to this assumption would be the production of a good requiring expenditure of labour only at the beginning of the production process, the rest being left to nature; as, for example, in the case of the planting of a tree. But even this would only completely conform to our assumption if the saplings changed hands every year, i.e., if one man held one-year saplings, another two-year saplings, and so on. This difficulty only arises because, for purposes of exposition, it is easier to treat the average length of production as if it were uniform for all processes. In the real world, of course, it is the very fact that the period between the expenditure of the original means of production and the completion of the consumers' goods is different for every original means of production used, which makes it necessary that the goods should pass through several hands before they are ready for consumption. We assume, therefore, that, for example, the value of all means of production coming to the market during one period is eight times as great as the value of the consumption goods produced during the same period, and the latter is sold for 1,000 units of money, say pounds sterling. We disregard the differences in value conditioned by interest, that is to say, we make the assumption that interest on capital employed, together with the remuneration of the original means of production, is paid out only in the highest stage of production. The whole process of production and the circulation of money connected with it can then be represented schematically as shown in Scheme A (see following page).

Such a table represents at once both the products of the various stages of production coming on to the market *simultaneously* with the consumption goods and the *successive* intermediary products from which the actual product finally emerges, since, in a stationary economy, these are the same. We exhibit, that is to say, the total supply of goods originating in one branch of production (or, if the scheme is applied to the whole economy, all branches of production), and coming on to the market in one period of time. The sums paid at the ninth stage of production for the original means of production correspond necessarily with the value of the consumption goods, and form the origin of the funds for which the consumption goods are sold.

Scheme A[54]

			£
Demand for consumption goods (= products of stage of production No. 1)		...	1,000

Demand for the products of the stages of production	No. 2	...	1,000
	No. 3	...	1,000
	No. 4	...	1,000
	No. 5	...	1,000
	No. 6	...	1,000
	No. 7	...	1,000
	No. 8	...	1,000
	No. 9	...	1,000

Total demand for produced means of production—8 x 1000 =   ...   8,000

Relation of the demand for consumption goods to the demand for produced means of production—1 : 8.

[54]If it were desired, in order to bring the scheme closer to reality, to demonstrate, instead of the average length of the production process, the various lengths of its particular branches, it should be represented somewhat as follows:

			£		£
Demand for consumption goods (= products of stage of production No. 1)		...	1,000		58.8
	No. 2	...	941.2		58.8
	No. 3	...	882.4		58.8
	No. 4	...	823.5		58.8
	No. 5	...	764.8		58.8
	No. 6	...	705.9	From which	58.8
	No. 7	...	647.6	we have to	58.8
	No. 8	...	588.2	deduct for	58.8
Demand for products of the stages of production	No. 9	...	529.4	original	58.8
	No. 10	...	470.6	means of	58.8
	No. 11	...	411.8	production	58.8
	No. 12	...	352.9		58.8
	No. 13	...	294.1		58.8
	No. 14	...	235.3		58.8
	No. 15	...	176.5		58.8
	No. 16	...	117.6		58.8
	No. 17	...	58.8		58.8

Total Demand for produced means of production   8,000.0

Total demand for original means of production   1,000.0

Relation of the demand for consumption goods to the demand for produced means of production—1 : 8.

Let us assume, then, that the owners of the original means of production spend from their total income of £1,000 only £900, and invest in production the remaining £100 thus saved. There is, therefore, £8,100 now available for the purchase of production goods, and the relation between the demand for consumption goods and the demand for production goods changes from 1:8 to 1:9.

In order that the increased sum of money now available for the purchase of means of production should be profitably utilized, the average number of stages of production must increase from eight to nine; the situation represented in Scheme A has therefore to be altered as shown in Scheme B, below:

Scheme B

(£100 is saved and invested.)

			£
Demand for consumption goods (= products of stage of production No. 1)		...	900
	No. 2	...	900
	No. 3	...	900
	No. 4	...	900
Demand for the products of the stages	No. 5	...	900
of production	No. 6	...	900
	No. 7	...	900
	No. 8	...	900
	No. 9	...	900
	No. 10	...	900
Total demand for produced means of production—9 x 900 =		...	8,100

Relation of the demand for consumption goods to the demand for produced means of production—1 : 9.

Scheme B[54]

---

[54] Such an exposition, more complete than the former, alters nothing of its results, but complicates considerably the clarity of the presentation.

Those readers who find this mode of arithmetical illustration difficult to follow are referred to my forthcoming work on *Prices and Production*, shortly to be published by Messrs Routledge, where the same thing is illustrated diagramatically. [*Prices and Production*, op. cit. –Ed.]

In this case also, the total sum which is spent in the last stage for the original means of production, and which is therefore available as income for the purchase of the product, coincides with the value of the product after the necessary adjustments have taken place. The allocation of the additional means of production has been effected by maintaining the equilibrium between costs of production and the prices of consumption goods in such a way that the money-stream has been lengthened and narrowed down correspondingly, i.e., the average number of the successive turnovers during the productive process has risen in the same ratio as the demand for means of production in relation to the demand for consumption goods has increased. If the supply of money remains unaltered this is necessarily connected with a fall in the prices of the factors of production, the unchanged amount of which (disregarding the increase of capital) has to be exchanged for £900; and a *still greater fall* in the prices of consumption goods, the volume of which has increased on account of the utilization of more roundabout methods of production while their total money value has diminished from £1,000 to £900.

This demonstrates at any rate the *possibility* that, by an increase in the money-stream going to production and a diminution of that going to consumption, production *can* still be organized in such a way that the products can be sold at remunerative prices. It remains to show that (1) with an unchanged amount of money, production will be governed by prices so that such an adjustment does take place, (2) that by such an adjustment of production the purpose of saving is achieved in the most favourable way, and (3) that on the other hand every change in the volume of currency, especially every monetary policy aiming at the stability of the prices of consumption goods (or any other prices) renders the adaptation of production to the new supply of saving more difficult and indeed frustrates more or less the end of saving itself.

VIII

In order to remain as faithful as possible to the example which Messrs Foster and Catchings have put in the foreground, let us consider the case of a joint stock company reinvesting a portion of its profits which was hitherto distributed. In what way will it utilize the additional capital? This utilization may be different in different individual cases, yet important conclusions may be drawn from a consideration of the general possibilities of additional investments.

In principle it is possible for a single enterprise—in contrast to the whole industry—to utilize the available amount of capital for extending production by retaining existing methods but employing larger quantities of *all* factors.[55] We can leave the possiblity of this out of consideration for the moment, as our undertaking could only get additional labour and other original means of production by drawing them away from other undertakings, by outbidding them. And this process will change the relative proportion of capital to the other factors in the other enterprise, and thus a transition of production to new methods will become necessary. This is clearly the general economic effect of the increase of capital, and it is this in which we are interested. For the sake of simplicity let us assume, then, that the transition has already taken place in the first enterprise which undertook the savings.

But if a 'linear' extension of production is ruled out, and the undertaking has to utilize its relative increase in capital supply for a transition to more capitalistic methods, there remain two main types of investment for the additional capital which have to be considered. These are usually distinguished as investment in fixed capital or durable producers' goods, and in circulating capital or non-durable producers' goods respectively. Up to now in following Messrs Foster and Catchings we have only considered investment in circulating capital, in future we shall have to distinguish between these two possibilities.

Whether in any given case investment in fixed capital or in circulating capital is the more profitable, and is therefore undertaken, depends on the technical conditions of the concrete case, and therefore cannot be decided a priori. For analytical purposes it is desirable to treat these two cases separately, both as regards the conditions which must be given in order to render more capitalistic methods profitable, and also as regards the effect on prices.

[55]In practice, such a *linear* extension of production will be of importance in so far as, by an increase in the supply of capital, not only will the share of capital in every branch of production increase, but there will be an increase in the relative size of more capitalistic branches of production as compared with less capitalistic ones, i.e., the former will employ *more* labour, and this extension of the whole undertaking can so far overshadow the increase in the relative share of capital as to create the impression of a linear (proportional) extension of the more capitalistic undertakings. Even if the proportion between capital and the original means of production employed remains absolutely constant, but the more capitalistic undertakings were extended at the expense of the less capitalistic ones (as may be the case with undertakings of average roundaboutness), this implies, from the point of view of the whole industry, a transition to more capitalistic methods.

IX

As regards investment in *fixed capital* (i.e., durable means of production), the case is relatively simple. Messrs Foster and Catchings leave this case entirely out of account (a fact on which, as we have already mentioned, Mr. A. B. Adams bases his criticism) and Mr. P. W. Martin applies a similar theory of his own expressly to the case of investment in circulating capital only.[56] What we shall have to say here, therefore, will hardly meet with much opposition, and for this reason it will be easier in this connection to develop the analysis which is relevant also for the subsequent investigation.

In order that new investment in fixed capital may be profitable, it is necessary that the increase in receipts from the increased product following the investment should be sufficient to cover the interest and depreciation of the invested capital. The rate of interest must be somewhat higher where the new investments are made than in the alternative employments which are open to them, but somewhat lower than the rate of interest paid hitherto. It is just the circumstance that the rate of interest has fallen and that the investment in question is the nearest in the scale of profitableness which determines that it, and no other, shall be undertaken. In judging its profitableness, account must be taken of the fact that the enlarged product following the new investment can only be sold in the long run at prices lower relatively to the prices of original means of production than hitherto. This is partly because, owing to the cooperation of new capital, more consumption goods will be produced from a given quantity of original means of production; and also because a greater amount of consumption goods must be sold against the income of the original means of production and of capital, and the increase in the income from the latter (if it occurs at all—if the increase in capital is not more than compensated by the fall in the interest rate) must always be relatively less than the increase of consumption goods.[57]

---

[56]Cf. *Unemployment and Purchasing Power*, op. cit., p. 15.

[57]The fall in the rate of interest necessitates ipso facto such a relative change in the price of means of production and of products because, in a state of equilibrium, the rate of interest must exactly correspond with the difference between the two. With regard to the relation between changes in the rate of interest and changes in relative prices, cf. the appendix to my essay, "Das intertemporale Gleichgewichtssystem der Preise und die Bewegungen des Geldwertes", *Weltwirtschaftliches Archiv*, vol. 28, July 1928. [See the translation of this important article, "Intertemporal Price Equilibrium and Movements in the Value of Money", in *Money, Capital, and Fluctuations: Early Essays*, op. cit., pp. 71–118. The significance of the article is discussed in Stephan Boehm, "Time and Equilibrium; Hayek's Notion of Intertemporal Equilibrium Reconsidered", in *Subjectivism, Intelligibility and*

If the quantity of money remains unchanged, the unavoidable fall in the relative prices of consumption goods will also manifest itself absolutely. It is in this way that the relative fall will establish itself at the moment when the new consumption goods come on to the market. If the supply of money is kept constant, this effect of every extension of production will be well known to producers and they will therefore *only choose such employments for the investment of new savings as remain profitable even if prices are expected to fall.* But these employments—and this, as we shall see presently, is the essential point—are the only ones through which the social advantages of saving can be realised without loss.

Even if the volume of money is increased so that the prices of consumption goods do not fall, a new equilibrium must inevitably be established between costs of production and the prices of products. This can come about—if a fall in the prices of consumption goods is excluded—in two ways: either by a rise in the prices of means of production; or by a return to the previous, shorter, less productive methods of production; or by both of these ways together. What actually happens depends on where and when the additional money is injected into the economic system. If the increase in the supply of money were only to take place at the time when the additional volume of consumption goods comes on to the market and in such a way as to render it directly available for the purchase of consumption goods,[58] the expectation of unchanged prices for products would result in a portion of the additional amount, rendered available for the purchase of means of production through saving, not being utilized for a lengthening of the production process, i.e., the formation of new capital; it would simply serve to drive up the prices of the means of production. Because of the expectation of stable prices for the products, *more* openings for the new savings will appear profitable than can actually be exploited with their aid. The rate of interest is only sufficient to limit alternatives to those most profitable when price-relations are also in equilibrium with it. Competitive selection must therefore take place in the market for the means of production, i.e., the prices of means of production must rise until only so many extensions of the productive process appear profitable at those prices

---

Economic Understanding: Essays in Honor of Ludwig M. Lachmann on his Eightieth Birthday, ed. Israel Kirzner (New York: New York University Press, 1986), pp. 16–29. —Ed.]

[58]This is the suggestion made by Messrs Foster and Catchings; we shall have occasion to go into this case more extensively in the last section, when we come to criticise their proposals for reform.

as can actually be carried out by the new savings. That simply means that a portion of the savings will not be utilized for the creation of capital, but merely for the purpose of increasing the prices of available means of production.

But the assumption that the supply of money will only be increased when the enlarged volume of consumption goods comes on to the market has little probability. In the first place, the fact that new savings offer possibilities for the extension of production will, as a rule (according to the prevalent opinion, quite justifiably), give rise to an increase in the volume of money in the form of producers' credits. On the other hand, the fact that, in spite of the more capitalistic and more productive methods, the prices of the products do not fall will provide an incentive to take up additional loans from the banks far beyond the sum voluntarily saved, and will thus increase the demand for means of production much more than would be justified by the new savings. The rise in the prices of these means of production conditioned by it will gradually cause the excessive price-margin between these goods and consumption goods to disappear (and thus take away the incentive for further extensions of credit); at the same time, more means of production than are justified by the new savings will be transferred for use in longer processes (i.e., more lengthy processes will be undertaken than can be carried out). In other words, it will be possible, through an increase in the volume of money, to draw away as many factors from the consumption goods industries, over and above the quota voluntarily saved, as to enable at first the commencement of all en- largements of fixed capital which appear profitable at the lower rate of interest having regard to the unchanged prices.

All these investments, however, can be carried on only so long as the new money used for extensions of production is not utilized by the owners of the factors of production, to whom it is paid, for the pur- chase of consumption goods or so long as the increase in the demand for consumption goods is offset by a progessive increase in the supply of new productive credits.[59] As soon as the increase in the volume of credits granted to producers is no longer sufficient to take away as many means of production from the provision of current consumption as would be required for the execution of all the projects which appear profitable under the lower rate of interest and the unchanged price relationship between consumption goods and means of production, then the increasing utilization of means of production for the provision of

---

[59]Cf. my work *Geldtheorie und Konjunkturtheorie* (Vienna: Springer, 1929). [See F. A. Hayek, *Monetary Theory and the Trade Cycle*, op. cit. —Ed.]

current needs through less lengthy processes of production will drive up the prices of means of production, both absolutely and relatively to consumption goods, and thus render unprofitable those extensions of production which only became possible through the policy of price stabilization.

As, in the case under consideration, we are dealing with extensions of durable plant, which as a rule must be left in their previous employments even if they become unprofitable (even if their quasi-rents fall to such a level as to drive their value much below the cost of production, and thus prevent their replacement), the adjustments necessary will only proceed very slowly and with great sacrifices of capital. But, apart from this loss of a portion of the savings, the final equilibrium of production will establish itself in that position where it would have been established right from the beginning had no increase in money supply intervened; that is to say, at that point where the diminution in the cost per unit of product brought about by the investment is just great enough to sell the larger quantity of the final product despite the fact that, owing to savings, only a smaller proportion of the total money-stream goes to purchase it than hitherto. Although the schematic representation given above is only completely applicable to the case (to which we shall return later) of investment in circulating capital, it is also true in the case of investment in fixed capital that the necessary fall in the price of the final product manifests itself not only in a fall of the price per unit (which must take place even if an unchanged money-stream goes to buy a larger product) but also in a diminution in the proportion of the total money-stream which is available for the purchase of consumption goods.

The difference between this case and that of investment in circulating capital lies in the fact that in the former case the demand for means of production in relation to the demand for consumption goods does not, in the long run, increase by the whole of the newly invested sum, but only by the amount necessary to keep the additional capital intact. So long as the production of additional capital is going on, the demand for consumption goods diminishes by the whole of the amount newly saved and invested.[60] The transference of factors of production for the production of new means of production which is conditioned by this

[60]In order to avoid too much complication in the exposition I disregard the case of an increase in the supply of capital leading to a more than proportional increase in the supply of fixed capital (or vice versa) which may occur owing to the fact that a fall in the rate of interest may render it profitable to transform already existing investments in circulating capital into fixed capital.

diminution is, however, partly temporary. As soon as the new durable means of production are ready, and the production of final products can be correspondingly increased with their aid, the sums available for their purchase in the hands of consumers are not diminished by the value of the newly invested capital, but only by that amount which is necessary for their upkeep and amortisation. But an amount of this magnitude will always have to be put aside by the entrepreneur and thus withdrawn from consumption.

Even if he can only proceed to a renewal of fixed capital (in the absence of new savings) when the old is fully amortised, the sums accumulating for amortisation will increase the current demand for means of production in the meantime for the purpose of producing new means of production. The entrepreneur must try to invest these sums to the best advantage until he needs them himself, and thus will increase the supply of capital and exercise a further pressure on interest rates. Without going into the complicated processes which are conditioned by the temporary accommodation of sums accumulated for amortisation, it may be said that they signify a temporary transformation of capital (mostly in circulating form), but they also form a current demand for the production of capital goods. As a result, an increase in fixed capital will have the same effects as if every single undertaking continuously renewed the wear and tear of its plant, i.e., spent uniformly a greater proportion of its receipts than before the investment in new capital on the purchase of intermediate products, and a smaller proportion on the purchase of original means of production. As this implies a corresponding diminution in the amounts available for the purchase of consumption goods, investment in fixed capital will therefore also have the effect of 'stretching' the money- stream, that is to say, it becomes longer and narrower; or, in the terminology of Messrs Foster and Catchings, the circuit velocity of money diminishes.

X

The same effects manifest themselves still more directly in the case of an investment of new savings in *circulating capital*. And yet, as the examples of Messrs Foster and Catchings, Mr. P. W. Martin, and Mr. A. B. Adams show, this necessary concomitant phenomenon of *every* increase of capital is, in just this case, very easily overlooked. The explanation lies in the fact that the case of a single enterprise, which can always utilize its increased circulating capital for a proportional increase of its labourers and other means of production, is applied directly to the economic system as a whole, although it should be clear that an increase in capital, whether fixed or circulating, can only show itself in the economic system as a whole in an increase in intermediate products in relation to original means of production.

One of the most frequent cases of an increase in circulating capital—it is the case which led Messrs Foster and Catchings and their adherents to overlook completely the capital function of the invested savings—is the case which has already been mentioned[61] of a relative extension of the more capitalistic branches of production at the expense of the less capitalistic ones. In this case, original means of production will be taken away from the latter and utilized in the former, without an increase in their fixed capital, so that at first the original means of production employed there increase relatively to the fixed capital. As has already been emphasised, it is not the increase in the volume of original means of production employed which is significant here, but the fact that they are now employed in a way which causes, on the average, a longer period of time to elapse between their employment and the emergence of their final product, and therefore more intermediary products to exist at any moment than before. It is just because an increase in the supply of capital enables relatively more roundabout processes to be undertaken that the more capitalistic undertakings can now employ more labour (and possibly more land).

At first the increased capital supply will result in the more capitalistic undertakings demanding more original means of production than hitherto, acquiring these by overbidding other undertakings. As more units of factors can only be acquired at a higher cost per unit, the extent to which they are able to do so depends on their expectations of an increase in total receipts from an increase in the volume of the product. In no case, however, will they be able to spend the total amount of new capital on increased employment of original means of production. Even to the extent that capital *is* used for that purpose in a single enterprise, this does not imply that part of the new capital is definitely used to remunerate original means of production. By exactly the same amount by which this enterprise increases its expenditure on original means of production because it expects a corresponding increase of its receipts, other enterprises will have to cut down expenditure on original means of production because their receipts will have undergone a corresponding decrease and will be able to invest that part as capital.

On the assumption, which we still adhere to, that the products of every stage of production come on to the market and are acquired there

---

[61]See Scheme A, note 54.

by the entrepreneur of the next stage, it is evident that only a portion of the newly invested savings can be spent on original means of production, while another and, in the modern, highly developed, economy, much greater portion must be used to acquire additional quantities of the products of the previous stage of production. This portion will be all the larger, the greater the number of the stages of production (represented by independent enterprises) and, as a rule, several times as large as the portion spent on wages etc.[62] It serves the purpose of providing all the stages of production (up to the last stage, where the final products of the original means of production now employed in the longer processes emerge) with a correspondingly larger amount of intermediate products; or, which means the same thing, it makes it possible for the additional means of production to be paid for continuously, period by period, so long as their additional product has not yet reached the final stage.

After what we have seen in the case of investment in fixed capital, we can formulate the problem before us by asking how, when new investment in circulating capital takes place, the price relations between production goods and consumption goods must adjust themselves in order that production will be extended to such, and only to such an extent that the new savings just suffice to carry out the enlarged processes?

Again we can start by assuming that, in the long run, the new capital investment must bring about a fall of the price of the products in relation to the prices of the means of production. If entrepreneurs expect—as, if the volume of money were kept constant, they ought to expect from experience—that the prices of the products will fall absolutely, then from the outset they will only extend production in such proportions as to ensure profitableness even if the relative prices of products (as opposed to the means of production) fall. This means that the increase in production will be limited, right from the beginning, to that extent which can permanently be maintained. If, however, un-

---

[62]While, in assuming only one stage of production, the value of all products at the end of the production process equals the value of the means of production employed; on the other hand, on the assumption that equal quantities of original means of production are employed at every stage (the case represented in this chapter, note 54), the value of the latter is one and one-half times as great if two, two and one-half times if four, and five and one-half times if ten stages of production are assumed, and so on. (Cf. Eugen Böhm-Bawerk, *Positive Theory of Capital* [1889], 4th German edition (Jena: Fischer, 1921), vol. 1, p. 397.) [Eugen Böhm-Bawerk [1889], *Positive Theory of Capital*, vol. 2 of *Capital and Interest* [1884–1912], 3 vols (South Holland, Ill.: Libertarian Press, 1959), p. 318. Hayek uses the same argument and citation in his critique of Keynes; see this volume, chapter 3, note 15. —Ed.]

changed prices are expected for the products, it would seem profitable at first to attempt a further extension of production; and that to the extent which would seem profitable at the present prices of the means of production. The latter will not increase at first by as much as will finally be necessary for the establishment of equilibrium; they will rise only gradually as the increased demand for original means of production is passed on from the higher to the lower stages. With the progressive increase in the prices of the means of production, not only that portion of the additional production which would not have been undertaken if falling prices had been expected will become unprofitable; but also—since too many means of production were used up, a greater scarcity ensues, and their prices will increase more than they otherwise would—some part of the production which would have been profitable but for the dissipation of a part of the supply of means of production. Every attempt to prevent the fall of prices by increasing the volume of money will have the effect of increasing production to an extent that it is impossible to maintain, and thus part of the savings will be wasted.

XI

Let us now consider the case—fundamental to Messrs Foster and Catchings's analysis—in which production is completely integrated vertically, the case in which all stages of one branch of production are united in one undertaking. In such circumstances there is no necessity to utilize certain parts of the money-stream for the purchase of intermediate products; only consumption goods proper on the one hand, and the original means of production on the other are exchanged against money. The examination of this case is essential to prove the validity of our thesis—partly because, in the existing economic order, the various stages of production are not always divided into separate undertakings, and therefore an increase in the number of stages need not necessarily bring about an increase in the number of *independent undertakings*, but chiefly because the lengthening of the production process need not manifest itself in an increase in the number of *distinguishable stages* (as for the sake of clarity of exposition we have assumed up to the present), but simply in the lengthening of a continuous production process.

It is however impossible for reasons which are obvious, but which were overlooked by their critics, to follow Messrs Foster and Catchings in their assumption that all the *various branches* of production are also united in a single enterprise. If that were so, there would be no inducement for that undertaking to save money, or to take up the money savings of private individuals; and there would thus be no opportunity for private individuals to invest their savings. If that undertaking is the only one of its kind, and therefore the only one using original means of production, it can—just as the dictator of a Socialist economy can—determine at will what proportion of the original means of production should go for the satisfaction of current consumption, and what proportion to the making or renewal of means of production. Only if, and in so far as, there is competition between the various branches of production for the supply of the means of production, is it necessary, in order to obtain the additional means of production requisite for an enlargement of capital equipment, to have the disposal of additional amounts of money (either saved for that purpose or newly created). Only in such circumstances does there exist, accordingly, any inducement to save.

As it is clearly inadmissible to start from an assumption which renders the phenomenon to be investigated (i.e., the saving of individuals and companies) totally meaningless,[63] we can go no further in our investigations than the case of the complete vertical integration of single branches of production. But here, after what has been demonstrated above, it can be shown without difficulty that, if a transformation of money savings into additional real capital is to come about, the investment must lead to a diminution in the money-stream available for the purchase of consumption goods[64] (i.e., to that slowing down of the "circuit velocity of money" of which Messrs Foster and Catchings are so afraid), and that savings can only be utilized to the best advantage when the supply of money remains unaltered and the price per unit of the enlarged volume of goods diminishes.

Let us assume, therefore, that such an undertaking comprising all stages of production in one branch extends its production by 'corporate saving' so that during the extension of capital equipment the sums necessary for this purpose are raised from profits (i.e., interest on capital and earnings of management). In this way it will be able to keep its demand for original means of production constant, although, owing to the transformation of production, it can temporarily only bring a smaller volume of ready consumption goods on to the market, and its current receipts must fall. It is a necessary condition of the longer duration of

---

[63]Messrs Foster and Catchings, it is true, expressly declare that their assumption about the number of undertakings is insignificant and in no way invalidates their reasoning (*Profits*, op. cit., p. 270). They did not put forward any proof, however, and the fact that, even in trying to justify it, they do not realize that savings would be entirely meaningless under these circumstances, is the best proof of how completely they misunderstand the real function of saving.

[64]At any rate for so long as the transition of production goes on.

the new production process that either the undertaking cannot for a short period bring any goods on to the market, or, if it apportions its sales uniformly through time, it can offer only a smaller amount of the finished product for a longer period. The savings accumulated through individual profits serve just this very purpose of making good the diminution of receipts and enabling it to undertake the more productive, but more lengthy process. It must not, therefore, devote the whole sum to obtain more original means of production than before, for part must be used for bridging over the time during which its receipts will fall below current expenditure. The time during which it will be able to cover the difference between outgoings and receipts by saving forms the limit to the possible lengthening of the production process.

As long as the new investment is going on, a larger sum of money will be expended on means of production than that which is received from the sale of consumption goods at the same time. That occurs, as Messrs Foster and Catchings repeatedly and correctly emphasize, by "money that is once used to bring about the production of goods being again used to bring about the production of goods before it is used to bring about the consumption of goods", that sums which represent the remuneration of capital and entrepreneurial services are utilized for the purchase of means of production instead of the purchase of consumption goods. What Messrs Foster and Catchings misunderstand is the function of and the necessity for this relative increase in the demand for production goods and the corresponding diminution in the sales of consumption goods. It is the natural and necessary corollary of saving, which, in terms of Crusoe-economics, consists in the fact that less consumption goods are produced and consumed than could be produced from the means of production employed. The simultaneous increase in the demand for original means of production, i.e., the increase in the sums spent in the last stage of production (from which the original factors are remunerated) during one economic period, does not imply that at a later stage the money demand for consumption goods has to be increased by a similar amount in order to enable the sale of the enlarged volume of finished goods. The increase in the demand for means of production originates from the *lengthening* of the production process; so long as this is going on, more means of production are produced at every stage than are consumed at the next; production will serve the double purpose of satisfying current demand with the older (and shorter) process, and future demand with the new (longer) process. The demand for means of production is therefore, so long as new saving is going on, greater in relation to the demand for consumption goods than in the absence of savings because (in contrast to the stationary economy where the product of the means of production used in every period equals the goods consumed in that period) *the product of the means of production applied during the saving period will be consumed during a period which is longer than the saving period itself.*[65]

In order that the means saved should really bring about that extension of productive equipment for which they are just sufficient, the expected prices must make just that extension seem profitable. But that is (as should be clear by now, without a repetition of what has been said before) only the case when the money available for the purchase of the larger product is not greater than the part of the current outlays which served for *its* production. And since longer processes are more productive, in order that this may be the case, the unit prices of the product must now be less. Every expectation of future receipts greater than those necessary to cover the smaller costs per unit will lead to such excessive extensions of production as will become unprofitable as soon as the relative prices are no longer disturbed by the injection of new money.

XII

There is no danger, therefore, that too much money will be spent on production in relation to the sums available for consumption so long as the relative diminution in the demand for consumption goods is of a permanent nature and the latter does not, as *must* be the case with changes in the relative demand brought about by changes in the volume of money, increase again and drive the prices of the original means of production to such a height that the completion of the more capitalistic processes becomes unprofitable. As it is not the absolute level of the prices of the product, but only their relative level in comparison with factor prices which determines the remunerativeness of production, it is, therefore, never the absolute size of the demand for consumption goods, but the relative size of the demands for the means of production to be used for the various methods of producing consumption goods that determines this relative profitableness. *In principle, therefore, any portion, however small, of the total money-stream ought to be sufficient to take up the consumption goods produced with the aid of the other portions, as long as, for any reason, the demand for consumption goods does not rise suddenly in relation to the*

---

[65]That is correctly recognised by Mr. A. B. Adams in his criticism mentioned above of Messrs Foster and Catchings in *Profits, Progress and Prosperity*, op. cit., where it is expressly stated (p. 18), "If the physical volume of current output of consumers' goods should equal the physical volume of all goods produced currently there could be no accumulation of permanent capital—there could be no real savings".

demand for means of production, in which case the disproportionate amount of intermediate products (disproportionate in relation to the new distribution of demand) can no longer be sold at prices which cover costs.

The problem is therefore never the absolute amount of money spent for consumption goods, but only the question whether the relative demand for the consumption goods is not *greater* in relation to the money-stream utilized for productive purposes than the current flow of consumption goods in relation to the simultaneous output of means of production. In this, and only in this case, will a disproportionate supply of means of production, and thus the impossibility of remunerative employment, arise, *not because the demand for consumption goods is too small, but on the contrary because it is too large and too urgent* to render the execution of lengthy roundabout processes profitable. The idea of a general overproduction in relation to the money incomes of the consumers as Messrs Foster and Catchings conceive it is as untenable in a money economy as under barter. A crisis occurs only when the available supply of intermediate products in all stages of production in relation to the supply of consumers goods is greater than the demand for the former in relation the demand for the latter. Apart from the case of spontaneous consumption of capital, this can only arise when either the *supply* of means of production or the *demand* for consumption goods has been artificially and temporarily extended by credit policy. In either case a price relation will arise between means of production and finished products which renders production unprofitable.

XIII

That concludes our criticism of the cases in which savings are supposed to involve trade depression if the supply of money is not increased. The whole question is very similar to the old problem whether, when productivity is increasing, prices should remain stable or fall. As Mr. A. H. Hansen has pointed out, the argument of Messrs Foster and Catchings is applicable not only to the effect of saving but also to all other cases of increasing productivity.[66] To this extent, both authors became the victims of that uncritical fear of any kind of fall in prices which is so widespread today, and which lends a cloak to all the more refined forms of inflationism—a fashion which is all the more regrettable

---

[66]*Business Cycle Theory*, op. cit., p. 44 [Alvin Hansen, op. cit; see this chapter, note 35, for more on Hansen. —Ed.]

since many of the best economists, A. Marshall,[67] N. G. Pierson,[68] W. Lexis,[69] F. Y. Edgeworth,[70] Professor Taussig[71] in the past, and more recently Professor Mises,[72] Dr. Haberler,[73] Professor Pigou,[74] and Mr. D. H. Robertson[75] have repeatedly emphasized the misconception underlying it.

But in the special case which Messrs Foster and Catchings have made the basis of their proposals for stabilization, their argument is based on

[67]Cf. his evidence before the Gold and Silver Commission of 1887, now reprinted in *Official Papers by Alfred Marshall*, ed. J. M. Keynes (London: Macmillan, 1926), especially p. 91.

[68]Cf. e.g., "Gold Scarcity", translated into German by R. Reisch, in the *Zeitschrift für Volkswirtschaft, Sozialpolitik und Verwaltung*, vol. 4, no. 1, 1895, esp. p. 23. [Nikolaas Pierson (1839–1909) was a Dutch economist who popularised the Austrian approach in Holland. Hayek chose a 1902 essay of his for inclusion in *Collectivist Economic Planning* (London: Routledge and Kegan Paul, 1935; reprinted, Clifton, N. J.: Kelley, 1975). —Ed.]

[69]On several occasions in connection with the bimetallist question, e. g. in the *Verhandlungen der deutschen Silberkomission* (Berlin, 1894). Similarly C. Helfferich, E. Nasse, and L. Bamberger. [Wilhelm Lexis (1837–1914) and Erwin Nasse (1829–1890) were German economists, and both participated in the founding of the *Verein für Sozialpolitik*. Nasse was president of the organization from 1874 until his death, and Lexis after 1891 served as editor of the journal *Jahrbücher für National Statistik*. Karl Helfferich (1872–1924), a German economist, was a defender of the gold standard—see T. E. Gregory's introduction in the translation of his *Money* (London: Benn, 1927; reprinted, New York: Kelley, 1969). Ludwig Bamberger (1823–1899), a German liberal politician, was a proponent of the gold standard and a fervent anti-bimetallist. —Ed.]

[70]Cf. "Thoughts on Monetary Reform", *Economic Journal*, vol. 5, September 1895, pp. 434–451, reprinted as "Questions Connected with Bimetallism", in *Papers Relating to Political Economy*, vol. 1 (London: Macmillan, 1925; reprinted, New York: Franklin, 1970), pp. 421–442. [See this volume, chapter 1, note 20, for more on Edgeworth. —Ed.]

[71]Cf. *The Silver Situation in the United States* (New York: G. P. Putnam's Sons, 1893), pp. 104–112. [See this volume, chapter 1, note 4, for more on Taussig. —Ed.]

[72]*Geldwertsstabilisierung und Konjunkturpolitik* (Jena: Gustav Fischer, 1928), p. 30.

[73]*Der Sinn der Indexzahlen* (Tübingen: J. C. B. Mohr (Paul Siebeck), 1927, pp. 112 et seq. [Gottfried Haberler (1900–) was a friend of Hayek's from their student days at Vienna. He introduced what is now known as the production possibilities frontier in his article on international trade, "The Theory of Comparative Costs and Its Use in the Defense of Free Trade" [1930], reprinted in *Selected Essays of Gottfried Haberler*, ed. Anthony Koo (Cambridge: MIT Press, 1985), pp. 3–19. He also introduced the "real-balance effect" (often called "the Pigou effect") before Pigou did, in an early edition of his *Prosperity and Depression*, 6th edition (Cambridge: Harvard University Press, 1964). *Der Sinn der Indexzahlen* is summarized in *Selected Essays*, op. cit. —Ed.]

[74]*Industrial Fluctuations* (London: Macmillan, 1929; reprinted, New York: Kelley, 1967), pp. 182 et. seq. and 255 et seq. [A. C. Pigou (1877–1959) was the successor to Marshall's chair at Cambridge. His central work was *The Economics of Welfare* [1920], 4th edition (London: Macmillan, 1932), in which the Cambridge variant of welfare economics, often called the "Old Welfare Economics", was articulated. —Ed.]

[75]*Money* (London: Bisbet, rev. ed., 1924; 4th edition, New York: Pitman, 1948).

a different and less excusable misconception. What they entirely lack is any understanding of the function of capital and interest. The gap in their analytical equipment in this respect goes so far that, in their exposition of the theory of price, while most of the general problems are very thoroughly and adequately treated, any examination of this question is utterly lacking, and in the alphabetical index of *Profits* "capital" is only mentioned as a source of income. I cannot help feeling that, if they had extended their investigations to this field, or even if they had merely thought it worth their while to make themselves familiar with the existing literature or a question so cogent to their problem, they would themselves have realized the untenable nature of their theory. In the literature of monetary theory (with the exception of the works of K. Wicksell and Professor Mises, which are probably inaccessible to them for linguistic reasons)[76] they will, of course, look in vain for the necessary explanation, for so many writers on this subject still labour under the sway of the dogma of the necessity for a stable price level, and this makes recognition of these interconnections extraordinarily difficult. But just as Mr. R. W. Souter, their prizewinning critic, recommended them to read Marshall, so I would recommend them, still more urgently, to make a thorough study of Böhm-Bawerk, whose main work, if only in the first edition, is available in English translation.[77]

XIV

We have repeatedly had occasion while examining the theory of Messrs Foster and Catchings to point to the effects which would ensue if the proposals based upon it were put into practice. But it may well be that the contrast between the real effects of such proposals and the expectations based upon them may not yet be sufficiently clear. And as similar demands are continually being brought forward everywhere for all kinds of reasons, it seems worth while finally attempting a systematic account of the actual consequences to be expected if they were really carried out.

It has already been explained that Messrs Foster and Catchings's proposals for reform involve increasing the volume of money, either

---

[76] [Hayek is referring to Ludwig von Mises, *Geldwertsstabilisierung und Konjunkturpolitik,* op. cit., as well as to his *Theory of Money and Credit,* op. cit., and to Knut Wicksell, *Lectures on Political Economy,* op. cit. See this volume, chapter 1, note 4, for more on Wicksell. —Ed.]

[77] [Eugen Böhm-Bawerk, *The Positive Theory of Capital* (London: Macmillan, 1891). —Ed.]

through consumers' credits or the financing of state expenditure, in order to bring about the sale at unchanged prices of a volume of products enlarged by an increase of saving. The effects of such increases of money spent on consumption can best be demonstrated by contrasting them with the effects of additional productive credits. We shall work under the assumption used in the previous analysis, where the different stages of production are in the hands of different undertakings. The application of this reasoning to that of the completely integrated branch of production should follow more or less of itself.

We may take as a starting-point the result of our previous demonstration of the effect of saving, the volume of money remaining unchanged (Scheme B). According to this the relation of the demand for consumers' goods to the demand for means of production from £1,000:£8,000 to £900:£8,100, or from 1:8 to 1:9, so that the number of stages increased correspondingly from 9 to 10. Now let us assume that, in accordance with the proposal of Messrs Foster and Catchings, at the moment when the enlarged product comes on to the market, the volume of money is increased by the same sum as the sums spent on production, i.e., by £100[78] and that this additional sum is spent exclusively on consumption goods. Because of this, the demand for consumption goods again increases from £900 to £1,000, while the sums available for means of production remain unchanged, so that the relation between the demand for the two groups of goods changes from £900:£8,100 to £1,000:8,100, i.e., the relative size of the demand for means of production in comparison with the demand for consumption goods falls from 9 times to 8.1 times the latter. The transformation of production conditioned by this, in the form of a shortening of the productive process, comes about in the manner represented in Scheme C (see following page). As the number of stages of production, under our assumption, must then be 8:1, the last stage (No. 10) must be represented by a value which is only one-tenth of the rest.

But this shortening of the production process to the point where it stood before the investment of new savings (see, for example, Scheme A) need not be the final effect, if the increase in money occurs only once and is not repeated again and again. The extension of production became possible because producers consumed, instead of one-ninth

---

[78]In fact we ought to take an increase of £200, since, as a consequence of saving, the difference between the sums spent on production and on consumption goods increases by that amount. As by taking this larger amount the effect demonstrated will only become more pronounced, it will suffice to regard the more simple case given in the text.

Scheme C
(£100 is added to the circulation as credit to consumers.)

			£
Demand for consumption goods (= products of stage of production No. 1) ...			1,000
	No. 2	...	1,000
	No. 3	...	1,000
	No. 4	...	1,000
Demand for the products of the stages	No. 5	...	1,000
of production	No. 6	...	1,000
	No. 7	...	1,000
	No. 8	...	1,000
	No. 9	...	1,000
	No. 10	...	100

Total demand for produced means of
production—8.1 x 1,000 =   ...   8,100

Demand for consumption goods in relation to the demand for produced means of production—1 : 8.1.

(Scheme A), only one-tenth (Scheme B) of their total receipts, and utilized the rest for the purpose of keeping their capital intact. In so far as they persist in their endeavour to keep their capital intact, in spite of the diminution of the purchasing power of those parts of their receipts which are conditioned by the appearance of new money, the demand for consumption goods in relation to that for means of production will again shift in favour of the latter as soon as the demand for the former is no longer artificially extended through additional spending power. To this extent the shortening of the production process and the devaluation of fixed plant connected with it will only be temporary; but this is contingent upon a cessation of the flow of additional money. What is important, however, is that (even in an expanding economic system) *such an inflationist enlargement of the demand for consumption goods must, in itself, bring about at once similar phenomena of crisis to those which are necessarily brought about in consequence of an increase in productive credits, as soon as the latter cease to increase or their rate of flow diminishes.*[79] This will be best

[79]It would be a mistake to argue against the representation of the effect of consumptive credits above by saying that the war-inflation was also brought about by additional expenditure on consumption, and yet did not lead to crisis, but, on the

understood if we represent this case schematically also. We again take Scheme B as our starting point, assuming that, in accordance with prevalent opinion, the extension of production is taken as a justification for an extension in money supply. This extension, however, takes the form of productive credits. For simplicity, we assume that the additional money injected in the form of productive credits amounts to £900, and, therefore, the relation between the demand for consumption goods and the demand for production goods alters, as compared with the case represented in Scheme B, from £900:£8,100 to £900:£9,000, or from 1:9 to 1:10.

The proportional increase in the demand for means of production as compared with the demand for consumption goods enables an extension of the production process as compared with the position in Scheme B, as shown in Scheme D (see following page).

This lengthening of the productive process, however, can continue only so long as the demand for means of production is kept at the same relative level through *still further* additions of producers' credits; i.e., so long and so far as the durable production goods produced on account of the temporary increase in the demand for means of production suffice to carry on production of this extent. As soon and in so far as neither of these two assumptions remains true, all consumers whose real income was diminished through the competition of the increased demand for means of production will attempt to bring their consumption up again to the previous level, and to utilize a corresponding portion of their money income for the purchase of consumption goods. But that means that the demand for consumption goods will increase again to more than one-tenth of the total demand for goods of every stage. Accordingly, only a smaller proportion of the total money-stream goes to buy produced means of production, and the changes in the

---

contrary, to a boom. The war-inflation could never have led to such an extension of production as it actually did had the additional credits only been given to undertakings in the form of proceeds for the sale of products, and not—whether in the form of prepayments or directly in productive credits—placed at their disposal in advance for the purpose of extending production. One should visualize what would have happened had the increase in the demand for consumption goods always preceded the increase in the sums available for the purchase of means of production. And one would soon realise that this would only have rendered production of the present extent unprofitable, and would have led to a diminution of the productive apparatus in the form of a consumption of capital. During the war, this phenomenon was also rendered invisible through the appearance of specious profits following currency depreciation, which caused entrepreneurs to overlook that they were, in fact, consuming capital.

Scheme D
(In the scheme depicted in Scheme B £900 is added as credits to producers, first stage.)

			£
Demand for consumption goods (= products of stage of production No. 1) ...			900
	No. 2	...	900
	No. 3	...	900
	No. 4	...	900
Demand for the products of the stages	No. 5	...	900
of production	No. 6	...	900
	No. 7	...	900
	No. 8	...	900
	No. 9	...	900
	No. 10	...	900
	No. 11	...	900

Total demand for produced means of production—10 x 900 = ... 9,000

Demand for consumption goods in relation to the demand for produced means of production—1 : 10.

structure of production shown in Scheme E (see following page) will occur.

Without any further change in the volume of money, and only because the increase in the form of productive credits has ceased, the whole production process, and thus the length of the circuit velocity of money, tends again to contract to the old level. This contraction, which naturally involves the loss of those means of production which are adapted to the longer processes, and which is directly occasioned by the rise in the price of the means of production brought about by an increase in the demand for consumption goods, which renders the longer processes unprofitable, is a typical phenomenon of any crisis. As is easily seen, it is of the same nature as the effects of a relative increase in the demand for consumption goods brought about by consumers' credits.

It is just because with *every* increase in the volume of money, whether it is made available first for consumption or first for production, the relative size of the demand for those means of production which already exists or which has been directly enlarged by an increase in money must eventually contract in relation to the demand for consumption goods,

Scheme E
(Same as Scheme D, second stage)

			£
Demand for consumption goods (= products of stage of production No. 1)		...	1,000

	No. 2	...	1,000
	No. 3	...	1,000
	No. 4	...	1,000
Demand for the products of the stages	No. 5	...	1,000
of production	No. 6	...	1,000
	No. 7	...	1,000
	No. 8	...	1,000
	No. 9	...	1,000
	No. 10	...	1,000

Total demand for produced means of production—9 x 1,000 =	...	9,000

Demand for consumption goods in relation to the demand for produced means of production—1 : 9.

that a more or less severe reaction will follow. This frantic game of now enlarging, now contracting the productive apparatus through increases in the volume of money injected, now on the production, now on the consumption side, is always going on under the present organization of currency. Both effects follow each other uninterruptedly and thus an extension or contraction of the productive process is brought about, according to whether credit-creation for productive purposes is accelerated or retarded. So long as the volume of money in circulation is continually changing, we cannot get rid of industrial fluctuations. In particular, every monetary policy which aims at stabilising the value of money and involves, therefore, an increase of its supply with every increase of production, must bring about those very fluctuations which it is trying to prevent.

But least of all is it possible to bring about stability by that "financing of consumption" which Messrs Foster and Catchings recommend, since there would be added to the contraction of production process which automatically follows from increase of productive credits a still further contraction because of the consumptive credits, and thus crises would be rendered exceptionally severe. Only if administered with extraordinary caution and superhuman ability could it, perhaps, be made to prevent crises: if the artificial increase in the demand for consumption goods brought about by those credits were made exactly to cancel the increase in the demand for means of production brought about by the investment of the current flow of savings, thus preserving constant the proportion between the two, this might happen. *But such a policy would effectively prevent any increase in capital equipment and completely frustrate any saving whatever.*[80] There can be no question, therefore, that in the long run, even a policy of this sort would bring about grave disturbances and the disorganization of the economic system as a whole. So that, we may say, in conclusion, that the execution of Messrs Foster and Catchings' proposals would not prevent, but considerably aggravate, crises; that is, it would punish every attempt at capital creation by a loss of a portion of the capital. Carried through to its logical conclusion, it would effectively prevent every real capital accumulation.

That this unavoidable, and, in my opinion, unquestionable effect has not as yet been emphasised in the discussion on Messrs Foster and Catchings is a disturbing indication of the insight into the significance of these problems existing in expert circles. The effect of their teaching on popular opinion is less remarkable when it is considered that proposals of a more or less inflationist tendency—less extreme, perhaps, but in substance exactly similar—are put forward today by economists of very high repute.[81] They are the prevalent fashion of contemporary economics. It is hoped that in exhibiting the objections to such proposals this essay will serve a purpose no less important than the refutation of Messrs Foster and Catchings. Against the popular fallacy that a general crisis can be averted by extension of credit, the same arguments are valid as those used in refuting the theories we have been studying. For the same reasons the great expectations attached to a postponement of public works to times of depression seem to me fallacious. In so far as they are financed by additional credits—and only then can they form an additional demand—they must bring about all those evil effects which, as we have seen, arise when money is increased for consumptive purposes. Indeed the whole expediency of such attempts to alleviate unemployment by relief works and so on is in the light of this analysis highly questionable. If an excessive extension of productive equipment has been once begun, and the impossibility of carrying it through has manifested itself in a crisis, the appearance of unemploy-

---

[80]See the remarks of A. B. Adams, quoted in this chapter, note 65.

[81]This was written in 1929! [Hayek draws attention to the date because by 1931, when this translation appeared, such proposals had become even more popular. —Ed.]

ment and the resulting diminution of the demand for consumption goods may be the only way to set free the means necessary to complete at least a part of the enlarged productive equipment. This can only be mentioned as a possibility. It is by no means asserted as self-evident, nor is any examination of its validity here attempted.

PART II

HAYEK'S EXCHANGES WITH KEYNES AND SRAFFA

THREE

REFLECTIONS ON THE PURE THEORY OF MONEY OF MR. J. M. KEYNES[1]

I

The appearance of any work by Mr. J. M. Keynes must always be a matter of importance: and the publication of the *Treatise on Money*[2] has long been awaited with intense interest by all economists. None the less, in the event, the *Treatise* proves to be so obviously—and, I think, admittedly—the expression of a transitory phase in a process of rapid intellectual development that its appearance cannot be said to have that definitive significance which at one time was expected of it. Indeed, so strongly does it bear the marks of the effect of recent discovery of certain lines of thought hitherto unfamiliar to the school to which Mr. Keynes belongs, that it would be decidedly unfair to regard it as anything else but experimental—a first attempt to amalgamate those new ideas with the monetary teaching traditional in Cambridge and pervading Mr. Keynes's own earlier contributions. That the new approach, which Mr. Keynes has adopted, which makes the rate of interest and its relation to saving and investing the central problem of monetary theory, is an enormous advance on this earlier position, and that it directs the attention to what is really essential, seems to me to be beyond doubt. And even if, to a Continental economist, this way of approach does not seem so novel as it does to the author, it must be admitted that he has made a more ambitious attempt to carry the analysis into the details and complications of the problem than any that has been attempted hitherto. Whether he has been successful here, whether he has not been seriously hampered by the fact that he has not devoted the same amount of effort to understanding those fundamental theorems of "real" economics on which alone any monetary explanation can be successfully built, as he

---

[1] [Published as "Reflections on the Pure Theory of Money of Mr. J. M. Keynes", *Economica*, vol. 11, no. 33, August 1931, pp. 270–295. —Ed.]

[2] J. M. Keynes, *A Treatise on Money*, 2 vols (London: Macmillan, 1930). [Reprinted as volumes 5 (subtitled *The Pure Theory of Money*) and 6 (subtitled *The Applied Theory of Money*) (1971) of *The Collected Writings of John Maynard Keynes*, op. cit. —Ed.]

has to subsidiary embellishments, are questions which will have to be examined.

That such a book is theoretically stimulating goes without saying. At the same time, it is difficult to suppress some concern as regards the immediate effect which its publication in its present form may have on the development of monetary theory. It was, no doubt, the urgency which he attributes to the practical proposals which he holds to be justified by his theoretical reasoning, which led Mr. Keynes to publish the work in what is avowedly an unfinished state. The proposals are indeed revolutionary, and cannot fail to attract the widest attention: They come from a writer who has established an almost unique and well-deserved reputation for courage and practical insight; they are expounded in passages in which the author displays all his astonishing qualities of learning, erudition and realistic knowledge, and in which every possible effort is made to verify the theoretical reasoning by reference to available statistical data. Moreover, most of the practical conclusions seem to harmonise with what seems to the man in the street to be the dictates of common sense, and the favourable impression thus created will probably not be diminished at all by the fact that they are based on a part of the work (Books 3 and 4) which is so highly technical and complicated that it must forever remain entirely unintelligible to those who are not experts. But it is this part on which everything else depends. It is here that all the force and all the weakness of the argument are concentrated, and it is here that the really original work is set forth. And here, unfortunately, the exposition is so difficult, unsystematic, and obscure, that it is extremely difficult for the fellow economist who disagrees with the conclusions to demonstrate exact point of disagreement and to state his objections. There are passages in which the inconsistent use of terms produces a degree of obscurity which, to anyone acquainted with Mr. Keynes's earlier work, is almost unbelievable. It is only with extreme caution and the greatest reserve that one can attempt to criticise, because one can never be sure whether one has understood Mr. Keynes aright.

For this reason, I propose in these reflections to neglect for the present the applications, which fill almost the whole of volume 2, and to concentrate entirely on the imperative task of examining these central difficulties. I address myself expressly to expert readers who have read the book in its entirety.[3]

---

[3]If at any point my own analysis seems to English readers to take too much for granted, perhaps I may be permitted to refer to my *Prices and Production* in chapters 2 and 3 of which I have attempted to provide a broad outline of the general theoretical

II

Book 1 gives a description and classification of the different kinds of money which in many respects is excellent. Where it gives rise to doubts or objections, the points of difference are not of sufficient consequence to make it necessary to give them space which will be much more urgently needed later on. The most interesting and important parts consist in the analysis of the factors which determine the amounts of money which are held by different members of the community, and the division of the total money in circulation into "income deposits" and "business deposits" according to the purpose for which it is held. This distinction, by the way, has turned up again and again in writings on money since the time of Adam Smith (whom Mr. Keynes quotes), but so far it has not proved of much value.

Book 2 is a highly interesting digression into the problem of the measurement of the value of money and forms in itself a systematic and excellent treatise on that controversial subject. Here it must be sufficient to say that it deals with the problem in the most up-to-date manner, treating index-numbers on the lines developed chiefly by Dr. Haberler in his *Sinn der Indexzahlen*,[4] as expressions of the changes in the price-sum of definite collections of commodities—its main addition to the existing knowledge of this subject being an excellent and very much needed criticism of certain attempts to base the method of index numbers on the theory of probability. For an understanding of what follows, I need only mention that Mr. Keynes distinguishes as relatively less important for the purposes of monetary theory the Currency Standard in its two forms, the Cash Transactions Standard and the Cash Balances Standard (and the infinite number of possible secondary price-levels corresponding, not to the general purchasing power of money as a whole, but to its purchasing power for special purposes), from the "Labour Power" of Money and the Purchasing Power of Money proper, which are fundamental in a sense in which price-levels based on other types of expenditure are not, because "human effort and human consumption are the ultimate matters from which alone economic transactions are capable of deriving any significance".[5]

---

considerations which seem to me indispensable in any approach to this problem. [F. A. Hayek, *Prices and Production*, op. cit. —Ed.]

[4][Gottfried Haberler, *Der Sinn der Indexzahlen*, op. cit. See this volume, chapter 2, note 73 for more on Haberler. —Ed.]

[5]*Treatise* [1930], op. cit., vol. 1, p. 134. [*A Treatise on Money*, op. cit., vol. 5, p. 120. —Ed.]

III

It is in Books 3 and 4 that Mr. Keynes proposes "a novel means of approach to the fundamental problem of monetary theory".[6] He begins with an elaborate catalogue of the terms and concepts he wants to use. And here, right at the beginning, we encounter a peculiarity which is likely to prove a stumbling-block to most readers, the concept of entrepreneur's profits. These are expressly excluded from the category of money income, and form a separate category of their own. I have no fundamental objection to this somewhat irritating distinction, and I agree perfectly when he defines profits by saying that "when profits are positive (or negative) entrepreneurs will—in so far as their freedom of action is not fettered by existing bargains with the factors of production which are for the time being irrevocable—seek to expand (or curtail) their scale of operations"[7] and hence depicts profits as the mainspring of change in the existing economic system. But I cannot agree with his explanation of why profits arise, nor with his implication that only changes in "total profits" in his sense can lead to an expansion or curtailment of output. For profits in his view are considered as a "purely monetary phenomenon" in the narrowest sense of that expression. The cause of the emergence of those profits which are "the mainspring of change" is not a "real" factor, not some maladjustment in the relative demand for and supply of cost goods and the irrespective products (i.e., of the relative supply of intermediate products in the successive stages of production) and, therefore, something which could arise also in a barter economy, but simply and solely spontaneous changes in the quantity and direction of the flow of money. Indeed, throughout the whole of his argument the flow of money is treated as if it were the only independent variable which could cause a positive or negative difference between the prices of the products and their respective costs. The structure of goods on which this flow impinges is assumed to be relatively rigid. In fact, of course, the original cause may just as well be a change in the relative supply of these classes of goods, which then, in turn, will affect the quantities of money expended on them.[8]

---

[6]*Ibid.*, Preface. [*Ibid.*, p. xvii. —Ed.]

[7][*Ibid.*, pp. 112–113. —Ed.]

[8]The difference between Mr. Keynes's viewpoint and my own here is not, as may seem in the first instance, due to any neglect on my part of the fact that Mr. Keynes is dealing only with a short-run problem. It is Mr. Keynes rather, with his implied assumption that the real factors are in equilibrium, who is unconsciously introducing a long-run view of the subject.

But though many readers will feel that Mr. Keynes's analysis of profit leaves out essential things, it is not at all easy to detect the flaw in his argument. His explanation seems to flow necessarily from the truism that profits can arise only if more money is received from the sale of goods than has been expended on their production. But, obvious as this is, the conclusion drawn from it becomes a fallacy if only the prices of finished consumption goods and the prices paid for the factors of production are contrasted. And, with the quite insufficient exception of *new* investment goods, this is exactly what Mr. Keynes does. As I shall repeatedly have occasion to point out, he treats the process of the current output of consumption goods as an integral whole in which only the prices paid at the beginning for the factors of production have any bearing on its profitableness. He seems to think that sufficient account of any change in the relative supply (and therefore in the value) of intermediate products in the successive stages of that process is provided for by his concept of (positive or negative) investment, i.e., the net addition to (or diminution from) the capital of the community. But this is by no means suffficient if only the total or net increment (or decrement) of investment goods in all stages is considered and treated as a whole, and the possibility of fluctuations between these stages is neglected; yet this is just what Mr. Keynes does. The fact that his whole concept of investment is ambiguous, and that its meaning is constantly shifting between the idea of any surplus beyond the reproduction of the identical capital goods which have been used up in current production and the idea of any addition to the total value of the capital goods, renders it still less adequate to account for that phenomenon.

When I come to the concept of investment I shall quote evidence of this confusion. For the present, however, let us assume that the concept of investment includes, as, in spite of some clearly contradictory statements of Mr. Keynes it probably should include, only the net addition to the value of all the existing capital goods. If we take a situation where, according to that criterion, no investment takes place, and therefore the total expenditure on the factors of production is to be counted as being directed towards the current production of consumers' goods, it is quite conceivable that—to take an extreme case—there may be no net difference between the total receipts for the output and the total payments for the factors of production, and no net profits for the entrepeneurs as a whole, *because* profits in the lower stages of production are exactly compensated by the losses in the higher stages. Yet, in that case, it will not be profitable for a time for entrepreneurs as a whole to continue to employ the same quantity of factors of production as before. We need only consider the quite conceivable case that in each of the successive stages of production there are more intermediate products than are needed for the reproduction of the intermediate products existing at the same moment in the following stage, so that, in the lower stages (i.e., those nearer consumption) there is a shortage, and in the higher stages there is an abundance, as compared with the current demand for consumers' goods. In this case, all the entrepreneurs in the higher stages of production will probably make losses; but even if these losses were exactly compensated, or more than compensated, by the profits made in the lower stages, in a large part of the complete process necessary for the continuous supply of consumption goods it will not pay to employ all the factors of production available. And while the losses of the producers of those stages are balanced by the profits of those finishing consumption goods, the diminution of their demand for the factors of production cannot be made up by the increased demand from the latter because these need mainly semi-finished goods and can use labour only in proportion to the quantitites of such goods which are available in the respective stages. In such a case, profits and losses are originally not the effect of a discrepancy between the receipts for consumption goods and the expenditure on the factors of production, and therefore they are not explained by Mr. Keynes's analysis. Or, rather, there are no total profits in Mr. Keynes's sense in this case, and yet there occur those very effects which he regards as only conceivable as the consequence of the emergence of net total profits or losses. The explanation of this is that while the definition of profits which I have quoted before serves very well when it is applied to individual profits, it becomes misleading when it is applied to entrepreneurs as a whole. The entrepreneurs making profits need not necessarily employ more original factors of production to expand their production, but may draw mainly on the existing stocks of intermediate products of the preceding stages while entrepreneurs suffering losses dismiss workmen.

But this is not all. Not only is it possible for the changes which Mr. Keynes attributes only to changes in "total profits" to occur when "total profits" in his sense are absent: It is also possible for "total profits" to emerge for causes other than those contemplated in his analysis. It is by no means necessary for "total profits" to be the effect of a difference between *current* receipts and *current* expenditure. Nor need every difference between current receipts and current expenditure lead to the emergence of "total profits". For even if there is neither positive nor negative investment, yet entrepreneurs may gain or lose in the aggregate because of changes of the value of capital which existed before—changes due to new additions to or subtractions from existing capital.[9] It is such changes in the value of existing intermediate products (or "investment", or capital, or whatever one likes to call it) which act as a balancing factor between current receipts and current expenditure. Or to put the same thing another way, profits cannot be explained as the difference between expenditure in one period and receipts in the *same* period or a period of equal length because *the result of the expenditure in one period will very often have to be sold in a period which is either longer or shorter than the first period.* It is indeed the essential characteristic of positive or negative investment that this must be the case.

It is not possible at this stage to show that a divergence between current expenditure and current receipts will always tend to cause changes in the value of existing capital which are by no means constituted by that difference, and that because of this, the effects of a difference between current receipts and current expenditure (i.e., profits in Mr. Keynes's sense) may lead to a change in the value of existing capital which may more than balance the money-profits. We shall have to deal with this matter in detail when we come to Mr. Keynes's explanation of the trade cycle, but before we can do that we shall have to analyse his concept of investment very closely. It should, however, already be clear that even if his concept of investment does not refer, as has been assumed, to changes in the value of existing capital but to changes in the physical quantitites of capital goods—and there can be no doubt that in many parts of his book Mr. Keynes uses it in this sense—this would not remedy the deficiencies of his analysis. At the same time there can be no doubt that it is the lack of a clear concept of investment—and of capital—which is the cause of this unsatisfactory account of profits.

There are other very mischievous peculiarities of this concept of profits which may be noted at this point. The derivation of profits from the difference between receipts for the total output and the expenditure on the factors of production implies that there exists some normal rate of remuneration of invested capital which is more stable than profits. Mr. Keynes does not explicitly state this, but he includes the remuneration of invested capital in his more comprehensive concept of the "money rate of efficiency earnings of the factors of production" in general, a concept on which I shall have more to say later on. But even if it be true, as it probably is, that the rate of remuneration of the original factors of production is relatively more rigid than profits, it is certainly

---

[9]Of course such changes need not only affect entrepreneurs. They may also affect other owners of capital.

not true in regard to the remuneration of invested capital. Mr. Keynes obviously arrives at this view by an artificial separation of the function of the entrepreneurs as owners of capital and their function as entrepreneurs in the narrow sense. But these two functions cannot be absolutely separated even in theory, because the essential function of the entrepreneurs, that of assuming risks, necessarily implies the ownership of capital. Moreover, *any new chance to make entrepreneurs' profits is identical with a change in the opportunities to invest capital, and will always be reflected in the earnings (and value) of capital invested.* (For similar reasons it seems to me also impossible to mark off entrepeneurs' profits as something fundamentally different from, say, the extra gain of a workman who moves first to a place where a scarcity of labour makes itself felt and, therefore, for some time obtains wages higher than the normal rate.)

Now this artificial separation of entrepreneurs' profits from the earnings of existing capital has very serious consequences for the further analysis of investment: It leads not to an explanation of the changes in the demand price offered by the entrepreneurs for new capital, but only to an explanation of changes in their aggregate demand for "factors of production" in general. But, surely, an explanation of the causes which make investment more or less attractive should form the basis of any analysis of investment. *Such an explanation can, however, only be reached by a close analysis of the factors determining the relative prices of capital goods in the different successive stages of production*—for the difference between these prices is the only source of interest. But this is excluded from the outset if only *total* profits are made the aim of the investigation. Mr. Keynes's aggregates conceal the most fundamental mechanisms of change.

IV

I pass now to the central and most obscure theme of the book, the description and explanation of the processes of investment. It seems to me that most of the difficulties which arise here are a consequence of the peculiar method of approach adopted by Mr. Keynes, who, from the outset, analyses complex dynamic processes without laying the necessary foundations by adequate static analysis of the fundamental process. Not only does he fail to concern himself with the conditions which must be given to secure the continuation of the existing capitalistic (i.e., roundabout) organisation of production—the creating an equilibrium between the depreciation and the renewal of existing capital—not only does he take the maintenance of the existing capital stock more or less as a matter of course (which it certainly is not—it requires quite definite relationships between the prices of consumption goods and the prices of capital goods to make it profitable to keep capital intact): He does not even explain the conditions of equilibrium at any given rate of saving, nor the effects of any change in the rate of saving. Only when money comes in as a disturbing factor by making the rate at which additional capital goods are produced different from the rate at which saving is taking place does he begin to be interested.

All this would do no harm if his analysis of this complicating moment were based on a clear and definite theory of capital and saving developed elsewhere, either by himself or by others. But this is obviously not the case. Moreover, he makes a satisfactory analysis of the whole process of investment still more difficult for himself by another peculiarity of his analysis, namely by completely separating the process of the reproduction of the old capital from the addition of new capital, and treating the former simply as a part of current production of consumption goods, in defiance of the obvious fact that the production of the same goods, whether they are destined for the replacement of or as additions to the old stock of capital, must be determined by the same set of conditions. New savings and new investment are treated as if they were something entirely different from the reinvestment of the quota of amortisation of old capital, and as if it were not the same market where the prices of capital goods needed for the current production of consumption goods and of additional capital goods are determined. Instead of a "horizontal" division between capital goods (or goods of higher stages or orders) and consumption goods (or goods of lower stages)—which one would have thought would have recommended itself on the ground that in each of these groups and sub-groups production will be regulated by similar conditions—Mr. Keynes attempts a kind of vertical division, counting that part of the production of capital goods which is necessary for the continuation of the current production of consumption goods as a part of the process of producing consumption goods, and only that part of the production of capital goods which *adds* to the existing stock of capital as production of investment goods. But this procedure involves him, as we shall see, in serious difficulties when he has to determine what is to be considered as additional capital—difficulties which he has not clearly solved. The question is whether any increase of the value of the existing capital is to be considered as such an addition—in this case, of course, such an addition could be brought about without any new production of such goods—or whether only additions to the physical quantities of capital goods are counted as such an addition—a method of computation which becomes clearly impossible when the old capital goods are not replaced by goods of exactly the same kind, but when a transition to more capitalistic methods brings it about that other goods are produced in place of those used up in production.

This continual attempt to elucidate special complications without first providing a sufficient basis in the form of an explanation of the more simple equilibrium relations becomes particularly noticeable in a later stage of the investigation when Mr. Keynes tries to incorporate into his system the ideas of Wicksell. In Wicksell's system these are necessary outgrowths of the most elaborate theory of capital we possess, that of Böhm-Bawerk.[10] It is a priori unlikely that an attempt to utilise the conclusions drawn from a certain theory without accepting that theory itself should be successful. But in the case of an author of Mr. Keynes's intellectual calibre, the attempt produces results which are truly remarkable.

Mr. Keynes ignores completely the general theoretical basis of Wicksell's theory. But, nonetheless, he seems to have felt that such a theoretical basis is wanting, and accordingly he has sat down to work one out for himself. But for all this, it still seems to him somewhat out of place in a treatise on money, so instead of presenting his theory of capital here, in the forefront of his exposition, where it would have figured to most advantage, he relegates it to a position in volume 2 and apologizes for inserting it.[11] But the most remarkable features of these chapters (27–29) is not that he supplies at least a part of the required theoretical foundation, but that he discovers anew certain essential elements of Böhm-Bawerk's theory of capital, especially what he calls (as has been done before in many discussions of Böhm-Bawerk's theory—I mention only Taussig's *Wages and Capital*[12] as one of the earliest and best

[10][See this volume, chapter 1, note 4 for more on Wicksell. Keynes mentions Wicksell at various points in the *Treatise* (e.g., vol. 5, pp. 139, 167, 176–178), but the reference is always to Wicksell's 1898 book, which was translated by Keynes's former student Richard F. Kahn as *Interest and Prices*, op. cit. In his earlier work, *Über Wert, Kapital und Rente*, translated as *Value, Capital and Rent* [1893] (London: Allen & Unwin, 1954), Wicksell had proposed a synthesis of the Walrasian general equilibrium approach with Böhm-Bawerk's theory of capital, a synthesis he carried to fruition in his two-volume work, *Vorlesungen über Nationalökonomie* [1901, 1906], translated as *Lectures on Political Economy*, op. cit. It is interesting to note that Keynes was an unenthusiastic reviewer of the translation of the *Lectures* for another press, Macmillan's, in the early 1930s; see his letter in *Economic Articles and Correspondence: Investment and Editorial*, Donald Moggridge, ed., vol. 12 (1983) of *The Collected Writings of John Maynard Keynes*, op. cit., pp. 862–865. Hayek's point in this section is that the monetary framework of *Interest and Prices* is erected upon a theory of capital found in Wicksell's earlier book, but reference to which is absent in Keynes's *Treatise*. —Ed.]

[11]*Treatise* (1930), op. cit., vol. 2, p. 95. [*A Treatise on Money*, op. cit., vol. 6, p. 85. —Ed.]

[12][Frank Taussig, *Wages and Capital* (New York: D. Appleton, 1896; reprinted, New York: Kelley, 1968). See this volume, chapter 1, note 4, for more on Taussig. —Ed.]

known instances) the "true wages fund"[13] and earlier[14] Böhm-Bawerk's formula for the relation between the average length of the roundabout process of production and the amount of capital.[15] Would not Mr. Keynes have made his task easier if he had not only accepted one of the descendants of Böhm-Bawerk's theory, but had also made himself acquainted with the substance of that theory itself?

V

We must now consider in more detail Mr. Keynes's analysis of the process of investment. Not the least difficult part of this task is to find out what is really meant by the expression investment as it is used here. It is certainly no accident that the inconsistencies of terminology, to which I have alluded before, become particularly frequent as soon as investment is referred to. I must mention here some of the most disturbing instances, as they will illustrate the difficulties in which every serious student of Mr. Keynes's book finds himself involved.

Perhaps the clearest expression of what Mr. Keynes thinks when he uses the term investment is to be found where he defines it as "the act of the entrepreneur whose function it is to make the decisions which determine the amount of the non-available output" consisting "in the positive act of starting or maintaining some process of production or of withholding liquid goods. It is measured by the net addition to wealth whether in the form of fixed capital, working capital, or liquid

---

[13] *Treatise* (1930), op. cit., vol. 2, pp. 127–129. [*A Treatise on Money*, op. cit., vol. 6, pp. 114–115. —Ed.]

[14] *Ibid.*, vol. 1, p. 308. [*Ibid.*, vol. 5, pp. 276–277. —Ed.]

[15] According to Böhm-Bawerk (*Positive Theory*, 3rd edition, p. 535, English translation p. 328) the stock of capital must be $(x+1)/2$ as great as the amount of consumption goods consumed during a period of time if x stands for the total length of the production process and if the original factors of production are applied at a steady rate. Mr. Keynes calls the magnitude which Böhm-Bawerk called x, $2r - 1$ and, as $[(2r - 1) + 1]/2 = r$, comes to the conclusion that the working capital (to which, for unaccountable reasons, he confines his formula) amounts to r times the earnings per unit of time. [Hayek refers to Böhm-Bawerk's *Positive Theory of Capital*, op. cit., p. 318. —Ed.]

capital".[16] It is perhaps somewhat misleading to use the term investment for the act as well as the result, and it might have been more appropriate to use in the former sense the term "investing". But that would not matter if Mr. Keynes would confine himself to these two senses, for it would not be difficult to keep them apart. But while the expression "net addition to wealth" in the passage just quoted clearly indicates that investment means the increment of the value of existing capital—since wealth cannot be measured otherwise than as value—somewhat earlier, when the term "value of investment" occurs for the first time,[17] it is expressly defined as "not the increment of value of the total capital, but the value of the increment of capital during any period". Now, in any case, this would be difficult as, if it is not assumed that the old capital is always replaced by goods of exactly the same kind so that it can be measured as a physical magnitude, it is impossible to see how the increment of capital can be determined otherwise than as an increment of the value of the total. But, to make the confusion complete, side by side with these two definitions of investment as the increment of the value of existing capital and the value of the increment, four pages after the passage just quoted, he defines the "Value of the Investment" (should the capital V or the second "the" explain the different definition?) not as an increment at all but as the "value of the aggregate of Real and Loan Capital" and contrasts it with the increment of investment which he now defines as "the net increase of the items belonging to the various categories which make up the aggregate of Real and Loan Capital" while "the value of the increment of investment" is now "the sum of the values of the additional items".[18]

These obscurities are not a matter of minor importance. It is because he has allowed them to arise that Mr. Keynes fails to realize the necessity of dealing with the all-important problem of changes in the value of existing capital; and this failure, as we have already seen, is the main cause of his unsatisfactory treatment of profit. It is also partly responsible for the deficiencies of his concept of capital. I have tried hard to discover what Mr. Keynes means by investment by examining the use he makes of it, but all in vain. It might be hoped to get a clearer definition by exclusion from the way in which he defines the "current output of consumption goods" for, as we shall see later, the amount of investment stands in a definite relation to the current output of

[16]*Treatise* (1930), op. cit., vol. 1, p. 172. [*A Treatise on Money*, op. cit., vol. 5, p. 155. —Ed.]

[17]*Ibid.*, vol. 1, p. 126. [*Ibid.*, vol. 5, p. 114. —Ed.]

[18][*Ibid.*, vol. 5, p. 117. —Ed.]

consumers' goods so that their aggregate cost is equal to the total money income of the community. But here the obscurities which obstruct the way are as great as elsewhere. While on page 135,[19] the cost of production of the current output of consumption goods is defined as total earnings *minus* that part of it which has been earned by the production of investment goods (which a few pages earlier[20] has been defined as "non-available output *plus* the increment of hoards"), there occurs on page 130 a definition of the "output of consumption goods during any period" as "the flow of available output *plus* the increment of Working Capital which will emerge as available output", i.e., as including part of the as yet non-available output which, in the passage quoted before, has been included in investment goods and therefore excluded from the current output of consumption goods. And still a few pages earlier[21] a "flow of consumers' goods" appears as part of the available output, while on the same page "the excess of the flow of increment to unfinished goods in process over the flow of finished goods emerging from the productive prices" (which, obviously, includes "the increment of Working Capital which will emerge as available output" which, in the passage quoted before, is part of the output of consumption goods) is now classed as non-available output. I am afraid it is not altogether my fault if at times I feel altogether helpless in this jungle of differing definitions.

VI

In the preceding sections we have made the acquaintance of the fundamental concepts which Mr. Keynes uses as tools in his analysis of the process of the circulation of money. Now we must turn to his picture of the process itself. The skeleton of his exposition is given in a few pages[22] in a series of algebraic equations which, however, are not only very difficult, but can only be correctly understood in connection with the whole of Book 3. In the diagram that follows, I have made an attempt to give a synoptic view of the process as Mr. Keynes depicts it, which, I hope, will give an adequate idea of the essential elements of his exposition.

---

[19][*Ibid.*, vol. 5, p. 121. —Ed.]

[20]*Ibid.*, vol. 1, p. 130. [*Ibid.*, vol. 5, p. 118. —Ed.]

[21]*Ibid.*, vol. 1, p. 127. [*Ibid.*, vol. 5, p. 115. —Ed.]

[22]*Ibid.*, vol. 1, pp. 135–140. [*Ibid.*, vol. 5, pp. 121–126. This is the part of the *Treatise* where Keynes's famous "fundamental equations" are revealed. —Ed.]

Diagrammatic Version of Mr. Keynes's Theory of the Circulation of Money[23]

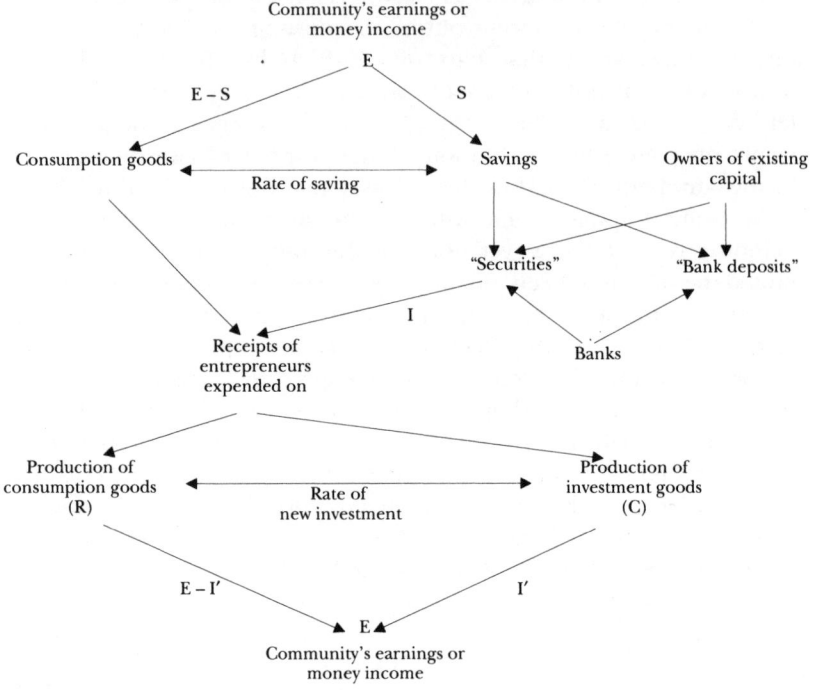

[23] The formulæ on which the above diagram is based are as follows:

$R + C = O$ (quantity of total current output)

$\dfrac{E}{O} = W_1$ (rate of efficiency earnings) $= \dfrac{W}{e}$ (rate of earnings per unit of human effort ÷ the co-efficient of efficiency)

Q_1 (Profit on consumption goods) $= (E - S) - (E - I') = I' - S$

P (Price level of consumption goods) $= \dfrac{E}{O} + \dfrac{I' - S}{R} = W_1 + \dfrac{Q_1}{R}$ \hfill (1)

Q_2 (Profit on investment goods) $I - I'$

P′ (Price level of investment goods*) $= \dfrac{E}{O} + \dfrac{I - I'}{C} = W_1 + \dfrac{Q}{C}$

Q (Profit on total output) $= (E - S) + I - E = I - S$

II (Price level of total output) $= \dfrac{E}{O} + \dfrac{I - S}{R} = W_1 + \dfrac{Q}{O}$ \hfill (2)

(The numbers in brackets denote Mr. Keynes's first and second fundamental equations respectively.)

E, which stands at the top and again at the bottom of the diagram, represents (according to the definition which opens Book 3) the total earnings of the factors of production. These are to be considered as identically one and the same thing as (*a*) the community's money income (which includes all wages in the widest sense of the word, the normal remuneration of the entrepreneurs, interest on capital, regular monopoly gains, rents, and the like) and (*b*) "the cost of production". Though the definition does not expressly say so, the use Mr. Keynes makes of the symbol E clearly shows that that "cost of production" refers to current output. But here the first difficulty arises. Is it necessarily true that the E, which was the cost of production of current output, is the same thing as the E which is earned during the period when this current output comes on to the market and which therefore is available to buy that current output? If we take the picture as a crosscut at any moment of time, there can be no doubt that the E at the top and the E at the bottom of our diagram, i.e., income available for the purchase of output and the earnings of the factors of production, will be identical, but that does not prove that the cost of *current output* need necessarily also be the same. Only if the picture were to be considered as representing the process in time as a kind of longitudinal section, and if then the two E's at the top and at the bottom (i.e., current money income and the remuneration of the factors of production which were earned from the production of the current output) were still equal, would the assumption made by Mr. Keynes be actually given. But this could only be true in a stationary state: and it is exactly for the analysis of a dynamic society that Mr. Keynes constructs his formulae. And in a dynamic society that assumption does not apply.

But whatever the relations of earnings to the cost of production of current output may be, there can be no doubt that Mr. Keynes is right when he emphasises the importance of the fact that the flow of the community's earnings of money income shows "a twofold division (1) into the parts which have been earned by the production of consumption-goods and investment-goods respectively and (2) into parts which

---

There is a disturbing lack of method in Mr. Keynes's choice of symbols, which makes it particularly difficult to follow his algebra. The reader should especially remember that while profits on the production of consumption goods, investment goods and total profits are denoted by Q_1, Q_2 and Q respectively, the symbols for the corresponding price-levels are chosen without any parallelism as P, P' and I and I', where the dash does not stand for a similar relation, but in the former case serves to mark off the price-level of investment goods from that of consumption goods, and in the second case to distinguish the cost of production of the increment of new investment goods (I') from its value (I).

* This formula is not given by Mr. Keynes.

are *expended* on consumption goods and savings respectively"[24] and that these two divisions need not be in the same proportion, and that any divergence between them will have important consequences.

Clearly recipients of income must make a choice: They may spend on consumption goods or they may refrain from doing so. In Mr. Keynes's terminology the latter operation constitutes saving. In so far as they do save in this sense, they have the further choice between what one would ordinarily call hoarding and investing or, as Mr. Keynes (because he has employed these more familiar terms for other concepts) chooses to call it, between "bank-deposits" and "securities".[25] In so far as the money saved is converted into "loan or real capital", i.e., is lent to entrepreneurs or used to buy investment goods, this means a choice for what Mr. Keynes calls "securities" while when it is held as money this means a choice for "bank deposits". This choice, however, is not only open to persons saving currently, but also to persons who have saved before and are therefore owners of the whole block of old capital. But even this is not yet the end. There is a third and most important factor which may affect the relation between what is currently saved and what becomes currently available for the purposes of investment: the banks. If the demand of the public for bank deposits increases either because the people who save invest only part of the amounts saved, or because the owners of old capital want to convert part of their "securities" into "bank deposits", the banks may create the additional deposits and use them to buy the "securities" which the public is less anxious to hold, and so make up for the difference between current saving and the buying of securities. The banking system may, of course, also create deposits to a greater or a lesser extent than would be necessary for this purpose and will then itself be one of the three factors causing the divergence between savings and investment in "securities".

On the other hand, entrepreneurs will receive money from two sources: either from the sale of the output of consumption goods, or

---

[24] *Treatise* (1930), op. cit., vol. 1, p. 134. [*A Treatise on Money*, op. cit., vol. 5, p. 121. —Ed.]

[25] *Ibid.*, vol. 1, p. 141. [*Ibid.*, vol. 5, p. 127. —Ed.] Some readers may find it confusing that Mr. Keynes uses "bank deposits" and "savings deposits" interchangeably in this connection without explaining why a few lines after having introduced the term "bank deposits" in a special technical sense, he substitutes "savings deposits" for it. But as savings deposits are defined (*Ibid.*, vol. 1, p. 36) [*Ibid.*, vol. 5, p. 31. —Ed.] as bank deposits "held, not for the purpose of making payments, but as a means of employing savings, i.e., as an investment", this substitution is quite consistent with the definition, though it is certainly irritating that the employment of savings "as an investment" in this sense is to be contrasted with their other possible use for "securities" which again means investment, but in another, special sense.

from the "sale" of "securities" (which means investment in the ordinary sense), which latter operation may take the form of selling investment goods they have produced or raising a loan for the purpose of holding old or producing new investment goods. I understand—I am not sure whether Mr. Keynes really intends to convey this impression—that the total received from these two sources will be equal to the value of new investment, but in this case it would be identical with the amount of the "securities", and there would then be no reason to introduce this latter term. If, however, I should be mistaken on that point, the symbol *I* (which stands for the value of new investments) would not belong to the place where I have inserted it in the diagram above.

In regard to this total of money at the disposal of entrepreneurs, these have a further and, as must be conceded to Mr. Keynes, to a certain extent independent choice: They have to decide what part of it shall be used for the current production of consumption goods and what part for the production of new investment goods. But their choice is by no means an arbitrary one; and the way in which changes in the two variables mentioned above and changes in technical knowledge and the relative demand for different consumption goods (those which require more or less capital for their production) influence the relative attractiveness of the two lines is the most important problem of all, a problem which can be solved only on the basis of a complete theory of capital. And it is just here, though, of course, Mr. Keynes devotes much effort to the discussion of this central problem, that the lack of an adequate theoretical basis and the consequent obscurities of his concept of "investment", which I have noted before, make themselves felt. The whole idea that it is possible to draw in the way he does a sharp line of distinction between the production of investment goods and the current production of consumption goods is misleading. *The alternative is not between producing consumption goods or producing investment goods, but between producing investment goods which will yield consumption goods at a more or less distant date in the future.* The process of investment does not consist in producing side by side with what is necessary to continue current production of consumption goods on the old methods, additional investment goods, but rather in producing *other* machinery, for the same purpose but of a greater degree of efficiency, to take the place of the inferior machinery etc., used up in the current production of consumption goods. And when the entrepreneurs decide to increase their investment, this does not necessarily mean that at that time more original factors of production than before are employed in the production of investment goods, but only that the new processes started will have the effect that, because of their longer duration, *after some time* a smaller proportion of the output will be "available" and a larger "non-available". Nor does it mean as a matter of course that even that part of the total amount spent on the factors of production which is not new investment but only reproduction of capital used up in the current production of consumption goods will become available after the usual time.

VII

But, in addition to all these obscurities which are a consequence of the ambiguity of the concept of investment employed by Mr. Keynes, and which, of course, disturb all the apparent neatness of his mathematical formulae, there is a further difficulty introduced with these formulae. In order to provide an explanation of the changes in the price-level (or rather price-levels) he needs, in addition to his symbols denoting amounts of money or money-values, symbols representing the physical quantities of the goods on which the money is spent. He therefore chooses his units of quantities of goods in such a way that "a unit of each has the same cost of production at the base date" and calls O "the total output of goods in terms of these units in a unit of time, R the volume of liquid Consumption-goods and Services flowing onto the market and purchased by the consumers, and C the net increment of investment, in the sense that $O = R + C$".[26] Now these sentences, which are all that is said in explanation of these important magnitudes, give rise to a good deal of doubt. Whatever "cost of production" in the first sentence means (I suppose it means money cost, in which case R would be identical with $E - I'$ and C with I' at the base date), *the fact that these units are based on a relation existing at an arbitrarily chosen base date makes them absolutely unsuitable for the explanation of any dynamic process.* There can be no doubt that any change of the proportion between what Mr. Keynes calls production of consumption goods and what he calls production of investment goods will be connected with changes of the quantities of the goods of both types which can be produced with the expenditure of a given amount of costs. *But if, as a consequence of such a change, the relative costs of consumption goods and investment goods change, this means that the measurement in units which are produced at equal cost at some base date is a measurement according to an entirely irrelevant criterion.* It would be nonsense to consider as equivalent a certain number of bottles and an automatic machine for producing bottles because, before the fall in the rate of interest made the use of such a machine profitable, it cost as much to produce the one as the other. But this is exactly what Mr.

[26]*Ibid.*, vol. 1, p. 135. [*Ibid.*, vol. 5, p. 122. —Ed.]

Keynes would be compelled to do if he only stuck to his definitions. But, of course, he does not, as is shown by the fact that he treats $(E/O)R$ as identical with $E - I'$ and $(E/O)C$ as identical with I' throughout periods of change—which would only be the case if his units of quantity were neither determined by equality of money cost at the base date (money cost without a fixed base would give no measure of quantities) nor, indeed, by any cost at the base date at all, but by some kind of variable "real cost". This is probably what Mr. Keynes has in mind most of the time, though he never says so—but I cannot see how it will help him in the end.

But not only does the division of O into its component parts R and C give rise to such difficulties. The use which is made of O alone is also not free from objections. We shall see in a moment that E/O (i.e., the total income divided by the total output) forms one of the terms of both his fundamental equations. Mr. Keynes calls this the "money rate of efficiency earnings of the factors of production", or more shortly the "money rate of efficiency earnings". Now let me remind the reader for a moment that E means, as identically one and the same thing, (1) the community's money income, (2) the earnings of the factors of production, and (3) the cost of production, and that it expressly includes interest on capital and therefore in any case interest earned on existing capital goods.[27] I must confess that I am absolutely unable to attach any useful meaning to his concept of "the money rate of efficiency earnings of the factors of production" if capital is to be included among the factors of production and if it is *ex hypothesi* assumed that the amount of capital and therefore its productivity is changing. If the units in which O is measured are in any sense cost units, it is surely clear that interest will not stand in the same relation to the cost of production of the capital goods as the remuneration of the other factors of production to their cost of production. Or does there lie at the basis of the concept some attempt to construct a common denominator of real cost so as to include "abstinence"?

Mr. Keynes shows a certain inclination to identify efficiency earnings with efficiency wages (as when he speaks about the prevailing type of

---

[27]On page 211 (*Ibid.*, vol. 1) [*Ibid.*, vol. 5, p. 189. —Ed.], it is expressly stated in connection with some special problem that "in this case interest is simply the money rate of earnings of one of the factors of production", but as E includes interest, and the money-rate of efficiency earnings of the factors of production is expressed by E/O this must be true generally and not only in that particular context.

contracts between entrepreneurs and the factors of production being that of efficiency-earnings rather than effort-earnings—what does efficiency-earnings or even effort-earnings mean in regard to capital?—or when he speaks about the rate of earnings per unit of human effort,[28] and in regard to wages the concept of efficiency of earnings certainly has some sense if it is identified, as it is on page 166, with piece wages. But even if we assume that all contracts with labour were on the basis of piece wages, it would by no means follow that so long as existing contracts continue, efficiency wages would always be E/O. Piece rates relate only to a single workman or perhaps a group of workmen and their respective immediate output, but never to output as a whole. If, at unchanged piece rates for the individual workmen, total output rises as a consequence of an improved organisation of the total process of production, E/O may change (because O is increased) without any corresponding change in the rate of money earnings of the individuals. A type of contract according to which the earnings of factors engaged in the higher stages of production automatically changed as their contribution to the output of the last stage changed not only does not exist, it is inconceivable. There is, therefore, no market where the "money rate of efficiency earnings of the factors of production" is determined, and no price or group of prices which would correspond to that concept. What it amounts to is, as Mr. Keynes himself states in several places,[29] nothing else but the average cost of production of some more or less arbitrarily chosen units of output (i.e., such units as had "equal costs at the base date") which will change with every change of the price of the units of the factors of production (including interest) as well as with every change in the organisation of production, and therefore with every change not only in the average price of the factors of production, but also with every change in their relative prices—changes which generally lead to a change in the methods of production and therefore in the amount of output produced with a given amount of factors of production. To call this the "money rate of efficiency earnings of the factors of production" and occasionally even simply "rate of earnings" can have no other effect than to convey the

[28]*Ibid.*, vol. 1, pp. 135, 153, 166 et seq. [*Ibid.*, vol. 5, pp. 122, 137–138, 149 et seq. —Ed.]

[29]*Ibid.*, vol. 1, p. 136. [*Ibid.*, vol. 5, p. 122. —Ed.]

misleading impression that this magnitude is determined solely by the existing contracts with the factors of production.

VIII

Mr. Keynes's picture of the circulation of money shows three points where spontaneous change may be initiated: (1) the rate of saving may change, i.e., the division of the total money income of the community into the parts which are spent on consumption goods and saving respectively; (2) the rate of investment may change, i.e., the proportion in which the factors of production are directed by entrepreneurs to the production of consumption goods and the production of additional investment goods respectively; (3) banks may pass on to investors more or less money than that part of the savings which is not directly invested (and that part of the old capital which is withdrawn from investment) but converted into bank deposits so that the total of money going to entrepreneurs as investment surpasses or falls short of total savings.

If only (1) changes, i.e., if the rate of saving changes without any corresponding change in (2) and (3) from the position existing before the change in (1) (which is to be taken as an equilibrium position) took place, the effect will be that producers of consumption goods receive so much more or less for their output than has been expended on its production as $E - S$ exceeds or falls short of $E - I'$. $(E - S) - (E - I')$ or $I' - S$, i.e., the difference between savings and the cost of investment, will be equal to the profits on the production of consumption goods; and as this magnitude is positive or negative entrepreneurs will be induced to expand or curtail output. Provided that (3) remains at the equilibrium position, i.e., that banks will pass on to the entrepreneurs exactly the amount which is saved and not invested directly, the effect on the production of investment goods will be exactly the reverse of the effect on the production of consumption goods. That is to say (positive or negative) profits made on the production of consumption goods will be exactly balanced by (negative or positive) profits on the production of investment goods. A change in (1) will, therefore, never give rise to total profits, but only to partial profits balanced by equal losses, and only lead to a shift between the production of consumption goods and the production of investment goods which will go on until profits on both sides disappear.

It is easily to be seen that the effect of changes of the type (2) will, if not accompanied by changes in either (1) or (3), be of exactly the same nature as of changes in (1). Positive profits on the one hand and negative profits on the other will soon show that the deviation from the equilibrium position existing before without a corresponding change in

(1) is unprofitable and will lead to a re-establishment of the former proportion between the production of consumption goods and the production of investment goods.

Only a change in (3) will lead to total profits. (This is also shown by the formula for total profits, namely $Q=I-S$.) Now the causes why I may be different from S are of a very complex nature, and are investigated by Mr. Keynes in very great detail. We shall have to discuss his analysis of this problem when we come to his theory of the bank rate. For present purposes, it will, however, be more convenient to take the possibility of such a divergence for granted, and only to mention that the fact that more (or less) money is being invested than is being saved is equivalent to so much money being added to (or withdrawn from) industrial circulation, so that the total of profits, or the difference between the expenditure and the receipts of the entrepreneurs, which is the essential element in the second term of the fundamental equations, will be equal to the net addition to (or subtraction from) the effective circulation. It is here, according to Mr. Keynes, that we find the monetary causes working for a change in the price-level; and he considers it the main advantage of his fundamental equations that they isolate this factor.

IX

The aim of the fundamental equations is to "exhibit the causal process, by which the price-level is determined, and the method of transition from one position of equilibrium to another".[30] What they say is essentially that the purchasing power of money (or the general price-level) will deviate from its "equilibrium position", i.e., the average cost of production of the unit of output, only if I' or I (if the price-level in general and not the purchasing power of money, or the price-level of consumption goods is concerned) is different from S. This has to be constantly kept in mind lest the reader be misled by occasional statements which convey the impression that this applies to every change in the price-level, and not only to changes relatively to cost of production[31] or that the "equilibrium position" is in any way definitely

---

[30] *Ibid.*, vol. 1, p. 135. [*Ibid.*, vol. 5, p. 120. —Ed.]

[31] Cf. e.g. on page 158 of *Treatise,* op. cit., vol. 1 [*A Treatise on Money,* op. cit., vol. 5, p. 142. —Ed.], where Mr. Keynes speaks simply of the "condition for the stability of the purchasing power" where he obviously does not mean absolute stability but permanent coincidence with the "equilibrium level".

determined by the existing contracts with the factors of production[32], and not simply the cost of production, or what means the same thing, the "money-rate of efficiency earnings of the factors of production".

The best short explanation of the meaning of the fundamental equations I can find is the following[33]: "Thus, the long period equilibrium norm of the Purchasing Power of Money is given by the money-rate of efficiency earnings of the Factors of Production; whilst the actual Purchasing Power oscillates below or above this equilibrium level according as the cost of current investment is running ahead of, or falling behind, savings.... A principal object of this Treatise is to show that we have here the clue to the way in which the fluctuations of the price-level actually come to pass, whether they are due to oscillations about a steady equilibrium or to a transition from one equilibrium to another.... Accordingly, therefore, as the banking system is allowing the rate of investment to exceed or fall behind the rate of saving, the price-level (assuming that there is no spontaneous change in the rate of efficiency-earnings) will rise or fall. If, however, the prevailing type of contract between the entrepreneurs and the factors of production is in terms of effort-earnings W and not in terms of efficiency-earnings W_1 (existing arrangements probably lie as a rule somewhere between the two) then it would be $(1/e)P$, which would tend to rise or fall, where, as before, e is the coefficient of efficiency".

This says quite clearly that not all changes of the price-level need to be started by a divergence between I' (or I) and S, but that it is only one particular cause of such changes, i.e., the changes in the amount of money in circulation, which is isolated by this form of equation. But the peculiar substitution of the misleading term "the money-rate of efficiency earnings of the Factors of Production" for simply money cost of production seems at places to mislead Mr. Keynes himself. I cannot see any reason whatever why, as indicated in the passage just quoted, and elaborated at length in a later section,[34] so long as the second term is in the equilibrium position, i.e., zero, the movement of the price-level should be at all dependent upon the prevailing type of contract with the factors of production. So long as the amount of money in circulation, or more exactly E, remains unchanged, the fluctuations in the price-level

[32]Cf. on page 138 of *Treatise*, op. cit., vol. 1 [*A Treatise on Money*, op. cit., vol. 5, pp. 124–125. —Ed.], where it is said that "these equations tell us that the price of consumption goods is equal to the rate of earnings of the factors of production *plus* the rate of profits per unit of output of consumption goods". —Ed.]

[33]*Treatise*, op. cit., vol. 1, pp. 152–153. [*A Treatise on Money*, op. cit., vol. 5, pp. 137–138. —Ed.]

[34]*Ibid.*, vol. 1, pp. 166–170. [*Ibid.*, vol. 5, pp. 149–153. —Ed.]

would by no means be determined by the existing contracts, but exclusively by the amount of factors of production available and changes in their efficiency, i.e., by the two factors affecting total output. All Mr. Keynes's reasoning on this point seems to be based on the assumption that existing contracts will be changed by entrepreneurs only under the inducement (or pressure) of positive (or negative) profits *created by a change in the second term*. But to me there seems, on the contrary, no doubt possible that if a change in the coefficient of efficiency (or the amount of the factors of production available) occurs, existing contracts will have to be changed unless there is a change in the second term. *The difference seems to lie in the fact that Mr. Keynes believes that it is possible to adapt the amount of money in circulation to what is necessary for the maintenance of existing contracts without upsetting the equilibrium between saving and investing.* But under the existing monetary organisation, where all changes in the quantity of money in circulation are brought about by more or less money being lent to entrepreneurs than is being saved, any change in the circulation *must* be accompanied by a divergence between saving and investing. I cannot see why "if such spontaneous changes in the rate of earnings as tend to occur require a supply of money which is incompatible with the ideas of the Currency Authority or with the limitations on its powers, then the latter will be compelled, in its endeavour to redress the situation, to bring influences to bear which will upset the equilibrium of Investment and Saving, and so induce the entrepreneurs to modify their offers to the factors of production in such a way as to counteract the spontaneous changes which have been occurring in the rates of earnings".[35] To me it seems rather that if the currency authority wished to adapt the supply of money to the changed requirements, it could do so only by upsetting the equilibrium between saving and investment. But Mr. Keynes later on expressly allows for such increases in the supply of money as correspond to the increase of output and regards them as not upsetting the equilibrium. But how can the money get into circulation without creating a discrepancy between saving and investment? Is there any justification for the assumption that under these conditions entrepreneurs will borrow more just to go on with current production and not use the additional money for new investment? And even if they do use it only to finance the increased production, does not even this mean new investment in the interval of time until the additional products reach the consumer?

It seems to me that by not clearly distinguishing between stable cost of production per unit of output, stable contracts with the factors of

---

[35]*Ibid.*, vol. 1, p. 167. [*Ibid.*, vol. 5, p. 150. —Ed.]

production, and stable total cost (i.e., an invariable E) Mr. Keynes is led to connect two things which have nothing to do with one another: on the one hand the maintenance of a price-level which will cover costs of production while contracts with the factors of production are more or less rigid, and on the other hand the maintenance of an equilibrium between saving and investment. But without changes in the quantity of money and therefore without a divergence between I' and S, not only the Purchasing Power of Money, but also the Labour Power of Money, and therefore contracts with the factors of production would have to change with every change in total output.

There can, of course, be no doubt that every divergence between I or I' and S is of enormous importance. But that importance does not lie in the direction of its influence on the fluctuations of the *price-level*, be it its absolute fluctuations or its fluctuations about an equilibrium position, determined by the existing contracts with the factors of production.

It is true that in this attempt to establish a direct connection between a divergence between I and S, or what amounts to the same thing, a divergence between the natural and the money rate of interest, and the changes in the price-level, Mr. Keynes is following the lead of Wicksell. But it is just on this point that—as has been shown by Mr. D. H. Robertson[36] among English economists, and by the present writer[37] on the Continent—Wicksell has claimed too much for his theory. And even if Mr. Keynes substitutes for the absolute stability of the price-level which Wicksell had in mind a not clearly defined equilibrium price-level, he is still searching for a more definite relation between the price-level and the difference between saving and investment than can be found.

X

So far we have been mainly concerned with the tools which Mr. Keynes has created for the explanation of dynamic processes and the trade cycle. It is intended to discuss his actual explanation, beginning with the theory of the bank rate and including the whole of Book 4, in a second part of this article.[38]

---

[36]Dennis Robertson, *Money* [1922], op. cit., p. 99. [See this volume, chapter 2, notes 21, 75, for more on Robertson. —Ed.]

[37]*Geldtheorie und Konjunkturtheorie* (Vienna and Leipzig: Hölder-Pichler-Tempsky, 1929), pp. 61, 131, et seq. [See F. A. Hayek, *Monetary Theory and the Trade Cycle*, op. cit. —Ed.]

[38]Considerations of space have compelled the splitting up of this article. But there are other reasons which make me welcome the opportunity of delaying the second part of my criticism. As I had to confess at the beginning of this article, it is sometimes extremely

There is just one word more I feel I should add at this point. It is very likely that in the preceding pages I have quite often clothed my comments in the form of a criticism where I should simply have asked for further explanation and that I have dwelt too much on minor inaccuracies of expression. I hope it will not be considered a sign of inadequate appreciation of what is undeniably in so many ways a magnificent performance that what I have had so far to say was almost exclusively critical. My aim has been throughout to contribute to the understanding of this unusually difficult and important book, and I hope that my endeavour in this direction will be the best proof of how important I consider it. It is even possible that in the end it will turn out that there exists less difference between Mr. Keynes's views and my own than I am at present inclined to assume. The difficulty may be only that Mr. Keynes has made it so extraordinarily hard really to follow his reasoning. I hope that the reviewer will be excused if, in a conscientious attempt to understand it, he may sometimes have been betrayed into impatience with the countless obstacles which the author has put in the way of a full understanding of his ideas.

---

difficult to find out exactly what the meaning of Mr. Keynes's concepts is. On several occasions I have had to point out that several conflicting definitions are given for the same concept, and on many other points I am by no means certain whether I have understood Mr. Keynes correctly. It is very difficult to follow his subsequent complicated analysis so long as these ambiguities are not cleared up. One has to distinguish at every point the different meanings the exposition assumes according as concepts like investment etc., are interpreted according to this or to that of the several possible meanings it is given. There have accumulated so many questions of this kind which Mr. Keynes could certainly clear up that it is probably wiser to stop for the moment in the hope that further elucidations will in the meanwhile provide a firmer basis on which discussion may proceed. (Part 2 of this article will probably appear in *Economica*, November, 1931. —Ed.) [The second half of the article, reprinted below as chapter 6, did not appear until the February 1932 issue. —Ed.]

FOUR

THE PURE THEORY OF MONEY.
A REPLY TO DR. HAYEK[1]
by J. M. Keynes

I

In an article recently published in *Economica*,[2] Dr. Hayek has invited me
to clear up some ambiguities of terminology which he finds in my
Treatise on Money, and also other matters. As he frankly says, he has
found his difference with me difficult to explain. He is sure that my
conclusions are wrong (though he does not clearly state which conclusions), but he finds it "extremely difficult to demonstrate the exact point
of disagreement and to state his objections". He feels that my analysis
leaves out essential things, but he declares that "it is not at all easy to
detect the flaw in the argument". What he has done, therefore, is to
pick over the precise words I have used with a view to discovering some
verbal contradiction or insidious ambiguity. I think I can show that most
of my alleged terminological inconsistencies are either non-existent or
irrelevant to my central theme. But when I have done this (which I will
attempt in some short notes at the end of this article), I feel sure that
I shall have made little or no progress towards convincing Dr. Hayek.
For it is not really my use of language or the fact that my treatment
falls far short of a complete analysis (as it certainly does) which is
troubling him. It is something much more fundamental. And after
reading his article carefully, I have no doubt at all what it is.

II

Dr. Hayek has seriously misapprehended the character of my conclusions. He thinks that my central contention is something different from
what it really is. I deduce this from two passages in his article. The first

---

[1] [J. M. Keynes, "The Pure Theory of Money. A Reply to Dr. Hayek", *Economica*, vol.
11, no. 34, November 1931, pp. 387–397. —Ed.]

[2] "Reflections on the Pure Theory of Money of Mr. J. M. Keynes", op. cit. [Reprinted
in this volume, chapter 3. —Ed.]

(the italics are mine) is as follows: "The fact that more (or less) money is being invested than is being saved *is equivalent to so much money being added to (or withdrawn from) industrial circulation,* so that *the total of profits,* or the difference between the expenditure and the receipts of the entrepreneurs, which is the essential element in the second term of the fundamental equations, *will be equal to the net addition to (or subtraction from) the effective circulation.* It is here, according to Mr. Keynes, that we find the monetary causes working for a change in the price level; and he considers it the main advantage of his fundamental equations that they isolate this factor".[3] The second passage is on page 292[4]: "The difference (between us) seems to lie in the fact that Mr. Keynes believes that it is possible to adapt the amount of money in circulation to what is necessary for the maintenance of existing contracts without upsetting the equilibrium between saving and investing. But under the existing monetary organisation, *where all changes in the quantity of money in circulation are brought about by more or less money being lent to entrepreneurs than is being saved,*[5] any change in the circulation *must* be accompanied by a difference between saving and investing".

These quotations may be supplemented by a passage from Dr. Hayek's *Prices and Production,* page 23, where he succinctly states his own theory: "it is perfectly clear that, in order that the supply and demand for real capital should be equalised, the banks must not lend more or less than has been deposited with them as savings. *And this means naturally that they must never change the amount of their circulation.* At the same time, it is no less clear that, in order that the price level may remain unchanged, the amount of money in circulation must change as the volume of production increases or decreases. The banks could *either* keep the demand for real capital within the limits set by the supply of savings, *or* keep the price level steady; but they cannot perform both functions at once."[6]

Now the passages which I have italicized in the first of these quotations are far removed from the theory of my *Treatise on Money.* It is essential to that theory to deny these propositions—which Dr. Hayek puts in *my* mouth and, to judge from the second and third quotations, believes himself. No wonder that he finds many of my conclusions inconsistent with them. So long as a problem of this major magnitude is not cleared up between us, what is the use of discussing "irritating" terminology, which might not bother Dr. Hayek at all if he were not, for

---

[3]Op. cit., p. 290. [This volume, chapter 3, p. 142. —Ed.]
[4][See this volume, p. 144. —Ed.]
[5]My italics.
[6]My italics. [F. A. Hayek, *Prices and Production,* op. cit., pp. 23–24. —Ed.]

these excellent other reasons, looking for trouble? Dr. Hayek has missed, or at least does not discuss, the critical point at which our arguments part company. Having passed this by, but finding himself being led down strange and distasteful paths, he tries to prevent himself from being dragged along any further by representing the molehills in the pathway as mountains.

Dr. Hayek holds himself, and implies that I also hold, that an act of monetary expansion—meaning by this a transference from the inactive deposits to the active deposits the total quantity of money being unchanged, or an increase in the total quantity of money the quantity of the inactive deposits being unchanged[7]—is not merely a possible cause of investment exceeding saving, but (1) that it is a necessary cause of this and (2) that the amount of the monetary expansion exactly measures the excess of investment over saving and hence is exactly equal to the amount of profits (in my terminology). Will Dr. Hayek reconsider two matters?—(i) What passage can he quote from my *Treatise* which justifies him in attributing the above theory to me? (ii) What proof can he offer which justifies him in holding it himself?

In my *Rejoinder* to Mr. D. H. Robertson, published in the *Economic Journal* for September, 1931, I have endeavoured to re-state in a clearer way what my own theory actually is.[8] If the total quantity of money be supposed constant, Dr. Hayek's theory comes to the same thing as the theory that the excess of saving over investment is measured by the increase of the inactive deposits, which, in the above article, I have attributed to "some readers" though I did not then know that Dr. Hayek was among them.

Since Dr. Hayek has not been alone amongst competent critics of my *Treatise* in falling into this misapprehension (or into some more subtle variation of it), it must be my own fault, at least in part. I suspect that it may be partly due to the fact that when I first began to work on Book 3 of my *Treatise* I believed something resembling this myself. My ceasing to believe it was the critical point in my own development and was the germ from which much of my eventual theory was worked out. It is extraordinary that I should not have made this clear, because I was

---

[7]This is what his words mean in the first passage quoted above, but in the passage I have quoted from *Prices and Production* Dr. Hayek simplifies this (*vide* the words italicised) into an increase in the total quantity of money, but perhaps certain qualifications are to be understood.

[8]J. M. Keynes, "A Rejoinder", *Economic Journal*, vol. 41, September 1931, pp. 412–423, and D. H. Robertson, "Mr. Keynes's Theory of Money", *ibid.*, pp. 395–411. See this volume, chapter 2, note 21, on Robertson.]

acutely conscious of the difference of general outlook which the change of view involved; and after I had adopted this new view, I was at great pains to bring the rest of my work into line with it. But traces of old trains of thought are not easily obliterated, and certain passages which I wrote some time ago may have been unconsciously cast into a mould less obviously inconsistent with my own former views than they would be if I were writing now.

Yet I doubt if it is all my fault. For anyone brought up in the old Quantity-of-Money, Velocity-of-Circulation schools of thought, whether it be Cambridge Quantity Equations or Fisher Quantity Equations, this seems to be, for some obscure reason, a difficult transition to make.[9] Indeed I found it so myself. If the true theory were what Dr. Hayek believes it to be, the transition would be easy. If, on the other hand, my theory is right, not only is the angle of approach different, but it is difficult to see just what the relationship is between the new view and the old. Thus those who are sufficiently steeped in the old point of view simply cannot bring themselves to believe that I am asking them to step into a new pair of trousers, and will insist on regarding it as nothing but an embroidered version of the old pair which they have been wearing for years. Even so, I could never have expected, if it had not been for more than one experience to the contrary, that a competent economist could read my *Treatise* carefully and leave it with the idea that it was *my view* that the difference between saving and investment could be exactly measured by changes in the quantity of money, whether it be in the inactive circulation or the active circulation or the total circulation, corrected or uncorrected for changes in the velocity of circulation or the volume of output or the number of times intermediate products change hands.

At any rate *this*—and not whether I may have used the word "investment" in a different sense in one chapter from what I have in another—is the issue which Dr. Hayek and I ought to debate. He has taken as the self-evident basis of this theory ("it is perfectly clear that" is his own phrase) a proposition which I deny. But we have not hitherto got to grips, because any denial of his own doctrine has seemed to him

---

[9][Keynes is referring to the quantity theory of money, which relates the quantity of money in an economy to the aggregate price level and income. The two approaches he mentions are due to Irving Fisher (1867–1947), an American economist and the author of *Purchasing Power of Money* [1911], 2nd edition (New York: Macmillan, 1922; reprinted, New York: Kelley, 1985), and Arthur Pigou (1877–1959), successor to Marshall's chair and author of "The Value of Money", *Quarterly Journal of Economics*, vol. 32, November 1917, pp. 38–65. See this volume, chapter 2, note 6, for more on Fisher, and chapter 2, note 74, for more on Pigou. —Ed.]

so unthinkable, that even thousands of words of mine directed to its refutation have been water off a duck's back, and whilst he notices that I hold conclusions inconsistent with it, he seems still unaware that I have disputed it from the outset.

The point, put very briefly, is, firstly, that money may be advanced to entrepreneurs (directly by the banks, or through the new issue market or by the sale by them of their existing assets) either to meet losses or to provide for new investment, and that statistics of the quantity of money do not enable us to distinguish between the two cases; and, secondly (to indicate a general principle by means of an illustration), that, if, desiring to be more liquid, I sell Consols[10] to my bank in exchange for a bank deposit and my bank does not choose to offset this transaction but allows its deposits to be correspondingly increased, the quantity of money is changed without anything having happened either to saving or to investment.

III

It will be worth while to pursue the matter a little further. For reading Dr. Hayek's *Economica* article in the light of his book *Prices and Production*, and re-reading Mr. Robertson's *Economic Journal* article in the light of Dr. Hayek's two contributions, I fancy that I see at last where the stumbling block really is. Let me try, therefore, to bring matters to an issue by stating what I believe to be Dr. Hayek's fundamental theory and by explaining how, if I am right that this is what he holds, it differs from my theory. I would add that Mr. Robertson's original theory was, I think, substantially the same as that which I am imputing to Dr. Hayek; though Mr. Robertson may have now moved somewhat away from it.

"Voluntary" saving, according to Dr. Hayek, always finds its way into investment. This is so because (in his view[11]) an increase of saving means (*cet. par.*) a net increase of purchasing power directed to the buying of what I call "investment goods" but which Dr. Hayek calls "intermediate

---

[10][Consols refers to consolidated fund stocks ('Consolidated Annuities') once issued by the British government. Irredeemable fixed-interest securities, the yield on consols were often viewed as a measure of the long-term interest rate. —Ed.]

[11]This is clearly assumed in pp. 45–46 of his *Prices and Production*, op. cit.. Dr. Hayek must have overlooked the fact that it is fundamental to my position to deny this, because, if he had noticed something so much opposed to his own theory, he must surely have criticized it. I need not pursue my reasons here, as it is precisely the same point which has been the subject of discussion between Mr. Robertson and myself in the September *Economic Journal.*

products" and Mr. Robertson calls "machines".[12] It does not, however, follow from this (Dr. Hayek continues) that voluntary saving and investment are always equal. For if the banking system increases the supply of money, additional funds will be available for investment in excess of the amount provided by voluntary saving, with the result that investment will exceed saving, and contrariwise if the banking system decreases the supply of money. Thus, in his view, a disequilibrium between saving and investment is *necessarily* the result of action on the part of the banking system,[13] and, if we start from a position of equilibrium, cannot possibly arise otherwise. Sometimes he assumes that the excess (or deficiency) of investment is exactly equal to the change in the quantity of money—though there are passages in his *Prices and Production* which seem to me to be inconsistent with this—in which case investment is equal to voluntary saving *plus* (or *minus*) the change in the quantity of money. Investment due to an increase in the quantity of money involves the public in a corresponding amount what may be called "forced" saving. Thus (to quote from Dr. Hayek's *Prices and Production*, "a transition to more or less capitalistic methods of production . . . may come about in one of two ways: either as a result of changes in the volume of voluntary saving (or its opposite), or as a result of a change in the quantity of money which alters the funds at the disposal of entrepreneurs for the purchase of producers' goods".[14] Thus it is only a departure on the part of the banking system from what Dr. Hayek calls neutrality, which is capable of upsetting the equilibrium between saving and investment, and holding this view Dr. Hayek naturally asks me: "How can the (new) money get into circulation without creating a discrepancy between saving and investment?"[15]

Thus Dr. Hayek conceives of the flow of purchasing power as being made up of the incomes (how defined I do not know, i. e., whether equal to my E or my E + Q or to neither) of the factors of production

[12]Dr. Hayek not only implies that an increase of purchasing power directed as the result of an increase of saving to the buying of intermediate products must be spent on *newly* produced intermediate products, but also on newly produced intermediate products *which would not have been produced otherwise*. At least I cannot make sense of Chapter 2 of his *Prices and Production* except on this assumption.

[13]It should be explained to those who have not read Dr. Hayek's book that he does not regard as "action" on the part of the banking system, i.e., as a departure by them from neutrality, changes in the quantity of money required to offset changes in the velocity of circulation or in the number of times that intermediate products change hands before reaching the consumer.

[14]Op. cit., p. 45.

[15]"Reflections", op. cit., p. 293. [See this volume, p. 144. —Ed.]

plus the new money[16] (if any) created by the banking system. This double stream is then divided between consumers' goods and producers' goods. If saving is increased, less purchasing power is directed towards consumers' goods with the result that their price falls. At the same time more purchasing power must be directed *pari passu* towards producers' goods with the result that—I am not sure at this point whether Dr. Hayek holds that their price rises or that the quantity produced is increased or that a different kind of producers' goods is produced, but the argument of *Prices and Production*, chapter 2, seems to require that there will be an output of a different kind of producers' goods.[17]

Dr. Hayek concludes—and indeed it follows if one allows him his initial assumptions—that the necessary condition of avoiding Credit Cycles is for the banking system to maintain the effective quantity of money (interpreting this in Dr. Hayek's quite intelligible sense) absolutely and for ever unaltered.

My analysis is quite different from this; as it necessarily must be, since, in my view, saving and investment (as I define them) can get out of gear without any change on the part of the banking system from "neutrality" as defined by Dr. Hayek, merely as a result of the public changing their rate of saving or the entrepreneurs changing their rate of investment, there being no automatic mechanism in the economic system (as Dr. Hayek's view would imply there must be) to keep the two rates equal, provided that the effective quantity of money is unchanged.

As I conceive it, a changing price-level—due to a change in the relation between saving and investment, costs of production being unchanged—merely *redistributes* purchasing power between those who are buying at the changed price-level and those who are selling at it, as compared with what would have happened if there had not been a change in the relation between saving and investment. I am not sure that Dr. Hayek sees clearly the *two* sides of the account. Has he, moreover, apprehended the significance of my equation $S + Q = I$, namely that savings *plus* profits are always exactly equal to the value of new investment? It follows from this that, if we define *Income* to include Profits, and Savings as being the excess of Income thus defined over expenditure on consumption, then Savings and the Value of Investment are identically the same thing. He appears to conceive of Savings and

---

[16]Beyond what is required to offset changes in the velocity of circulation and in the number of times that intermediate products change hands.

[17]*Vide* page 45: "A transition to more capitalistic methods of production will take place if the total demand for producers' goods (expressed in money) increases relatively to the demand for consumers' goods."

Investment as not being identical and yet shrinks from defining them accordingly.

Dr. Hayek and Mr. Robertson both make use of the term "saving" or "voluntary saving". But though they criticise my definition of "saving", I am not aware that they have precisely defined it themselves. I think that it might help the debate to get on if Dr. Hayek would consider exactly what he means by "voluntary saving" on page 45 of his *Prices and Production*. It is argued that it is paradoxical on my part to exclude windfall profits and losses from my definition of income. But I suggest that it is still more paradoxical to include them in income; for in this case, given the value of the current output of investment goods, the amount of the community's income depends on how much it is saving, since any increase (or decrease) in "voluntary" saving will have the effect of decreasing (or increasing) the community's income by an equal amount.

IV

The reader will perceive that I have been drifting into a review of Dr. Hayek's *Prices and Production*. And this being so, I should like, if the Editor will allow me, to consider this book a little further. The book, as it stands, seems to me to be one of the most frightful muddles I have ever read, with scarcely a sound proposition in it beginning with page 45, and yet it remains a book of some interest, which is likely to leave its mark on the mind of the reader. It is an extraordinary example of how, starting with a mistake, a remorseless logician can end up in Bedlam. Yet Dr. Hayek has seen a vision, and though when he woke up he has made nonsense of his story by giving the wrong names to the objects which occur in it, his Khubla Khan is not without inspiration and must set the reader thinking with the germs of an idea in his head.

My notion of the real nature of the contribution to economic theory which Dr. Hayek is making brings me back, however, to what seems to me to be the underlying cause of the second vein of discontent with myself running through Dr. Hayek's *Economica* article. Dr. Hayek complains that I do not myself propound any satisfactory theory of capital and interest and that I do not build on any existing theory. He means by this, I take it, the theory of capital accumulation relatively to the rate of consumption and the factors which determine the natural rate of interest. This is quite true; and I agree with Dr. Hayek that a development of this theory would be highly relevant to my treatment of monetary matters and likely to throw light into dark corners. It is very possible that, looking back after a satisfactory theory has been completed, we shall see that the ideas which Böhm-Bawerk was driving at lie at the heart of the problem and that the neglect of him by English pre-war economists was as mistaken as their neglect of Wicksell.[18] But there is no such theory at present and, as Dr. Hayek would agree, a thorough treatment of it might lead one rather a long way from monetary theory. Nevertheless, substantially I concede Dr. Hayek's point. I agree with him that a clear account of the factors determining the natural rate of interest ought to have a place in a completed *Treatise on Money*, and that it is lacking in mine; and I can only plead that I had much to say for which such a theory is not required and that my own ideas about it were still too much in embryo to deserve publication. Later on, I will endeavour to make good this deficiency.

Now it is precisely to this theory that Dr. Hayek seems to me to be attempting to contribute in Lecture 2 of his *Prices and Production*. In this lecture he has been proceeding, so far as I can make out, on some such tacit assumption as that at every moment of time the market rate of interest is equal to what the natural rate of interest would be if the prevailing relationship of capital to consumption were to be permanent, and if entrepreneurs were acting on this latter assumption, without other errors of forecasting; and he then considers what would happen in an economic organization satisfying the above assumption when the rate of new investment in fact fluctuates.

At least, I have found no other interpretation which makes sense of the argument, or leaves it anything but a series of baffling *non-sequiturs*. If I am wrong, I hope that some authority, such as Professor Robbins,[19] who is confident that he understands what Dr. Hayek means in pages 45–64 of his book, will act as an interpreter. If I am right, it would follow that Dr. Hayek is *not* here dealing with the case, with which I was mainly preoccupied, of what happens when the market rate of interest departs from the natural rate, and that our theories occupy—as I believe they do—different *terrains*. A little consideration of his problem, however, brings out the point that the term "natural rate of interest" is not altogether free from ambiguity. I have defined it by reference to the rate which would at any moment equalize saving and investment, after taking account of the existing psychology of the market, including errors of forecasting, and irrespective of whether or not the then prevailing rate of investment is expected to be permanent. We might call this the "short-period" natural rate. But clearly there is also the other type,

---

[18][For more on Wicksell, see this volume, chapter 3, note 10. —Ed.]

[19][Lionel Robbins wrote the Foreword to *Prices and Production*. For more on Robbins see this volume, chapter 1, notes 15–17. —Ed.]

namely that envisaged by Dr. Hayek, which we might call the "long-period" natural rate. It seems to me that Dr. Hayek's methods may be suitable for analysing some of the conditions which determine this "long-period" natural rate of interest.

I am in full agreement, also, with Dr. Hayek's rebuttal of John Stuart Mill's well-known dictum that "there cannot, in short, be intrinsically a more insignificant thing, in the economy of society, than money",[20] which he expresses admirably in the following passage from his last lecture: "it means also that the task of monetary theory is a much wider one than is commonly assumed; its task is nothing less than to cover a second time the whole field which is treated by pure theory under the assumption of barter, and to investigate what changes in the conclusions of pure theory are made necessary by the introduction of indirect exchange. The first step towards a solution of this problem is to release monetary theory from the bonds which a too narrow conception of its task has created."[21]

V

There remain Dr. Hayek's criticisms of my use of terms, on which I offer the following notes:

(1) It is not the case, as Dr. Hayek alleges on the top of page 274,[22] that I contrast with the prices paid for the factors of production only the prices of finished consumption goods. Dr. Hayek forgets that "new investment goods" include, on my definition, unfinished consumption goods. Nevertheless, Mr. Hawtrey[23] has pointed out to me that changes in the values of unfinished goods largely cancel out in my price-level of output. "It is only", he points out, "in the case where the increment of investment includes some net addition to the stock of unfinished products the price-level is influenced in the *contrary* direction to the prices of intermediate products. Practically we can treat Mr. Keynes's price-level as the price-level of finished goods, subject only to a slight

---

[20][John Stuart Mill (1806–1873), British moral philosopher and economist. The reference is to a passage from Mill's *Principles of Political Economy* [1848; 7th edition, 1871] (Fairfield, N. J.: Kelley, 1987), p. 488. —Ed.]

[21]*Prices and Production*, op. cit., p. 110.

[22]"Reflections", op. cit., p. 274. [See this volume, p. 125. —Ed.]

[23][Ralph George Hawtrey (1879–1975), British Treasury official. In what turned into a lengthy correspondence, Hawtrey provided Keynes with a critical assessment of the *Treatise* just prior to its publication. See *The General Theory and After: Part I—Preparation*, op. cit., pp. 126–173. —Ed.]

correction for unfinished products in certain cases". Thus this point deserved more explanation than I gave it in my book.

(2) Is Dr. Hayek's point at the bottom of page 275 and the top of page 276[24] that I ought to include in my Q_2 profits arising from the ownership of old capital goods which have risen in value as well as those arising from currently produced capital goods? For certain purposes I should see no objection to amalgamating the two types of profit; but for other purposes, in particular where we are dealing with the price-level of output (which by its very nature distinguishes new capital from old capital) it is obviously necessary to distinguish them.

(3) It is not the case that I separate the process of the reproduction of the old capital from the addition of new capital (p. 278).[25] I reckon the wearing out of old capital as "disinvestment" and its replacement as "investment", and allow for this in reaching my totals of net output and of net investment.

(4) In the first paragraph of page 279[26] Dr. Hayek perhaps overlooks my distinction between the *cost* of investment and the *value* of investment. But both here and elsewhere (p. 281[27]) Dr. Hayek also criticises the conception of "quantity of capital" as being invalid on the ground that the different types of specific goods constituting capital are not always identical, and when non-identical are non-commensurable. But this is simply the same problem as that of the conception of "price-level" and the associated conception of real-wages when the complex of goods refers to changes in its make-up. This I have discussed at great length in Book II of my *Treatise*, and it arises of course in all types of monetary theory alike.

(5) An examination of the context to which Dr. Hayek refers in the first half of page 281[28] shows that the one refers to the value of current investment, and the other to the value of total investment.

(6) I confess to the verbal confusion of which Dr. Hayek complains at the bottom of page 281[29]. The object of the definition on page 130,[30] as can be seen from the context, is to distinguish between "output" of consumption-goods, as defined on page 127[31] and, by implication, on

[24]"Reflections", op. cit. [See this volume, pp. 126–127. —Ed.]
[25]*Ibid.* [See this volume, p. 129. —Ed.]
[26]*Ibid.*
[27]*Ibid.* [See this volume, p. 132. —Ed.]
[28]*Ibid.*
[29]*Ibid.* [See this volume, pp. 132–133. —Ed.]
[30]*Treatise* (1930), op. cit. [*A Treatise on Money*, op. cit., p. 117. —Ed.]
[31]*Ibid.* [*Ibid.*, vol. 5, pp. 114–115. —Ed.]

page 135,[32] which includes only finished consumption-goods coming on the market, from the *production* of consumption-goods which represents the work done during any period on goods which will eventually emerge as consumption-goods. Unluckily, while I speak of the *production* of consumption-goods in the first section of the paragraph in question, in the second sentence I speak of "*that* of consumption-goods",[33] not noticing that grammatically *that* refers back to the expression "output or production", used four lines previously in connection with "capital goods". If Dr. Hayek will read "the production of consumption-goods" (instead of "that of consumption-goods") in the second sentence of the paragraph as well as in the first sentence his mind will be at rest. This is a slip of the pen which may, I fear, have held up many readers for a moment. But that it should have left Dr. Hayek in a permanent confusion as to what I mean by "output of consumption-goods" on page 135[34] and throughout my book is a symptom, I feel, of how thick a bank of fog still separates his mind from mine.

---

[32]*Ibid.* [*Ibid.*, vol. 5, p. 121. —Ed.]
[33]*Ibid.* [*Ibid.*, vol. 5, pp. 117–118. —Ed.]
[34]*Ibid.* [*Ibid.*, vol. 5, p. 121. —Ed.]

FIVE

A REJOINDER TO MR. KEYNES[1]

As I have received the text of the preceding note too late to complete in time for this issue of *Economica* the second part of my more systematic Reflections, in the preparation of which I had hoped to profit from Mr. Keynes's explanations, I shall confine myself here to some direct comments on the preceding note and reserve the treatment of all problems which I had not yet taken up in my main article for its second part.[2] Unfortunately, Mr. Keynes's answer does not seem to me to clear up many of the difficulties I have pointed out, or indeed to improve the basis for further discussion. Instead of devoting his answer mainly to clearing up the ambiguities which I have indicated carefully and in detail, and the existence of which he cannot deny, he replies chiefly by a sweeping accusation of confusion, not in my critical article, but in another work, and even here I am unable to reply as he does not specify my confusions in any single case. I am bound to say that while I am very ready and indeed eager seriously to consider any definite criticism which Mr. Keynes may care to make, I cannot see what possible end is served by an unproved condemnation of my views in general. I cannot believe Mr. Keynes wishes to give the impression that he is trying to distract the attention of the reader from the objections which have been raised against his analysis by abusing his opponent, and I can only hope that after my critical article has appeared in its entirety he will not only try to refute my objection somewhat more specifically, but also to substantiate his counter-criticism.

For the present, I can only draw his attention anew to certain apparent confusions in his exposition and terminology which he has not cleared up in his reply; and which in spite of what he has said still seem to me to lie at the root of his general position. It is a regrettable fact that in none of the cases in which I have shown that several interpretations of the meaning of his exposition are possible has he explained

---

[1][F. A. Hayek, "A Rejoinder to Mr. Keynes", *Economica*, vol. 11, November 1931, pp. 398–403. —Ed.]

[2][Hayek is referring to the second part of his review article, "Reflections on the Pure Theory of Money of Mr. J. M. Keynes (*continued*)", which is reprinted as chapter 6, this volume. —Ed.]

decisively which of these interpretations is to be considered as authoritative. He has failed to elucidate his concept of Investment. I am as much at a loss as ever to see what it means exactly (cf. p. 280 of my article[3]). The same thing is true of his concept of profits. Indeed, until he has elucidated the concept of investment I do not see how he can be clear in his use of the term profit. Is it a change in the value of existing capital investment or is it profit? Again, is interest regularly part of the "rate of efficiency earnings of the factors of production"? If so, how is the average between the earnings of capital and of the other factors of production to be arrived at? If not (as one would assume from the passage on p. 211 of vol. 1 of the *Treatise*[4]) where else does interest come into the picture? Investment necessarily implies that the result of the expenditure of one period has often to be sold in a period which is either shorter or longer than that period (cf. p. 276[5] of my article). The E which represents cost of production of current output need not be identical with the E that stands for current income. How is this fact taken into account in the fundamental equations? Is the formula which I have substituted for P', for which Mr. Keynes gives no formula, a correct interpretation of his intentions (p. 283 of my article[6])? All these are questions which must be answered if Mr. Keynes wants the reader to understand what he means. I should have expected that an author who has been shown that almost all his fundamental concepts are ambiguous, and that some are even defined in several flatly contradictory ways, would have been more anxious to make clear in exactly what sense he wants them to be understood. Is it not the least we can ask from him that at any rate at this stage he should commit himself to a definite and unequivocal definition of his concepts?

But to come to what Mr. Keynes considers, probably justly, to be the main point of our differences. It is quite true that while I have pointed out that Mr. Keynes does not consistently adhere to the idea that a discrepancy between saving and investing[7] can only arise as a consequence of a change in the effective quantity of money, I have assumed that this is essentially what he means when he speaks about money

---

[3]["Reflections on the Pure Theory of Money of Mr. J. M. Keynes", op. cit.; reprinted as chapter 3, this volume. —Ed.]

[4]*Treatise*, op. cit. [*A Treatise on Money*, op. cit., vol. 5, pp. 188–189. —Ed.]

[5]"Reflections", op. cit. [See this volume, p. 127. —Ed.]

[6]*Ibid.* [See this volume, p. 134. —Ed.]

[7]If it is not accompanied by an exactly reverse discrepancy between the demand for consumption goods and the cost of current output of consumption goods, in which case, of course, it is nothing but the only effective method of bringing about a shift between the production of consumption goods and the production of investment goods.

exceeding (or falling short of) investment. I have been compelled to do so because I have been unable, and indeed still am unable, to detect in his *Treatise* or his subsequent elucidations any other tenable explanation of this phenomenon, and because I refused to believe, as I am afraid I must now believe, that Mr. Keynes could possibly consider his analysis of the relation between profits and investment an independent and sufficient explanation of how this discrepancy arises.

As I understand him now, his position is that an excess of saving over investment will arise when part of the saving, instead of being used for new investments, is used to make up for losses.[8] Let us take the simplest case which according to his assumption would fall into this category. If an entrepreneur who fails to earn his expected normal entrepreneur's wages cuts down his personal expenditure accordingly—to the extent to which his expenditure fell below his "normal" wage, this would constitute saving in Mr. Keynes's terminology[9]—and continues to pay out on costs of current output as much as before, then these "savings" would not lead to corresponding investing. This is no doubt true as a consequence of the definition of the concept chosen, but it explains neither how the excess of saving over investing, nor how the windfall losses arose, but only that both are *ex definitione* identical. To say that the excess of saving over investment is the cause of the losses (or the reverse) has no sense whatever. There exists only the kind of disequilibrium which has been supposed to exist at the outset when the hypothesis that the entrepreneurs were making windfall losses was introduced, and he does not adduce any reason for assuming that the original and unspecified cause of the losses would be eliminated by the banking system making up for the difference by lending more to investors. And, what is worse, this description of the relation between "profits", "money", and "investment" respectively in no way explains how it is possible that "windfall profits"

---

[8]The second of the two cases to which he refers (this volume, p. 151) is adduced to show that a change in the quantity of money may take place without any influence on either saving or investment. But this it does not prove, for a sale of securities to a bank in order to use the proceeds to improve liquidity (i.e., to hoard) does not change the effective quantity of money (in the sense of the concept on which we seem to be agreed, cf. p. 153, this volume).

[9]*Treatise*, op. cit., vol. 1, p. 139. [*A Treatise on Money*, op. cit., vol. 5, p. 125. This page in the *Treatise* is where Keynes likens consumption spending out of entrepreneurial profits to an inexhaustible "widow's cruse", doubtless his most famous Biblical allusion. —Ed.] That a man, who does not spend more than he earns, though he had expected to earn more, should be said to perform saving, can hardly be called anything but an abuse of ordinary language. The question whether there is any reason to desire that any *new* investment should correspond to such "saving" I shall investigate in some detail in the second part of my article.

as a difference between "saving" and "investing" can arise so long as the effective quantity does not change. So long as the money goes somewhere and is not hoarded and no new money is added (and this is what is meant by the assumption that the effective quantity of money is constant) it is difficult to see how there can arise that difference between the total expenditure and the total receipts of entrepreneurs which alone can create total profits in Mr. Keynes's sense.[10]

But what does it actually mean if part of current savings is used to make up for losses in the production of consumption goods—either directly by the method assumed above or indirectly by the entrepreneurs who suffer losses selling part of their illiquid assets to the savers? It must mean that though the production of consumers' goods has become less profitable, and that though at the same time the rate of interest has fallen so that the production of investment goods has become relatively more attractive than the production of consumption goods, yet entrepreneurs continue to produce the two types of goods in the same proportion as before. What justification can there be for this assumption? Mr. Keynes's assertion that there is no automatic mechanism in the economic system to keep the rate of saving and the rate of investing equal[11] might with equal justification be extended to the more general contention that there is no automatic mechanism in the economic system to adapt production to any other shift in demand. I begin to wonder whether Mr. Keynes has ever reflected upon the function of the rate of interest in a society where there is no banking system.

All this, of course, is just another consequence of the fact which I have noted already in my original article, that Mr. Keynes seems never to have been concerned to study the fundamental non-monetary problems of capitalistic production. He now contends that we have no satisfactory theory of capital. To a certain extent, I should be quite willing to concede this point. But the obvious answer, of course, is that even if we have no quite satisfactory theory we do at least possess a far better one than that on which he is content to rely, namely that of Böhm-Bawerk and Wicksell. That he neglects this theory, not because he thinks it is wrong, but simply because he has never bothered to make himself acquainted with it, is amply proved by the fact that he finds

---

[10]The only reason why entrepreneurs as a group could make profits in the ordinary sense of the word under this assumption would be because of changes in the value of existing capital, that balancing factor between current receipts and current expenditure which I have dealt with on p. 276 of my article ["Reflections", op. cit. —Ed.], but this phenomenon Mr. Keynes consistently neglects.

[11]This volume, p. 153.

unintelligible my attempt to develop certain corollaries of this theory—corollaries which are not only essential for the very problem we are discussing, but which, as experience has shown me, are immediately intelligible to every student who has ever studied Böhm-Bawerk or Wicksell seriously.

To reply on just one special point. I cannot see any difficulty in defining saving (or "voluntary" saving, which, of course, in Mr. Keynes's sense is the *only* saving because "forced saving" is only investment in excess of saving) in the old-fashioned way as refraining from any expenditure on consumption which would be possible without diminution of the value of the existing capital.[12] His objection to it[13] is in the first place based on the a priori assumption that an increase of saving and the consequent lowering of interest will have no effect on the current output of investment goods. This is an entirely arbitrary assumption. I think that if Mr. Keynes had for a moment reflected on what happens normally when saving increases and no special circumstances prevent investment from increasing at any equal rate (and, I think, even he cannot deny that this is sometimes the case) he could not have failed to see that only special monetary factors (hoarding or a direct increase or decrease of the quantity of money) could prevent such

---

[12]Immediately before the passage corresponding to the one on page 45 to which Mr. Keynes refers above, in the German edition of *Prices and Production* which appeared some weeks ago, and which was therefore finished long before I saw Mr. Keynes's note, I have inserted an additional paragraph which might clear up some of his doubts on my concept of saving and which, therefore, it might be useful to reproduce here in English: "Whether production will retain its present capitalistic structure will therefore depend upon whether the proportion between the amount of money used to demand producers' goods and the amount of money used to demand consumers' goods remains the same. How any change of this proportion will lead to a change of the capitalistic structure of production will be shown in following paragraphs of this chapter and in the following chapter. There is, however, one more point which needs some clearing up before we can enter upon that discussion. One might be tempted to consider any new investment in a firm as a net increase of the means available for production, and to overlook the fact that in the normal course of business always a great number of firms not only make no profit but suffer actual losses, and are therefore unable to reinvest in its production constantly an amount equivalent to the cost of their current output. This will, for instance, be regularly the case in industries which decline as a consequence of a change in technique or in fashion. In this case, in order to maintain the relative demand for producers' goods at its existing level it is necessary that these losses be made up by new savings, for instance from the industries which gain in consequence of the same change. Only the part of the current savings which exceeds the amount necessary to make up for these losses, or net savings, must therefore be considered as an addition to the demand for producers' goods, and where I use the expression savings in the following pages this means always only net savings in this sense". *Preise und Produktion* (Vienna: Springer, 1931), p. 49.

[13]This volume, pp. 152–154.

a change in saving from exerting a direct influence in the same direction on the rate of investing. But even granted (*posito, non concesso*) that this is not the case, it is not clear why the total income (*including* profits) should fall as a consequence of saving. When producers of consumption goods suffer losses because buyers save part of what they used to spend on consumption goods, but go on to produce the same amount as before and make up the losses by borrowing from the savers, it is impossible to see how total income (in the wider sense) should be decreased.

With Mr. Keynes's concept of the natural rate of interest and several other closely related matters which are touched upon in his note I shall deal in the second part of my main article.[14]

Addendum:The Early Hayek-Keynes Correspondence[15]

1. Keynes to Hayek, December 10, 1931[16]

Dear Hayek,

I wonder if you could elucidate for me a little further the definition of saving which you give on page 402 of the *Economica* for November, where you say that saving consists in 'refraining from any expenditure on consumption which would be possible without diminution of the value of the existing capital'.

I should find this clearer if you could give me a formula which shows how saving is *measured*. Also, what is the difference between 'voluntary saving' and 'forced saving' in *your* terminology?

Yours sincerely,
J. M. Keynes

---

[14][See chapter 6, this volume. —Ed.]

[15][A month after the publication in November, 1931, of the Comment and Reply that are reprinted as chapters 4 and 5 in this volume, letters were exchanged between Hayek and Keynes. They are printed here, as well as a short note from Keynes to Piero Sraffa and Richard Kahn, commenting on his exchange with Hayek. —Ed.]

[16][In *The General Theory and After: Part I, Preparation*, op. cit., p. 257. —Ed.]

2. Hayek to Keynes, December 15, 1931[17]

Dear Keynes,

While a quite satisfactory algebraic expression of saving would be rather complicated because the concept of 'maintaining the existing capital' would make it necessary to bring in a measure of the existing capital, i.e., the average investment period, I think that for our purposes the following definition will be sufficient:

Of the total money receipts of all members of the society or the effective circulation (amount *times* velocity) M a certain proportion pM must be constantly reinvested in order to maintain the existing capital constant. $(1 - p)M$ is therefore available for the purchase of consumers' goods. If $(1 - p)M$ is actually spent on consumers' goods, there is no (positive or negative) saving, but if a smaller amount $(1 - p - s)M$ is spent on consumers' goods, sM, the amount saved, may or may not be used to increase the total amount of new and renewed investment to $(p+s)M$, only sM being *new* investment. If sM is not used for new investment but is hoarded, the effective circulation decreases by exactly the same amount by which *new* investment falls short of saving. But if on top of the increase of investment made possible by the saving it is further increased by additional money being lent to producers to the amount of aM, then investment will exceed saving by $(p+s+a)M - (p+s)M = aM$. If, however, the new money is added at a time when only a part of the current savings, isM, is being invested, then the excess of investment over saving will be only $(p+is+a)M - (p+s)M = (is+a - s)M$. It is aM or $(is+a - s)M$ which I have called 'forced savings' in contrast to sM, the voluntary saving.

I entirely agree with you that it would be better not to use the word saving in connection with what I have called 'forced saving' but only to speak of investment in excess of saving. Unfortunately, however, the fact that you use 'saving' and 'investment' in a different sense has now made it difficult for me to adopt what is obviously the better terminology without creating confusion. It is essentially the different meaning of these concepts which is at the basis of our difference and it will be one of the main contentions of the second part of my article that while it is essential for an equilibrium that saving and investment in my sense should correspond, there seems to me to exist no reason whatever why saving and investment in your sense should correspond.

Yours sincerely,
F. A. Hayek

---

[17][*Ibid.*, pp. 257–258. —Ed.]

3. Keynes to Hayek, December 16, 1931[18]

Dear Hayek,

Many thanks for your letter, which makes things a good deal clearer to me.

There are, however, two expressions as to which I should like still further explanation.

When, at the beginning of your second paragraph, you spoke of 'velocity', could you give me your precise definition of this; since I reckon that there are now nine senses in which contemporary economists use this term, some of them differing but slightly and subtly from one another.

Secondly, when you speak of the existing capital being maintained constant, do you mean the money value of the existing capital, or its physical equivalent?

Yours sincerely,
J. M. Keynes

4. Hayek to Keynes, December 19, 1931[19]

Dear Keynes,

I have used the term 'velocity' only as a short and, as I thought, in this connection unequivocal explanation of what I meant by total effective circulation, but I do not normally work with this concept at all. My approach to the problem is rather on the lines of the cash-balances concept as developed by Mises in his *Theorie des Geldes und der Umlaufsmittel* (1912).

When I speak of maintaining capital intact I do, of course, *not* mean the money value of capital. To give an exact definition, which would hold under all circumstances, would take a great deal of space, but if we make the simplifying assumption that the total of original factors of production available remains unchanged, then it could be said that total capital, in order to remain constant, should always correspond to the product of these factors during a certain number of years, which is just another form of saying that the average period of production remains the same. My attention has just been drawn to the fact that a discussion of this problem, which on the whole agrees with my views, is given by Professor Pigou in the fourth chapter of the third edition of his *Economics of Welfare*.

Yours sincerely,
F. A. Hayek

---

[18][*Ibid.*, p. 258. —Ed.]
[19][*Ibid.*, p. 259. —Ed.]

5. Keynes to Hayek, December 23, 1931[20]

Dear Hayek,

Thanks for your letter of December 19. I am sorry to be so tiresome, but what I really wanted to get at was the exact significance you attach to 'effective circulation'. Do you mean by this what the Americans call the aggregate of bank debits, that is to say, turnover of cash, or do you mean something different from this?

Yours sincerely,
J. M. Keynes

6. Hayek to Keynes, December 25, 1931[21]

Dear Keynes,

I am sorry I have misunderstood your question. 'The total effective circulation' as I understand it and as I thought you understood it on page 393 of your *Economica* article where you speak of the 'quite intelligible sense' in which I use this concept, is simply the total of all money payments effected (in cash, bank deposits, or whatever other form) during any arbitrary period of time.

Yours sincerely,
F. A. Hayek

7. Keynes to Hayek, December 25, 1931[22]

That is what I thought you meant and that is just my difficulty. For by the 'effective circulation of M' in your first letter of Dec. 15 you seemed, judging by the context, to mean something which corresponded in some sense to what one might call 'aggregate income', which is not the same thing as aggregate money turnover. If M means money turnover, why must 'a certain proportion pM be constantly reinvested in order to maintain the existing capital constant'? I am not able to perceive any particular relation between aggregate money turnover and the amount of capital replenishment required to keep capital constant.

J. M. K.

[20][*Ibid.*, pp. 259. —Ed.]
[21][*Ibid.*, p. 259–260. —Ed.]
[22][*Ibid.*, p. 260. —Ed.]

8. Hayek to Keynes, January 7, 1932[23]

Dear Keynes,

Returning from the meeting in Reading and a few days stay in [the] country I find your letter of December 25th. The question which you put in it is, indeed, of the most central importance and if I had thought that you had any difficulties about this point I should have long ago tried to make it clearer. When, however, you wrote on p. 397 of your *Economica* article that you consider the replacement of 'disinvestment' as 'investment' I thought you saw the point.

If we take a stationary society where there is no saving and no net investment (in your sense) a constant process of reproduction of existing capital will go on which is necessary in order to maintain its amount constant. In the case of circulating capital this will mean that its total amount will have to be replaced at least once during every year, and in the case of fixed capital that a certain proportion of the total existing capital which wears out during each year will have to be replaced. If we take the simplest case to which I have unfortunately confined myself too much in *Price[s] and Production,* i.e., the case where all the existing capital owes its existence to one of the reasons which make the existence of capital necessary, namely to the *duration of the process of production*—the other cause being the *durability of many instruments* of production—and where, therefore all capital is 'circulating capital' in the usual sense of this word—which is very misleading because this circulating capital is different from fixed capital only from the point of view of an individual and not for society as a whole—it is fairly clear that a continuous process of production requires—in every stage a constant disinvestment and reinvestment so that, if we assume that goods pass from one stage of production to the next every period of time, there will be a constant stream of money directed to intermediate products which will be roughly as many times greater than the stream of money directed against consumption goods as the average number of periods of time which elapse between the application of the original factors of production and the completion of the consumption goods. (I apologize for this terrible 'German' sentence.) The proportion between the demand for consumption goods and the demand for intermediate products will however exactly correspond to the average length of the production process only on the assumption that the goods pass from one stage to the next in equal intervals corresponding to the unit period. What it will actually be depends upon the given organization of industry, but given this organization it will change with every change in the amount of capital existing—or, what means the same thing, the average length of the production period—and will remain different so long as the amount of capital remains at its new level (and not only so long as the amount of capital is changing).

The situation is not fundamentally different if we take the other ideal case where the existence of capital is entirely due to the other of the two causes, the durability of the instruments. If we assume that the actual process of production of the instruments as well as of the finished consumption goods takes no appreciable time so that only 'fixed' capital and no 'circulating' capital is existing, then it is again clear that, in order to maintain capital constant, such proportion of the existing machinery as wears out during a period will have to be replaced. In a stationary society this proportion will be determined by the amount of capital and its lifetime, and since the amount of capital existing at a moment of time will itself of necessity be equal to the discounted value of a year's output of consumers' goods *times* the average lifetime of the machines, the annual demand for machines will stand in a proportion to the annual output of consumers' goods which is determined by the average duration of the machines.

The problem becomes, of course, a little more complicated if one combines, as one has to do to come nearer to reality, the two factors determining the existence of capital. The simplest way out seems to me to be to reduce both factors, 'duration of the process' in the narrower sense and the duration of the instruments, to the concept of the average length of the production process in a wider sense as the common denominator. I am conscious that I have treated the durability factor lightly too in *Prices and Production*, but I did so because I hoped to make it less difficult and because I assumed a greater familiarity with Böhm-Bawerk's concepts of the average length of production than I ought obviously to have done. I have, however, treated these problems at somewhat greater length in sections IX–XI of my "Paradox of Saving".

Yours very truly,
F. A. Hayek

9. Keynes to Hayek, January 12, 1932[24]

Dear Hayek,

Thank you for taking so much trouble about my questions.

The point you go into was not really the one that bothered me. I quite follow the point as to the proportion of income required to make good depreciation. But incidentally in the course of what you say, you do I think make clear what assumptions underlay your conclusion.

I might put it like this. It is clear to me that in a stable society the amount required to make good depreciation is a standard proportion of the annual income. If therefore it be assumed that the cash turnover bears a fixed relation to the annual income, then I can follow that in a completely stable society, in which moreover the volume of cash turnover bears a fixed proportion to the annual income, the allowance for depreciation will bear a fixed proportion to the cash turnover. I take it from what you say that your article is intended to be subject to these assumptions.

---

[24][*Ibid.*, pp. 262–263. —Ed.]

So far so good. But I should still need to know if your definition of saving is to be of general application, what would happen in a progressive society or in a society where, e.g., new inventions are liable to cause obsolescence of existing plant (as distinct from depreciation) and where there is no stable relationship between cash turnover and the national income (e.g., 1931 the relationship between the two, here or in America, was widely different from what it was in 1929).

Yours sincerely,
J. M. Keynes

10. Hayek to Keynes, January 23, 1932[25]

Dear Keynes,

I have had a slight attack of influenza which made me unable to do any serious work. You will, therefore, excuse, if the answer to your last letter has again been delayed.

If you drop the simplifying assumption of constancy of my 'coefficient of money transactions' then, indeed, a purely monetary definition of saving becomes impossible. In order to know what *new* investment is necessary to offset the individual decisions of income receivers in regard to what part of their income they spend on consumption, a rather detailed analysis of what happens to the real structure of production in any given case becomes necessary.

To take the case of obsolescence which you raise, i.e., losses in capital value due to new inventions, the question how much new investment should correspond to a given amount of saving in your sense (i.e., gross saving) can only be answered on the basis of a quite unequivocal concept of what constituted new investment. I suggest that it is a more satisfactory way of approach to drop the distinction between new investment and reinvestment in that connection entirely and to start from the proportion between consumption and total investment which would have had to exist if the structure of production existing before that change were to be maintained permanently. Total investment in that sense includes not only, as you seem to suggest in your letter, the quota of income required to make good depreciation of fixed capital, but also the constant reinvestment of all the circulating capital. And, perhaps still more important, if the 'coefficient of money transactions' changes it need not mean a constant money stream for investment purposes. If any given firm which before used annually to buy a certain amount of machines in replacement of old ones decides to produce these machines in its own factories, the amount of money used to buy investment goods will decrease but the total amount of investment will not have changed. In such conditions it is impossible to measure investment in merely monetary terms and the only measure of the amount of investment going on is the average time for which the total of all factors of production is being invested. It is, of course, one of the most difficult tasks of monetary theory to determine what monetary changes become necessary to offset changes in the organization of business.

The main problems, however, are two: What are the effects of changes in that proportion supposed that the money supply is so adjusted that total incomes are constant, and, secondly, what is the effect of changes in total incomes. The essential part of my theory is that the fluctuations in the proportions between income and total investment and the consequent changes in what I have called the structure of production which constitute the business cycle and, in particular, changes in favour of income relatively to investment which lead to a destruction of capital and a crisis. Even changes in total incomes will affect production mainly via their effect on this proportion, though in a system where prices are very rigid it will of course have serious consequences even if it would leave the proportion unchanged.

To return to the particular case of obsolescence which I set out to discuss, if in any particular industry some firms find themselves unable to earn a sufficient amortization quota on the cost of their fixed capital because some other firms, equipped with more modern machinery undercut them—and this seems to me essentially to be what obsolescence means—the effect will be that these firms have to cut down their investment. If at the same time nobody else would invest more than is necessary to maintain his capital this would mean that the demand for investment goods would be permanently reduced to that extent. In so far as however, e.g., the firms using the new machinery are able to make new investment out of their extraordinary profits, these investments will at first be required to keep total capital constant and in this sense constitute no net addition to investment and make no increase of the total output of capital goods necessary. The output on investment goods will in this case not have changed and yet there will be no excess of saving over investment since the savings of the one group of people have been required to make up for the capital losses of another group of people. To require that in such a case the production of investment goods should actually increase by the full amount of savings, as you seem to do, seems to me to invite trouble, since there is no reason why this increased proportion of investment relatively to consumption would be maintained.

I am dealing with this aspect of the problem in the second part of my 'Reflections' of which I have just read the proofs.

Yours sincerely,
F. A. Hayek

11. Keynes to Piero Sraffa and R. F. Kahn, February 1, 1932[26]

What is the next move? I feel that the abyss yawns—and so do I. Yet I can't help feeling that there *is* something interesting in it.

12. Keynes to Hayek, February 11, 1932[27]

Dear Hayek,

I should have acknowledged before now your letter of January 23, but I have been much occupied on matters other than those of pure theory.

Your letter helps me very much towards getting at what is in your mind. I think you have now told me all that I am entitled to ask by way of correspondence. The matter could not be carried further except by an extension of your argument to a more actual case than the simplified one we have been discussing. And that is obviously a matter for a book rather than for correspondence.

But I am left with the feeling that I very seldom know, when I read your stuff, exactly what simplified assumptions you introduce or what effect it would have on the argument if these simplified assumptions were to be removed. This is more important when one is considering practical applications, than if one regards oneself as at the beginning of a long theoretical enquiry, in the earlier stages of which the use of simplified assumptions is desirable.

Going back to the point at which our correspondence started, I am left where I began, namely in doubt as to just what you mean by voluntary saving and forced saving as applied to the actual world we live in; though I think I understand now what you mean by them in certain special cases, and this of course gives me some sort of general idea as to the sort of thing you have in mind.

Many thanks for answering me so fully.

Yours sincerely,
J. M. Keynes

13. Keynes to Hayek, March 29, 1932[28]

Dear Hayek,

I will certainly reserve you space in this June *Journal* for a reply to Sraffa. But let it be no longer than it need be. It is the trouble of controversy—from an editor's point of view—that it is without end. Your MS should reach me not later than May 1.

[26][*Ibid.*, p. 265. —Ed.]
[27][*Ibid.*, p. 265. —Ed.]
[28][*Ibid.*, p. 266. —Ed.]

Having been much occupied in other directions, I have not yet studied your *Economica* article as closely as I shall. But, unless it be on one or two points which can perhaps be dealt with in isolation from the main issue, I doubt if I shall return to the charge in *Economica*. I am trying to re-shape and improve my central position, and that is probably a better way to spend one's time than in controversy.

Yours sincerely,
J. M. Keynes

REFLECTIONS ON THE PURE THEORY OF MONEY OF MR. J. M. KEYNES (continued)[1]

XI

Towards the end of his summary of the argument contained in those sections of the *Treatise* which were discussed in the first part of this article, Mr. Keynes writes: "If the banking system controls the terms of credit in such a way that savings are equal to the value of new investment, then the average price-level of output as a whole is stable and corresponds to the average rate of remuneration of the factors of production. If the terms of credit are easier than this equilibrium level, prices will rise, profits will be made....And if the terms of credit are stiffer than the equilibrium level, prices will fall, losses will be made. ...Booms or slumps are simply the expression of the results of an oscillation of the terms of credit about their equilibrium position."[2] This brings us to the first and, in many respects, the most important question we have to consider in this second article, viz., Mr. Keynes's theory of the Bank Rate.

The fundamental concept, upon which his analysis of this subject is based, is Wicksell's idea of a natural, or equilibrium, rate of interest, i.e., the rate at which the amount of new investment corresponds to the amount of current savings—a definition of Wicksell's concept on which, probably, all his followers would agree.[3] Indeed, when reading Mr. Keynes's exposition, any student brought up on Wicksell's teaching will find himself on what appears to be quite familiar ground until, his suspicions having been aroused by the conclusions, he discovers that, behind the verbal identity of the definition, there lurks (because of Mr.

---

[1][F. A. Hayek, "Reflections on the Pure Theory of Money of Mr. J. M. Keynes *(continued)*", *Economica*, vol. 12, no. 35, February 1932, pp. 22–44. —Ed.] The first part of these "Reflections" was published in *Economica*, no. 33, August 1931. See also Mr. Keynes's reply and the author's rejoinder in *Economica*, no. 34, November 1931. [See preceding three chapters. —Ed.]

[2]*A Treatise on Money*, op. cit., vol. 1, pp. 183–184. [*A Treatise on Money*, op. cit., vol. 5, p. 165. —Ed.]

[3][See this volume, chapter 1, note 4, and chapter 3, note 10 for more on Wicksell. —Ed.]

Keynes's peculiar definition of saving and investment) a fundamental difference. For the meaning attached by Mr. Keynes to the terms "saving" and "investment" differs from that usually associated with them. Hence the rate of interest which will equilibrate "savings" and "investment" in Mr. Keynes's sense is quite different from the rate which would keep them in equilibrium in the ordinary sense.

The most characteristic trait of Mr. Keynes's explanation of a deviation of the actual short-term rate of interest from the "natural" or equilibrium rate is his insistence on the fact that this may happen independently of whether the effective quantity of money does, or does not, change. He emphasises this point so strongly that he could scarcely expect any reader to overlook the fact that he wishes to demonstrate it. But, at the same time, while he certainly *wants* to establish this proposition, I cannot find any proof of it in the *Treatise*. Indeed, at all the critical points, the assumption seems to creep in that this divergence is made possible by the necessary change in the supply of money.[4]

It is quite certain that his reason for believing that a difference between saving and investment can arise without the banks changing their circulation does not become clear in the first section of the relevant chapter. In this section he distinguishes three different strands of thought in the traditional doctrine—only the first and third of which are relevant to this point, so that the second, which is concerned with the effect of the Bank Rate on international capital movements, may be neglected here. According to Mr. Keynes, the first of these strands of thought "regards Bank Rate merely as a means of regulating the *quantity* of bank money"[5] while the third strand "conceives of Bank Rate as influencing in some way the rate of investment and, perhaps, in the case of Wicksell and Cassel, as influencing the rate of investment relatively to that of saving".[6] But, as Mr. Keynes himself sees in one place,[7] there is no necessary conflict between these two theories. The obvious relation between them, which would suggest itself to any reader of Wicksell—a view which was certainly held by Wicksell himself—is

---

[4]I do not refer here to certain passages (e.g., vol. 1, pp. 198, 272, vol. 2, 100) [*A Treatise on Money*, op. cit., vol. 5, pp. 177, 243–244; vol. 6, p. 89. —Ed.] where this assumption is quite explicitly expressed; these are probably accounted for by the fact that Mr. Keynes actually believed something of this sort when he first began working on Book 3 of the *Treatise* (see his reply to the first part of this article, p. 389) [this volume, p. 149. —Ed.]

[5]*Treatise*, op. cit., vol. 1, p. 187. [*A Treatise on Money*, op. cit., vol. 5, p. 168. —Ed.]

[6]*Ibid.*, p. 190. [*Ibid.*, p. 170–171. —Ed.]

[7]*Ibid.*, p. 197. [*Ibid.*, p. 176–177. —Ed.]

that since, under the existing monetary system, changes in the amount of money in circulation are brought about mainly by the banks expanding or contracting their loans, and since money so borrowed at interest is used mainly for purposes of investment, any addition to the supply of money, not offset by a reverse change in the velocity of circulation, is likely to cause a corresponding excess of investment over saving; and any decrease will cause a corresponding excess of saving over investment. But Mr. Keynes believes that Wicksell's theory was something different from this and, in fact, rather like his own, apparently because Wicksell thought that one and the same rate of interest may serve both to make saving and investment equal *and* to keep the general price-level steady. As I have already stated, however, this is a point on which, in my view, Wicksell was wrong. But there can be no doubt that Wicksell was emphatically of the opinion that the possibility of there being a divergence between the market rate and the equilibrium rate of interest is entirely due to the "elasticity of the monetary system"[8], i.e., to the possibility of adding money to, or withdrawing it from, circulation.

XII

Mr. Keynes's own exposition of the General Theory of the Bank Rate[9] does not, by any means, solve the problem of how a divergence between the Bank Rate and the equilibrium rate should affect prices and production otherwise than by means of a change in the supply of money. Nowhere more than here, is one conscious of the lack of a satisfactory theory as to the effects of a change in the equilibrium rate; and of the confusion which results from the fundamentally different treatment of fixed and working capital. In most parts of his analysis, one is not clear whether he is speaking of the effects of *any* change in the Bank Rate, or whether what he says applies only to the effect of the Bank Rate being different from the market rate; nowhere does he make it clear that a central bank is in a position to determine the rate only because it is in a position to increase or decrease the amount of money in circulation.

But the least satisfactory part of this section is the oversimplified account of how a change in Bank Rate affects investment or, rather, the

---

[8]See *Geldzins und Güterpreise*, op. cit., p. 101; *Vorlesungen*, op. cit., vol. 2, p. 221. [Translated as *Interest and Prices*, op. cit., and *Lectures on Political Economy*, op. cit. —Ed.]

[9]*Treatise*, op. cit., vol. 1, pp. 200–209. [*A Treatise on Money*, op. cit., vol. 5, pp. 179–187. —Ed.]

value of *fixed* capital—since, for some unexplained reason, he here substitutes this latter concept for the former. This explanation consists merely in pointing out that, since "a change in Bank Rate is not calculated to have any effect (except, perhaps, a remote effect of the second order of magnitude) on the prospective yield of fixed capital" and since the conceivable effect on the price of that yield may be neglected, the only "immediate, direct and obvious effect" of a change in the Bank Rate on the value of fixed capital will be that its given yield will be capitalised at the new rate of interest.[10] But capitalisation is not so directly an *effect* of the rate of interest; it would be truer to say that both are effects of one common cause, viz., the scarcity or abundance of means available for investment, relative to the demand for those means. Only by changing this relative scarcity will a change in the Bank Rate also change the demand price for the services of fixed capital. If a change in the Bank Rate corresponds to a change in the equilibrium rate it is only an expression of that relative scarcity which has come about independently of this action. But if it means a movement away from the equilibrium rate, it will become effective and influence the value of fixed capital only in so far as it brings about a change in the amount of funds available for investment.

It is not difficult to see why Mr. Keynes came to neglect this obvious fact. For it is scarcely possible to see how a change in the rate of interest operates at all if one neglects, as Mr. Keynes neglects in this connection, the part played by the circulating capital which co-operates with the fixed capital; only in this way can one see how a change in the amount of free capital will affect the value of invested capital. To over-emphasise the distinction between fixed and circulating capital, which is, at best, merely one of degree, and not by any means of fundamental importance, is a common trait of English economic theory and has probably contributed more than any other cause to the unsatisfactory state of the English theory of capital at the present time. In connection with the present problem it is to be noted that his neglect of working capital not only prevents him from seeing in what way a change in the rate of interest affects the value of fixed capital, but also leads him to a quite erroneous statement about the degree and uniformity of that effect. It is simply not true to state that a change in the rate of interest will have no noticeable effect on the yield of fixed capital; this would be to ignore the effect of such a change on the distribution of circulating capital. The return attributable to any piece of fixed capital, any plant, machinery etc., is, in the short run, essentially a residuum after

---

[10] *Ibid.*, p. 202. [*Ibid.*, p. 181. —Ed.]

operating costs are deducted from the price obtained for the output, and once a given amount has been irrevocably sunk in fixed capital, even the total output obtained with the help of that fixed capital will vary considerably, according to the amount of circulating capital which it pays at the given prices, to use in co-operation with the fixed capital. Any change in the rate of interest will, obviously, materially alter the relative profitableness of the employment of circulating capital in the different stages of production, according as an investment for a longer or shorter period is involved; so that it will always cause shifts in the use of that circulating capital between the different stages of production, and bring about changes in the marginal productivity (the "real yield") of the fixed capital which *cannot* be so shifted. As the price of the complementary working capital changes, the yield and the price of fixed capital will, therefore, vary; and this variation may be different in the different stages of production. The change in the price of working capital, however, will be determined by the change in the total means available for investment in all kinds of capital goods ("intermediate products"), whether of durable or non-durable nature. Any increase of means available for such investment will necessarily tend to lower the marginal productivity of any further investment of capital, i.e., lower the margins of profit derived from the difference between the prices of the intermediate products and the final products by raising the prices of the former relatively to the prices of the latter.

It would appear that Mr. Keynes's failure to see these interrelations is due to the fact that he does not clearly distinguish, in the passage referred to above, between the *gross* and the *net* yield of fixed capital. If he had concentrated on the effects of a change in the rate of interest on the net yield as being the only relevant phenomenon, he could hardly have failed to see that the effect of such a change on fixed capital is not quite as direct and uniform as he supposes; and he would certainly have remembered also that there exists a tendency for the net money yield of real capital and the rate of interest to become equal. Thus the process of capitalisation at any given rate of interest means merely that, while money is obtainable at a rate of interest lower than the rate of yield on existing capital, borrowed money will be used to purchase capital goods until their price is so enhanced that the rate of yield is lowered to equal the rate of interest; and vice versa.

XIII

Although these deficiencies account for the fact that Mr. Keynes has not seen what I think is the true effect of a divergence between Bank Rate and equilibrium rate of interest, their existence does not give an

REFLECTIONS ON THE PURE THEORY OF MONEY OF MR. J. M. KEYNES

explanation of Mr. Keynes's own solution to this problem. This has to be sought elsewhere, viz., as already indicated, in Mr. Keynes's peculiar concept of saving. He believes that, in order to maintain equilibrium, new investment must be equal not only to that part of the money income of all individuals which *exceeds* what they spend on consumers' goods *plus* what must be re-invested in order to maintain existing capital equipment (which would constitute saving in the ordinary sense of the word); but also to that portion of entrepreneurs' "normal" incomes by which their actual income (and, therefore, their expenditure on consumption goods) has fallen short of that "normal" income. In other words, if entrepreneurs are experiencing losses (i.e., are earning less than the normal rate), and make up for such losses either by cutting down their own consumption *pari passu*, or by borrowing a corresponding amount from the savers, then, argues Mr. Keynes, not only do these sums make replacement of the old capital possible, but there should also be a further amount of *new* investment corresponding to these sums.[11] And as Mr. Keynes obviously thinks that saving (i.e., the refraining from buying consumers' goods) may, in many cases, actually cause some entrepreneurs to suffer losses which will absorb some of the savings which would otherwise have gone to new investment, this special concept of saving probably explains why he suspects almost *any* increase in saving of being conducive to the creation of a dangerous excess of saving over investment.

In order to arrive at a clearer understanding of this point, let us try to see what usually happens when people begin to save. The first effect will be that *less* consumers' goods are sold at existing prices. This does not mean that their prices must fall, still less that their prices must decline in proportion to the decrease in demand. Actually, the first effect will probably be that the sellers of consumers' goods, being unable to retail as much as before at existing prices, will, rather than sell at a loss, decide to increase temporarily their holdings of these goods and to slow down the process of production.[12] This is not only to be expected

---

[11]As regards the inclusion of such sums in Mr. Keynes's concept of saving, cf. *Treatise*, vol. 1, p. 139 [*A Treatise on Money*, op. cit., vol. 5, p. 125. —Ed.], and my Rejoinder, op. cit., p. 400 [this volume, p. 161. —Ed.]. That Mr. Keynes actually wants additional new investments to correspond to savings in this sense, has now become quite clear from his definition of net investment, to be found at the top of page 397 of the same issue of *Economica* [this volume, p. 157].

[12]This tendency is likely to be modified only to the extent that the cost of carrying goods makes it advisable to reduce prices so as to dispose of them more quickly. But it must be remembered that these costs, also, will be reduced as a consequence of the fall of interest and that this will act as an inducement to merchants to carry larger stocks.

for psychological reasons, but it is important to note here that this action on the part of entrepreneurs is not only in their own interest, but is necessary in order to make the desire to save effective. Saving must involve a reduction in consumption, in order that there may be accumulated, in finished or semi-finished form, a stock of consumers' goods, which will serve to bridge the gap between the time when the last products of the former (shorter) process of production are consumed and the time when the first products of the new, more capitalistic, process reach the market.[13] And by holding their goods for some time, entrepreneurs will probably be able (if the saving has led to new investment) to dispose of them at the former price.

If, however, we assume that, for some reason or other, producers of consumers' goods prefer to go on producing at full capacity, selling at a loss in the hope that the demand will ultimately revive and that they will suffer smaller losses than a reduction of output might have involved, then, as Mr. Keynes rightly points out, if production is to be maintained at the same level, they must make up for their losses in one of four possible ways: they must cut down their own expenditure (or, in Mr. Keynes's terminology, they must *save* in order to cover their losses); reduce their bank balances; borrow from the people who save; or sell to these people other capital, such as securities. According to Mr. Keynes, it is in these cases that investment will remain below saving and it is, therefore, these cases which we must consider more closely.

The task of finding out whether, in any given situation, saving will or will not exactly correspond to investment in Mr. Keynes's sense, is rendered somewhat difficult because, as I have repeatedly pointed out, he has not provided us with a clear and unequivocal definition of what he means by "investment". But, for the present purpose, we can surmount the difficulty by simply taking his account of what happens when investment falls short of saving and then investigating whether these effects manifest themselves in our particular case. Now, the effect of an excess of saving over investment, according to Mr. Keynes, will be that total incomes will not be sufficient to purchase total output at prices which cover costs. (If I and I'= S, then the rate of efficiency earnings, $W_1 = E/O$, is constant and identical with P and II, the price level of consumption goods and the price level of output as a whole,

---

[13]Cf. *Treatise*, op. cit., vol. 1, p. 283. [*A Treatise on Money*, op. cit., vol. 5, p. 254. —Ed.], and my *Prices and Production*, op. cit., p. 79.

respectively.)[14] The question now is whether an excess of saving over investment in Mr. Keynes's sense, caused by a part of savings being used to cover losses in any of the above-mentioned ways, will cause total incomes to fall below total cost of production.

The answer to this question seems to me to be an emphatic negative. Two cases are conceivable according to the way in which production is financed by producers of consumption goods who do not reduce their output but suffer losses and go on producing as much as before. When the same output of consumption goods is made possible by the decreased expenditure of the entrepreneurs, incomes derived from the production of consumption goods will not fall off by more than the initial decline in the demand for consumption goods, as the decreased consumption of the entrepreneurs will to the same extent offset the effects of the initial decrease on incomes. In the other case, where producers of consumption goods do not reduce their own consumption but cover their losses by borrowing or selling capital assets, clearly the income derived from the production of consumption goods will not decline at all.[15] In the former case, therefore, the total income-stream will remain the same as when an amount equal to the new savings is being used for new investment and, in the latter case, the same will be true provided that the excess (if any) of saving over what has been lent or paid to the losing entrepreneurs is used for new investment. Mr. Keynes, however, seems to believe that a reduction in entrepreneurs' expenditure on consumption goods constitutes a net decrease in the demand for these goods, different from, and in addition to, that shift of incomes from producers of consumption goods to producers of capital goods, which will always be the initial effect of an increase in saving; and that, in order to prevent undesirable disturbances, this reduction in consumption should be offset by a corresponding amount of additional new investment, to be made possible by increased loans from the banks.

Let us, for the moment, concentrate on this example in which the entrepreneur, who is making losses, cuts down his consumption, this being the only available means of maintaining his capital and of recovering it for re-investment. If, in spite of the fact that he is making losses, he re-invests it in the same line of production, instead of

---

[14][See this volume, chapter 3, note 23, for definitions of these terms. —Ed.]

[15]I neglect in this connection, as Mr. Keynes neglects, the third possible case where entrepreneurs reduce their balances in order to continue production. The effect here would, obviously, be similar to that of an increase in the quantity of money.

shifting it to some more profitable employment, then his sacrifice will be in vain because, after the next turn-over of this capital, he will be face to face with a new loss equal in amount to the old. What is wanted in order to make effective not only his efforts to maintain his capital,but also the initial saving, is a reduction in his output, in order to set free the factors which are needed for the new investment. But so long as he insists upon maintaining his output at the old level, his saving (in Mr. Keynes's sense) not only cannot, but certainly *should not*, give rise to any new investment. In the other case, where the losing entrepreneur obtains from other savers the capital necessary to make up for his losses, it is, no doubt, true that these individual savings are wasted, i.e., make no increase of the capital equipment possible. But this is so only because it is *assumed* that the losing entrepreneur is consuming his capital and (since the savings of other people are required to compensate for this) is thus preventing any net saving. But since, on balance, there is no excess of incomes over net earnings, *there is no reason why any new investment should take place;* this is also shown by the fact that, because the production of consumption goods is going on at an unchanged rate, no factors of production can be set free for use in the production of new investment goods. *Any attempt to bring about an increase in investment to correspond to this "saving" which is already required to maintain the old capital would have exactly the same effect as any other attempt to raise investment above net saving; inflation, forced saving, misdirection of production and, finally, a crisis.* It must be remembered that, so long as entrepreneurs insist on producing consumption goods at the old rate, and selling them below normal cost, no restriction of consumption and, therefore, no real saving is effected; and no stock of consumption goods will be accumulated to bridge the time gap to which we referred above.[16]

At the same time, it is, of course, true that under Mr. Keynes's assumption saving will lead to a fall in the general price level, because this assumption implies that, in spite of the decreased demand for the available part of the output, the money which is not spent on consumers' goods is injected into a higher stage of the process of production of these consumers' goods in order to maintain the output and price there. The only effect of saving, on this assumption, would therefore be that the money would, as it were, skip the last stage of the productive process (consumers' goods), and go directly to the higher stage to maintain the demand there; and the consequence would be that no increase in demand would occur anywhere to offset the decreased

[16][See this chapter, p. 180. —Ed.]

demand for consumers' goods, and there would be no rise of other prices to compensate for the effect produced on the price level by the fall in the price of consumption goods.

All this is however true only because it is *assumed* from the outset that, in spite of the fact that investment in the production of consumption goods has become less profitable (or even, perhaps, a losing proposition), entrepreneurs insist on investing just as much here as before and (in so far as they do not provide the capital themselves by reducing their consumption) offer to the savers better terms than the producers of capital goods. I cannot help feeling that Mr. Keynes has been misled here by his treatment of interest as part of the "rate of efficiency earnings of the factors of production" which he considers to be fixed by existing contracts, so that capitalists will get the same return wherever they invest and only the incomes of entrepreneurs will be affected. In any case, it seems to me that a complete neglect of the part played by rate of interest is involved in the assumption that, after investment in the production of consumption goods has become relatively less profitable, some other openings for investment which are now more profitable will not be found.

The most curious fact is that, from the outset, all of Mr. Keynes's reasoning which aims at proving that an increase in saving will not lead to an increase in investment is based on the assumption that, in spite of the decrease in the demand for consumption goods, the available output is not reduced; this means, simply, that he assumes from the outset what he wants to prove. This could be shown by many quotations from the *Treatise* and it would be seen that some of his most baffling conclusions, such as the famous analogy between profits and the widow's cruse and losses and the Danaid jar, are expressly based on the assumption "merely (*sic!*) that entrepreneurs are continuing to produce the same output of investment goods as before".[17] But in his recent Rejoinder to Mr. D. H. Robertson,[18] Mr. Keynes admits that he did not, in his book, deal in detail "with the train of events which ensues when, as a consequence of making losses, entrepreneurs reduce their output".[19] This is really a most surprising admission from an author who has set out to study the shifts between available and non-available output and wants to "prove" that saving will not lead to the necessary shifts.

---

[17] *Treatise*, op. cit., vol. 1, pp. 139–140. [*A Treatise on Money*, op. cit., vol. 5, p. 126. —Ed.]

[18] [J. M. Keynes, "A Rejoinder", op. cit. The passage quoted is found in footnote 1, p. 418. See also D. H. Robertson, "Mr. Keynes's Theory of Money", op. cit., pp. 395–411. —Ed.]

[19] Keynes, "A Rejoinder", op. cit., p. 412.

To sum up the somewhat prolonged discussion of this point; in none of the cases which we have considered will there occur those effects which should follow if saving and investment (in the ordinary sense) diverge, viz., total income exceeding or falling short of the cost of total output; and *there is no reason why saving and new investment, in Mr. Keynes's sense, should correspond.* By arbitrarily changing the meaning of familiar concepts, Mr. Keynes has succeeded in making plausible a proposition which nobody would accept were it stated in ordinary terms. In the form stated by Mr. Keynes, this proposition certainly has nothing to do with Wicksell's theory, nor can Wicksell be held responsible for Mr. Keynes's interpretation.

XIV

The point discussed in the last section shows what is, obviously, the main reason for Mr. Keynes's belief that a divergence between saving and investment may arise without a change in the amount of the effective circulation. But there are two further reasons given in the *Treatise*. One of these, although it is (as Mr. Keynes himself points out) of but negligible importance, is indeed a conceivable case in which such a divergence may arise for non-monetary reasons; while the other, which is, no doubt, of great importance, clearly relies on a change in the effective circulation. I shall try to dispose of the less important point here and deal more thoroughly with the second in the next section.

The conceivable case in which saving might exceed investment without a change in the effective circulation is where part of the savings might be permanently absorbed by the security market. If this occurred to any considerable extent, i.e., if Mr. Keynes's Business-deposits B or that part of his Financial Circulation which serves to effect the transfer of securities were to vary by large amounts, this would indeed mean that a corresponding part of the savings would not lead to new investment because of the "Financial Circulation stealing resources from the Industrial Circulation".[20] But since Mr. Keynes himself argues[21] that the *absolute* variability of Business-deposits B is, as a rule, only small in proportion to the total quantity of money, and since his utterances have even been interpreted, probably justly, as a denial of the view that

---

[20] *Treatise*, op. cit., vol. 1, p. 254. [*A Treatise on Money*, op. cit., vol. 5, p. 226. —Ed.]
[21] *Ibid.*, 244, 249, 256, 267. [*Ibid.*, pp. 218, 223, 229, 239. —Ed.]

security speculation can absorb any credit,[22] we could safely ignore this possibility if Mr. Keynes's later exposition, particularly his Rejoinder to Mr. D. H. Robertson, did not create the impression that he is now inclined to attach more importance to this point. The particular case, in which security transactions seem to assume this new importance to him, is, however, one of the cases already discussed in the last section, and not one of the typical cases which might, at first thought, spring to the mind. It is the case in which the producers of consumption goods cover the losses, which they have suffered as a result of the increased saving, by selling securities. In this case, it might be said that the fall in prices is due to the fact that the money saved finds its way to the producers of consumption goods via the purchase of securities instead of via the purchase of consumption goods, so that a security transaction has taken the place of a commodity transaction and the total stream of money directed to the purchase of commodities (and, therefore, the price level of those commodities) has fallen. What I think about this case has already been said in the last section.

XV

The last and, perhaps, the most important cause of a disequilibrium between saving and investment, given by Mr. Keynes, is a change in the effective circulation—not a change in the *amount* of money, but merely in its effectiveness or in the velocity of circulation. Just as the potential saver has to make a double choice and decide, firstly, whether he will save at all and, secondly, whether he will invest or hoard what he has saved, so there are, also, two ways in which his decisions may cause savings to exceed investment: Either because he saves more than entrepreneurs are willing to use for new investment or because he hoards his savings instead of making them available for investment. The first factor, which is the one discussed above in section XIII and which is only very inadequately characterised in the preceding sentence, is christened by Mr. Keynes "the excess saving factor", while he calls the second, which we must now study, "the excess bearish factor".[23] As already indicated, the problem to be studied here is the problem of hoarding; not, however, the hoarding of cash but the much more complicated and interesting problem of "hoarding" in a society where

---

[22][Professor J. H. Williams, "The Monetary Doctrine of J. M. Keynes", *Quarterly Journal of Economics*, vol. 45, August 1931, pp. 547–587. —Ed.]

[23]*Treatise*, op. cit., vol. 1, p. 145. [*A Treatise on Money*, op. cit., vol. 5, p. 130. —Ed.]

all current money consists of bank deposits.[24]

It is undeniably true that economists in general still make too much use of the assumption that saving means, in the first instance, that people accumulate cash which they will soon bring to their bank if they do not invest it otherwise. Little attention has been given to the fact that, since a large part of our current money is now in the form of bank deposits, there is no need for people to bring their savings to the bank; and that, therefore, an increase in the amount of money left at the banks as savings need not increase the power or willingness of the banks to lend. This is particularly true if people leave their savings on current account—as is often the case where interest is paid on these; and to a considerable extent, also, if they transfer them from current account to deposit account, since this will increase the lending power of the bank only in proportion to the difference, if any, between the percentage of reserve held against current accounts and deposit accounts respectively.[25] One of the great merits of Mr. D. H. Robertson's work is that he has forcefully drawn attention to this fact—the existence of which makes any practical solution to these problems extremely difficult. I think, however, that it should be theoretically clear that what happens in such a case is essentially the same thing as hoarding (i.e., a decrease in the velocity of circulation of money) and that these particular considerations only show that the practical importance of this phenomenon is much greater than most economists used to suppose.

Mr. Keynes's elaboration of this contribution of Mr. Robertson is, in many respects, the most interesting part of his theoretical analysis. His contribution consists mainly of a detailed analysis of the causes which will lead people to prefer hoarding to investment or vice versa; and, since this depends mainly on the people's expectations about the future price of securities, the analysis becomes an extensive study of the relations between bank credit and the stock market. And even if Mr.

---

[24]It should be remembered throughout the following discussion, that, in Mr. Keynes's theoretical exposition, it is assumed that bank deposits are the only form of money in general circulation and that the cash, held by the banks as reserve against these deposits, never enters the general circulation (pp. 182–183, this volume]).

[25]If, for instance, the reserve held against current accounts (demand deposits) is 9 per cent and the reserve held against deposit accounts (time deposits) is only 3 per cent, then the transfer of any given amount from current account to deposit account will free two-thirds of the reserves formerly held and enable the bank to create additional demand deposits equal to two-thirds of the amount transferred to deposit account. Mr. Keynes would, therefore, be quite consistent if he thought it desirable that banks should not be compelled to hold any reserves against deposit accounts (*Treatise*, op. cit., vol. 2, p. 13). [*A Treatise on Money*, op. cit., vol. 6, pp. 11–12. —Ed.]

Keynes is not quite clear, and his solution of the problem not quite satisfactory, there is no doubt that he is here breaking new ground and that he has opened up new vistas.

At the same time, his exposition of this point, which is contained mainly in chapter 10 (section III) and chapter 15, is by no means less difficult than the parts of his discussion to which we have already referred, and I doubt whether anybody could gather, from the text of the *Treatise* alone, the exact meaning of the author's theory on this point. For my own part, I must confess that it is only after studying the further elucidation of this point, provided by the author in his Rejoinder to Mr. D. H. Robertson, that I venture to believe that I see what he is driving at. For the purpose of this discussion, therefore, I shall use his exposition in this rejoinder as much as the original text of the *Treatise*.

Before we can enter upon a discussion of the main problem, how-ever, we must acquaint ourselves with the author's special terminology which, in this connection, is as rich and varied as elsewhere. As men-tioned,[26] his initial terms for the alternatives which are commonly called "hoarding" and "investing" are "bank deposits" and "securities". But, instead of "bank deposits" (or "savings deposits" or "inactive de-posits"), the terms "liquid assets", "hoarded money", or "hoards" are fre-quently used, while the "securities" become "non-liquid assets". "Active deposits" correspond, of course, to "current accounts" or "demand deposits".

Only a part of the total savings-deposits, viz., "savings deposits B", is an alternative to securities in the sense that the holder takes an adverse view of the prospects of the money value of securities. It constitutes what Mr. Keynes calls the "bear position", "a 'bear' being, therefore, one who, at the moment, prefers to avoid securities and to lend cash; while a 'bull' is one who prefers to hold securities and borrow cash. The former anticipates that securities will fall in cash value and the latter that they will rise".[27] This is quite clear; but when Mr. Keynes goes on to elaborate his concept of the "state of preference for savings deposits" or "state or degree of bearishness" or "degree of propensity to hoard", particularly in his *Economic Journal* article,[28] we find suddenly that it depends not on the expectations with regard to the future price of securities, but on the present price of securities, in the sense that, at any moment of time, a curve expressing the "degree of propensity

---

[26]*Economica*, no. 33, op. cit., p. 184. [See this volume, p. 136. —Ed.]

[27]*Treatise*, op. cit., vol. 1, p. 250. [*A Treatise on Money*, op. cit., vol. 5, p. 224. —Ed.]

[28]J. M. Keynes, "A Rejoinder", op. cit.

to hoard" could be drawn in a system of co-ordinates where the ordinate expresses the "price of non-liquid assets in terms of liquid assets" and the abscissa the quantity of "inactive deposits" or "liquid assets" held by the community.[29] This curve which, according to the explanation give on pages 250–251 of the *Treatise*,[30] probably has a shape somewhat similar to a parabola with an axis parallel to the abscissa and convex towards the ordinate (though the case discussed here may be one of a shift, or change in the shape, of the curve) is therefore based on the assumption that, within certain limits, in a given situation any *fall* in the price of securities will cause a *decrease* in the propensity to hoard or, in other words, that any such fall in the price level of securities will strengthen the expectation of a future rise. To me, it seems very doubtful whether any change in present security prices will lead, immediately, to a reverse change in the expectations concerning future price movements.

This demand curve for securities or non-liquid assets assumes importance in connection with Mr. Keynes's further assumption that the banking system is in a position to determine the amount of savings deposits, and that "given the volume of savings deposits created by the banking system, the price level of investment goods"[31] (whether new or old) is solely determined by the disposition of the public towards

---

[29] *Ibid.*, p. 412.

[30] *Treatise*, op. cit., vol. 1. [*A Treatise on Money*, op. cit., vol. 5, pp. 224–225. —Ed.]

[31] There is considerable obscurity and contradiction with regard to the relation between the price level of "investment goods" and the price level of "securities". In the passage quoted in the text (and in many other places as, for example, at the top of page 418 in the *Economic Journal* article) the two are, obviously, treated as identical and the sub-section which deals with the determination of the prices of "securities", from which this passage is taken, is headed "The Price-Level of New Investment-goods" (p. 140). [*A Treatise on Money*, vol. 5, p. 127. —Ed.] Here "securities" are expressly defined as "loan or real capital" (p. 141) [*Ibid.*, vol. 5, p. 127. —Ed.] and the conclusion of the section is summarised in the following sentence: "The price level of investments as a whole and hence of new investments, is that price level at which the desire of the public to hold savings deposits is equal to the amount of savings deposits which the banking system is willing and able to create." [*Ibid.*, vol. 5, p. 129. —Ed.] Essentially the same statement is made on page 413 of Mr. Keynes's *Economic Journal* article, regarding the determination of the price of "non-liquid assets" which, as we know, is only another name for "securities". But on page 253 [*Ibid.*, vol. 5, p. 226. —Ed.] it is said that, when security prices are rising, "this is *likely*—in general, but not necessarily—to stimulate a rise in P', the price level of *new* investment", and on page 249 [*Ibid.*, vol. 5, p. 222. —Ed.] the following statement occurs: "Nor does the price of existing securities depend at all closely, over short periods, either on the cost of production *or on the price* of new *fixed* capital" (my italics). This last passage is the more remarkable in view of the fact that, in the sections dealing with the effect of the bank rate on investment, the effect on the production of fixed capital was alone considered—to the exclusion of all other kinds of investment goods (p. 202). [*Ibid.*, vol. 5, p. 180. —Ed.]

"hoarding money". If we concede both assumptions: The direct dependence of the demand for securities on their present price, and the power of the banking system to determine the volume of savings deposits, then, indeed, this conclusion certainly follows. But both assumptions are highly questionable.

To the former, it need only be answered that any fall in the price of securities is just as likely to create a fear of a further fall as the expectation of a rise. The second is more difficult to refute because, so far as I can see, Mr. Keynes has merely stated it without making any attempt to prove it. It depends, obviously, on the assumption (which, curiously enough, smacks of the fundamental error of the adherents of the banking principle) that the amount of money (or "deposits") required by the industrial circulation is determined independently of the terms on which the banking system is willing to lend; so that any excess of deposits created by the banking system beyond this given amount will necessarily go into "hoards", while any deficiency will come out of these hoards and leave the general industrial circulation unaffected.[32] But this position is not only untenable (which hardly needs proving); it is, also, a curious contradiction of other parts of Mr. Keynes's argument. What can the banking system do to keep savings deposits constant if the public become "bullish" and reduce their savings deposits in order to buy securities? Certainly a reduction in the rate of interest will serve only to stimulate the bull movement. And how could the banking system have any influence on investment at all if all deposits it creates in excess of the given "requirements" of industry become inactive?

The cloud which envelops this part of the activities of the banking system becomes even thicker when Mr. Keynes discusses the function of the banks as intermediaries in the situation in which "two opinions develop between different schools of the public, the one favouring bank deposits more than before and the other favouring securities".[33] The banking system can do this "by creating deposits, not against securities, but against short-term advances" ("brokers' loans").[34] Now, to take only one case in which, according to Mr. Keynes, an increase in savings deposits may take place at the expense of the Industrial Circulation: viz.,

---

[32]"The amount of inactive deposits or hoards actually held, is determined by the banking system, since it is equal to the excess of total bank money created over what is required for the active deposits", J. M. Keynes, "A Rejoinder", op. cit., p. 413. See also pp. 414, 415, and 419.

[33]Treatise, op. cit., vol. 1, pp. 143, 251. [A Treatise on Money, op. cit., vol. 5, pp. 129, 224. —Ed.]

[34]Ibid. [Ibid. —Ed.]

an abnormal rise in savings deposits accompanied by a rise in security prices; this may indicate a *difference* of opinion as to the prospects of securities, the party on the "bull" tack in effect buying securities and borrowing money via the banking system from the party on the "bear" tack.[35] I am not sure whether, at this point, Mr. Keynes has in mind the fact that the banks re-lend these savings deposits as "loans for account of others" or whether he thinks that the increase in savings deposits will lead the banks to grant additional credits to speculators on their own account. But, be this as it may, I cannot see how this process can, on balance, decrease the amount of active deposits. So long as the preference of one party for savings deposits is offset by a corresponding additional lending to the party preferring securities, any increase in inactive deposits involved in this process will *not* mean a corresponding decrease in active deposits.

On the whole, this discussion of the relation between the Industrial and the Financial Circulations accomplishes little beyond showing that any increase in inactive deposits at the expense of active deposits will lead to an excess of saving over investment and that these changes are likely to be affected by changes in expectations as to the future course of security values—a result which is not particularly surprising. What Mr. Keynes says besides this (in particular his obiter dictum on the duty of a Central Bank[36]) is so closely bound up with the obscurities just mentioned that it is scarcely possible to follow its meaning.

The "excess bearish factor" discussed in this section is the last of the different causes of "the mysterious difference between saving and investment" which Mr. Keynes discusses. The last major subject of his theoretical analysis which we shall discuss here is the interaction of these different factors during the credit cycle. Before we turn to this problem, however, a few remarks may be made on a point which fits in better here than at any other place in these Reflections.

XVI

The point in question concerns a statement so extraordinary that, if it were not clearly in his book in black and white, one would not believe Mr. Keynes to be capable of making it. In the historical illustrations given in vol. 2, he devotes a whole section to what he calls "the Gibson Paradox", i.e., "the extraordinarily close correlation over a period of more than one hundred years between the rate of interest, as measured

---

[35] *Ibid.*, vol. 1, p. 251. [*Ibid.*, vol. 5, p. 224. —Ed.]
[36] *Ibid.*, vol. 1, pp. 254–256. [*Ibid.*, vol. 5, pp. 227–228. —Ed.]

by the yield of Consols, and the level of prices as measured by the Wholesale Index number".[37] Mr. Keynes reproaches economists in general for not having recognised the significance of this phenomenon and urges that it provides a verification of his theory. Without his theory, he contends, it is incapable of explanation, particularly not by "Professor Irving Fisher's well-known theorem as to the relation between the rate of interest and the appreciation or depreciation of the value of money".[38] According to this theorem, he suggests, we should expect just the contrary. Surely this is a definite fallacy, for it can be shown quite easily that this alleged paradox is nothing but an example of Professor Fisher's theorem. In the case of a sum of money, borrowed today and repayable a year hence, Mr. Keynes thinks that, "if real interest is 5 per cent per annum and the value of money is falling 2 per cent per annum, the lender requires the repayment of 107 a year hence in return for 100 loaned today".[39] But the movements to which Mr. Gibson calls attention, so far from being compensatory, are in fact aggravating in their effect on the relation between lender and borrower; so that the purchaser of long-dated securities will, if prices rise 2 per cent per annum, in a year's time possess a sum which is worth 2 per cent less in money terms, money itself being 2 per cent less valuable, so that he is 4 per cent worse off than before. Now this is exactly what one would expect according to Professor Fisher's theorem, because, in the case of long-dated securities, a sale before the date when they become due is not the fulfillment of a contract in which the owner as lender would be in a position to ask for some compensation for the anticipated fall in the value of money; but, *on the contrary, the buyer is in the position of the lender, who (since the amount of the ultimate repayment is given) will naturally offer less if he expects the value of money to fall.* Only if the present holder, at the time when he bought the securities, foresaw the fall in the value of money (and if he found somebody who also foresaw it and was ready to sell) would he have been able to protect himself by offering less for a security which represented a claim to fixed payments in a depreciating money. But I find it utterly impossible to understand why one should expect, as Mr. Keynes obviously does, that a man holding a fixed-interest

---

[37] *Treatise*, op. cit., vol. 2, p. 198. [*A Treatise on Money*, op. cit., vol. 6, p. 177. A. H. Gibson identified a high correlation between interest rates and the price level in "The Future Course of High Class Investment Values", *The Bankers', Insurance Managers', and Agents' Magazine*, January 1923, pp. 15–34. —Ed.]

[38] *Treatise*, op. cit., vol. 2, p. 202. [*A Treatise on Money*, op. cit., vol. 6, p. 181. See this volume, chapter 4, note 8 for more on Fisher. —Ed.]

[39] [*A Treatise on Money*, op. cit., vol. 6, p. 181. —Ed.]

security should be in a position to ask more interest if the value of money falls. "Gibson's Paradox" is, therefore, no paradox at all and proves nothing in favour of Mr. Keynes's theory.[40]

XVII

Within the limits of this article, it is impossible to deal, in the same detail with which the fundamental concepts have been discussed, with the last major subject upon which I wish to touch: viz., the explanation of the credit cycle. It is only natural that, when one tries to use all these concepts as tools for the purpose for which they were forged, all the difficulties which have been pointed out not only recur but increase. To show in detail how they affect the results would require a discussion many times longer than that contained in the respective sections of the *Treatise*. All I can do is to take up a few central points and leave unexamined not only the more intricate problems which arise out of the combination of difficulties already noted but also some further important problems connected with the traditional English concept of capital, particularly the over-emphasised distinction between fixed and circulating capital, an adequate discussion of which would require a separate article.

The first point which must strike any reader conversant with the writings of Wicksell and of what Mr. Keynes calls the Neo-Wicksell school is how little use he finally makes of the effects of a monetary disequilibrium on *real* investment—which he has been at such pains to develop. What he is really interested in is merely the shifts in the money-streams and the consequent changes in price levels. It seems never to have occurred to him that the artificial stimulus to investment, which makes it exceed current saving, may cause a dis-equilibrium in the real structure of production which, sooner or later, must lead to a reaction. Like so many others who hold a purely monetary theory of the trade cycle (as, for example, Mr. R. G. Hawtrey in this country and Dr. L. A. Hahn in Germany[41]), he seems to believe that, if the existing monetary organisation did not make it impossible, the boom

---

[40]While reading the proofs of this article I notice that Professor Irving Fisher himself, in his new *Theory of Interest* (New York: Macmillan, 1930; reprinted, Porcupine Press, 1977), pp. 417ff, uses the very same figures of Mr. Gibson which are used by Mr. Keynes as evidence confirming his theory.

[41][See this volume, chapter 4, footnote 17 for more on Hawtrey. Albert Hahn (1889–1968) was a German trade-cycle theorist and author of *Volkswirtschaftlichen Theorie des Bankkredits* (Tübingen: Mohr, 1920; 3rd edition, 1930). —Ed.]

could be perpetuated by indefinite inflation. Though the term "over-investment" occurs again and again, its implications are never explored beyond the first conclusion that, so long as total incomes less the amount saved exceed the cost of the available output of consumers' goods (because investment is in excess of saving), the price level will have a tendency to rise. In Mr. Keynes's explanation of the cycle, the main characteristic of the boom is taken to be not the increase in investment, but this consequent increase in the prices of consumers' goods and the profit which is therefore obtained. Direct inflation for consumption purposes would, therefore, create a boom quite as effectively as would an excess of investment over saving. Hence he was quite consistent when, despairing of a revival of investment brought about by cheap money, he advocated, in his well-known broadcast address,[42] the direct stimulation of the expenditure of consumers on the lines suggested by other purchasing-power theorists such as Messrs Abbati, Martin, and Foster and Catchings;[43] for, on his theory, the effects of cheap money and increased buying of consumers are equivalent.

Since, according to this theory, it is the excess of the demand for consumers' goods over the costs of the available supply which constitutes the boom, this boom will last only so long as demand keeps ahead of supply and will end either when the demand ceases to increase or when the supply, stimulated by the abnormal profits, catches up with demand. Then the prices of consumers' goods will fall back to costs and the boom will be at an end, though it need not necessarily be followed by a depression; yet, in practice, deflationary tendencies are usually set up which will reverse the process.

This seems to me to be, in broad outline, Mr. Keynes's explanation of the cycle. In essence it is not only relatively simple, but also much less different from the current explanations than its author seems to think; though it is, of course, much more complicated in its details. To me, however, it seems to suffer from exactly the same deficiencies as all the other, less elaborate, purchasing-power theories of the cycle.

---

[42]Cf. his *Essays in Persuasion*, 1931, pp. 148 ff. [The radio address "Saving and Spending" is reprinted in J. M. Keynes, *Essays in Persuasion* [1931], volume 9 (1972) of *The Collected Writings of John Maynard Keynes*, op. cit., pp. 135–141. —Ed.]

[43]Alfred H. Abbati (1889–?) was the author of *The Unclaimed Wealth: How Money Stops Production* (London: Allen & Unwin, 1924) and of *The Final Buyer* (London: P. S. King, 1928). See this volume, chapter 2, note 22 for more on P. W. Martin. William Trufant Foster (1879–1950), economist and director of the Pollak Foundation for Economic Research, and Waddill Catchings (1879–1967), American lawyer, banker, and economist, founder of the Pollak Foundation. See this volume, chapter 2 for more on Foster and Catchings. —Ed.]

The main objections to these theories—I cannot go into details here and must beg permission, therefore, to refer to my other attempts to do so[44]—seem to me to be three in number. *Firstly*, that the original increase in investment can be maintained only so long as it is more profitable to increase the output of capital goods than to bid up the prices of the factors of production in the effort to satisfy the increased demands for consumers' goods. *Secondly*, that the increase in the demand for consumers' goods, if not offset by a new increase in the amount of money available for investment purposes, so far from giving a new stimulus to investment, will, on the contrary, lead to a decrease in investment because of its effect on the prices of the factors of production. *Thirdly*, that the very fact that processes of investment have been begun but have become unprofitable as a result of the rise in the price of the factors and must therefore be discontinued, is, of itself, a sufficient cause to produce a decrease of general activity and employment (in short, a depression) without any new monetary cause (deflation). In so far as deflation is brought about—as it may well be—by this change in the prospects of investment, it is a secondary or induced phenomenon caused by the more fundamental, real, disequilibrium which cannot be removed by new inflation, but only by the slow and painful process of readjustment of the structure of production. While Mr. Keynes has occasional glimpses of the alternative character of an increase in the output of consumers' goods and investment goods,[45] he does not follow up this idea; and, in my view, it is this alone which could lead him to the true explanation of the crisis. But it is not surprising that he fails to do so, for it is precisely in the elucidation of these interrelations that the tools he has created become an altogether inadequate and unsuitable equipment. The achievement of this object is, indeed, impossible with his present concepts of capital and "investment" and without a clear notion of the change in the structure of production involved in any transition to more or less capitalistic methods. An adequate criticism of Mr. Keynes's explanation of the cycle would, therefore, require a somewhat elaborate description of that

---

[44]Cf. my *Prices and Production*, op. cit.; and "The 'Paradox' of Saving", *Economica*, no. 32, May 1931. ["The 'Paradox' of Saving" is reprinted in this volume, chapter 2 above. —Ed.]

[45]For example, when he says (p. 289) [*A Treatise on Money*, op. cit., vol. 5, p. 259. —Ed.], that "the incentive to an increased output of capital goods should diminish, just as the incentive to the production of consumption goods increases", or again in the passage at the top of page 310 [*Ibid.*, vol. 5, p. 278. —Ed.], which clearly implies that it is the quick, and therefore less capitalistic, production of consumers' goods which has become relatively more profitable as a consequence of their higher prices.

process. This I have tried to give in the places referred to. All I shall attempt here will be some further explanation of the three points already mentioned.

XVIII

From Mr. Keynes's Reply to the first part of these Reflections,[46] I gather that he considers what I have called changes in the structure of production (i.e., the lengthening or shortening of the average period of production) to be a long-run phenomenon which may, therefore, be neglected in the analysis of a short-period phenomenon, such as the trade cycle. I am afraid that this contention merely proves that Mr. Keynes has not yet fully realised that *any* change in the amount of capital per head of working population is equivalent to a change in the average length of the roundabout process of production and that, therefore, all his demonstrations of the change in the amount of capital during the cycle prove my point[47]. Any increase in investment means that, on the average, a longer time will elapse between the application of the factors and the completion of the process and, what is particularly important in this connection, the period is not lengthened only while *new* investment is going on; it will have to be permanently longer if the increased capital is to be maintained, i.e., *total* investment (new and renewed) will have to be constantly greater than before. But if the increase of investment is not the consequence of a voluntary decision to reduce the possible level of consumption for this purpose, there is no reason why it should be permanent and the very increase in the demand for consumers' goods which Mr. Keynes has described will put an end to it as soon as the banking system ceases to provide additional cheap means for investment. Here his exclusive insistence on new investment and his neglect of the process of reinvestment makes him overlook the all-important fact that an increase in the demand for consumers' goods will not only tend to stop new investment, but may make a complete reorganisation of the existing structure of production inevitable—which would involve considerable disturbances and would render it impossible, temporarily, to employ all labour.

So long as the absolute rise in the price of consumption goods is relatively smaller than the rise in the price of investment goods due to a continued expansion of credit, it is true that the upward phase of the

---

[46]See J. M. Keynes, "The Pure Theory of Money: A Reply to Dr. Hayek", op. cit., p. 395. [This volume, p. 156. —Ed.]

[47]See *Treatise*, op. cit., vol. 2, chapters 27–29.

cycle will continue. But as soon as the rise in the former overtakes the rise in the latter, this will certainly not mean that "the upward phase of the cycle will have made its appearance".[48] On the contrary it must mean a period of declining investment.[49] And, as all inductive evidence shows, it is the decline in investment (or in the production of producers' goods) and not the impossibility of selling consumers' goods at remunerative prices, which characterises the beginning of the slump. Indeed, it is the experience of all depressions and especially of the present one, that the sale of consumption goods are maintained until long after the crisis; industries making consumption goods are the only ones which are prosperous and even able to absorb, and return profits on, new capital during the depression. The decrease in consumption comes only as a result of unemployment in the heavy industries, and since it was the increased demand for the products of the industries making goods for consumption which made the production of investment goods unprofitable, by driving up the prices of the factors of production, it is only by such a decline that equilibrium can be restored.

If the real trouble is that the proportion of the total output which, as a consequence of entrepreneurs' decisions, has become "non-available" is too great relative to what consumers are demanding to have "available"; and if, therefore, the production of "non-available" output has to be cut down, then, certainly, the resulting unemployment is due to more deep-seated causes than mere deflation and can be cured only by such a reduction of consumption relative to saving as will correspond to the existing proportion between "available" and "non-available" output; or by adapting this latter proportion to the former, i.e., by returning to less capitalistic methods of production and thus reducing total output. I do not deny that, during this process, a tendency towards deflation will regularly arise; this will particularly be the case when the crisis leads to frequent failures and so increases the risks of lending. It may become very serious if attempts artificially to "maintain purchasing power" delay the process of readjustment—as has probably been the case during the

---

[48]*Ibid.*, p. 283. [*Ibid.*, vol. 5, p. 254. —Ed.]

[49]Something like this seems to be going on at the present time in Russia where, after the burden imposed by the Five Years' Plan on the consumer was found to be intolerable, the authorities have decided to change their arrangements and speed up the output of consumers' goods. I should not have been surprised if this had led to unemployment just as in a capitalistic society; and in fact, if I have been informed correctly, this has already taken place. This does not, however, lead to an increase in the figure for unemployment, but only in the numbers of so-called unemployable—since workmen are only dismissed on the pretence of inefficiency.

present crisis. This deflation is, however, a secondary phenomenon in the sense that it is caused by the instability in the real situation; the tendency will persist so long as the real causes are not removed. Any attempt to combat the crisis by credit expansion will, therefore, not only be merely the treatment of symptoms as causes, but may also prolong the depression by delaying the inevitable real adjustments. It is not difficult to understand, in the light of these considerations, why the easy-money policy which was adopted immediately after the crash of 1929 was of no effect.

It is, unfortunately, to these secondary complications that Mr. Keynes, in common with many other contemporary economists, directs most attention. This is not to say that he has not made valuable suggestions for treating these secondary complications. But, as I suggested at the beginning of these Reflections, his neglect of the more fundamental "real" phenomena has prevented him from reaching a satisfactory explanation of the more deep-seated causes of depression.

SEVEN

DR. HAYEK ON MONEY AND CAPITAL[1]
by Piero Sraffa

To deal with the theory of money, from its doctrinal history down to the inevitable practical proposals, touching upon some of the most perplexing parts of the subject, and all this in four lectures,[2] must have been a feat of endurance on the part of the audience as much as of the lecturer. For, however peculiar, and probably unprecedented, their conclusions may be, there is one respect in which the lectures collected in this volume fully uphold the tradition which modern writers on money are rapidly establishing, that of unintelligibility. The fault must lie in the subject itself, or in the theories which are directed to elucidate it, for this notoriously is the case even with writers otherwise the most lucid. And Dr. Hayek himself in an excellent introductory lecture, in which he traces in the history of thought the sources of his own doctrine, is a model of clearness.

Taken as a whole, there is this to be said in favour of the book—that it is highly provocative. Its one definite contribution is the emphasis it puts on the study of the effects of monetary changes on the relative prices of commodities, rather than on movements of the general price level on which attention has almost exclusively been focussed by the old quantity theory. But in every other respect the inescapable conclusion is that it can only add to the prevailing confusion of thought on the subject.

The starting-point and the object of Dr. Hayek's inquiry is what he calls "neutral money"; that is to say, a kind of money which leaves production and the relative prices of goods, including the rate of interest, "undisturbed", exactly as they would be if there were no money at all.

This method of approach might have something to recommend it, provided it were constantly kept in mind that a state of things in which money is "neutral" is identical with a state in which there is no money at all: As Dr. Hayek once says, if we "eliminate all monetary influences

---

[1] [Pierro Sraffa, "Dr. Hayek on Money and Capital", *Economic Journal*, vol. 42, March 1932, pp. 42–53. —Ed.]

[2] F. A. Hayek, *Prices and Production*, op. cit.

on production...we may treat money as non-existent".[3] Thus the parallel inquiry into "neutral money" and various kinds of real money would resolve itself into a comparison between the conditions of a specified non-monetary economy and those of various monetary systems.

We therefore might expect that Dr. Hayek would, in discussing a number of assumed cases in which equilibrium is disturbed, compare the results in a moneyless economy with the corresponding results obtained under various monetary systems, or policies. This would bring out which are the essential characteristics common to every kind of money, as well as their differences, thus supplying the elements for an estimate of the merits of alternative policies.

But the reader soon realises that Dr. Hayek completely forgets to deal with the task which he has set himself, and that he is only concerned with the wholly different problem of proving that only one particular banking policy (that which maintains constant under all circumstances the quantity of money multiplied by its velocity of circulation) succeeds in giving full effect to the "voluntary decisions of individuals", especially in regard to saving, whilst under any other policy these decisions are "distorted" by the "artificial" interference of banks. Being entirely unaware that it may be doubted whether under a system of barter the decisions of individuals would have their full effects, once he has satisfied himself that a policy of constant money would achieve this result, he identifies it with "neutral money"; and finally, feeling entitled to describe that policy as "natural", he takes it for granted that it will be found desirable by every right-thinking person. So that "neutral" money, from being in the first lecture the object of theoretical analysis,[4] is shown in the body of the book to be "not merely entirely harmless, but in fact the only means of avoiding misdirections of production",[5] and in the end becomes "our maxim of policy".[6]

If Dr. Hayek had adhered to his original intention, he would have seen at once that the differences between a monetary and a non-monetary economy can only be found in those characteristics which are set forth at the beginning of every textbook on money. That is to say, that money is not only the medium of exchange, but also a store of value, and the standard in terms of which debts, and other legal obligations, habits, opinions, conventions, in short all kinds of relations between men, are more or less rigidly fixed. As a result, when the price

[3]*Ibid.*, p. 109.
[4]*Ibid.*, p. 28.
[5]*Ibid.*, p. 89.
[6]*Ibid.*, p. 106.

of one or more commodities changes, these relations change in terms of such commodities; while if they had been fixed in commodities, in some specified way, they would have changed differently, or not at all. Upon this basis it would be possible to find the monetary policy the effects of which are the nearest to a given non-monetary system.

It would be idle to rehearse these platitudes had not Dr. Hayek completely ignored them in his arguments. The money which he contemplates is in effect used purely and simply as a medium of exchange. There are no debts, no money-contracts, no wage-agreements, no sticky prices in his suppositions. Thus he is able to neglect altogether the most obvious effects of a general fall, or rise, of prices. This attitude, which amounts to assuming away the very object of the inquiry, appears to originate in a well-founded objection to the vagueness of the conception of "the general price-level" understood as anything different from one out of many possible index-numbers of prices, and in the opinion that such a conception can have no place in a theory of money. Such a theory, according to him, ought simply to consider the influence of money on the relative prices of commodities—which is excellent, provided that money itself is one of the commodities under consideration; but Dr. Hayek goes further and rejects not only the notion of general price level but every notion of the value of money in any sense whatever.[7] Having thus reduced money to utter insignificance, it is easy for Dr. Hayek to prove to his own satisfaction that, if its quantity is kept constant,[8] money is "neutral" in the sense that after a disturbance, such as an increase of saving, the new equilibrium of production and of relative prices is reached as smoothly as if no money existed. And, since he also impartially deprives money of its essence when he considers alternative monetary policies, it is inevitable that money should again be found to be "neutral", and the effects should be identical, that is to say, equally immaterial. But Dr. Hayek invariably finds, when he comes to compare the effects of alternative policies in regulating this emasculated money, that there is an all-important difference in the result, and that it is "neutral" only if it is kept constant in quantity, whilst if the quantity is changed, the most disastrous effects follow.

The reader is forced to conclude that these alleged differences can only arise either from an error of reasoning, or from the unwitting

[7]See, for example, *ibid.*, pp. 7 and 27.

[8]I follow Dr. Hayek's practice of using "the quantity of money" as short for "the quantity of money multiplied by its velocity in circulation"; although it is a dangerous omission which leads him to overlook that the velocity is bound to change as the direct result of a change in prices.

introduction, in working out the effects of one of the two systems compared, of some irrelevant non-monetary consideration, which produces the difference attributed to the properties of the system itself. The task of the critic, therefore, is the somewhat monotonous one of discovering, for each step of Dr. Hayek's parallel analysis, which is the error or irrelevancy which causes the difference. This will be done only for one or two of these cases in the course of the present review. But from the beginning it is clear that a methodical criticism could not leave a brick standing in the logical structure built up by Dr. Hayek.

A considerable part of the book is taken up by preliminaries about the relations between the quantity of capital and the length of the process of production and about the proportions in which the flow of money is divided between the purchase of consumers' goods and the purchase of producers' goods. Dr. Hayek as it were builds up a terrific steamhammer in order to crack a nut—and then he does not crack it. Since we are primarily concerned in this review with the nut that is not cracked, we need not spend time criticising the hammer. The part which its description plays in the book is little more than that of obscuring the main issue; a maze of contradictions makes the reader so completely dizzy that when he reaches the discussion of money he may out of despair be prepared to believe anything.[9]

The only point that need be retained is that Dr. Hayek conceives of saving as an increase in the proportion of the total flow of money that is directed to the purchase of producers' goods, as opposed to the proportion that is directed to the purchase of consumers' goods. When we start from the usual point of view, which regards consumers as deciding to save a part of their *net* income, the accumulation of capital proceeds, and no equilibrium can be established, until the consumers revert to the practice of consuming the whole of their net income. But when we start, with Dr. Hayek, from the *gross* receipts, saving means a decision to change the proportions in which those receipts are spent on

---

[9]The essential contradiction is that Dr. Hayek must both assume that the "consumers" are the same individuals as the "entrepreneurs", and that they are distinct. For only if they are identical can the consumers' decisions to save take the form of a decision to alter the "proportions" in which the total gross receipts are divided between the purchase of consumers' goods and the purchase of producers' goods; and only if they are distinct has the contrast between "credits to producers", which are used to buy producers' goods, and "credits to consumers", which are used to buy consumers' goods, any definite meaning. As a result we are alternately told that the "decisions to save" are taken by "the consumers" (op. cit., p. 46), by "the entrepreneurs" (p. 45), or even by "the industries" (p. 58). This makes a pair with the kindred though distinct contradiction of assuming in the same context that intermediate products never change hands against money (p. 38), and that they change hands against money in equal intervals of time (pp. 41–42).

producers' and consumers' goods; accumulation then proceeds for a limited period, after which equilibrium is reached, although the new proportions are permanently maintained; though this, it may be noticed, applies only to a very peculiar case, and not, as Dr. Hayek seems to believe, in general; but since, even within the limits of that case, Dr. Hayek's further conclusions appear to be invalid, the point need not detain us any longer.[10]

The central topic of the book is the analysis of the accumulation of capital in a monetary economy. Accumulation, Dr. Hayek says, can take place in two ways: "either as a result of changes in the volume of voluntary saving, or as a result of a change in the quantity of money which alters the funds at the disposal of the entrepreneurs for the purchase of producers' goods".[11]

If savings are "voluntary", consumers place certain sums of money in the hands of the entrepreneurs, who use them for lengthening the process of production, and thus capital accumulates. Skipping over the difficulties of the transition, Dr. Hayek concludes that the accumulation comes to a stop when saving ceases, and a new equilibrium is reached, where the same quantity of labour uses a larger quantity of capital, the output of consumption goods is larger and all prices, he assumes, are lower. The effect thus realized "is one which fulfils the object of saving and investing, and is identical with the effect which would have been produced if the savings were made in kind instead of in money".[12]

His next case is that of "forced saving". If, when no savings are being made, the banks expand the circulation, by means of "credits granted to producers", the initial effects will be the same as those of voluntary saving: The entrepreneurs will use the additional funds placed at their disposal to lengthen the process of production, and capital will be accumulated. An appropriate degree of inflation through loans "to producers" will bring about exactly the same results as voluntary saving; and a new situation will be reached, similar to it in all respects, except that all prices will be higher; higher, that is to say, as compared with the similar situation due to voluntary savings, but not necessarily, it should be noticed, as compared with the initial situation; on this latter basis, some prices may be higher and some lower.

---

[10]The extreme instance of integrated firms (pp. 59–60), if nothing else, should have warned Dr. Hayek that his method is not applicable in general, and put him on the track to finding its limits, which are extremely narrow; for in that case he is driven to assume that the money saved is hoarded for a time, thus directly contradicting his postulate that the quantity of money multiplied by its velocity is constant.

[11][Op. cit., p. 45. —Ed.]

[12]Op. cit., p. 49.

It would appear that the parallelism is due to our having ignored the secondary effects of a general fall or rise of prices. But Dr. Hayek has undertaken to avoid the concept of "value of money"; and at the same time he must impress us with the benefits of voluntary saving, and the evils of inflation. He therefore accepts the above conclusions, as far as they go, and must now try to find in a different set of considerations the reasons why inflation has not the same effects as saving.

The true difference between the two cases is, according to him, that the change in the structure of production brought about by saving is permanent, being due to the "voluntary decisions of individuals"; whereas the same change, if due to inflation, is "forced", and therefore the consumers, as soon as inflation ceases and their freedom of action is restored, will proceed to consume all the capital accumulated against their will, and re-establish the initial position.

That the position reached as the result of "voluntary saving" will be one of equilibrium (under Dr. Hayek's tacit assumption that the consequent fall in the rate of interest is irrelevant to the equilibrium) is clear enough; though the conclusion is not strengthened by the curious reason he gives for it.[13]

But equally stable would be that position if brought about by inflation; and Dr. Hayek fails to prove the contrary. In the case of inflation, just as in that of saving, the accumulation of capital takes place through a reduction of consumption. "But now this sacrifice is not voluntary, and is not made by those who will reap the benefit from the new invest-ments. . . . There can be no doubt that, if their money receipts should rise again [and this rise is bound to happen, as Dr. Hayek promises to prove] they would immediately attempt to expand consumption to the usual proportion", that is to say, capital will be reduced to its former amount; "such a transition to less capitalistic methods of production necessarily takes the form of an economic crisis".[14]

As a moment's reflection will show, "there can be no doubt" that nothing of the sort will happen. One class has, for a time, robbed another class of a part of their incomes; and has saved the plunder.

---

[13]The reason given is that "since, after the change had been completed, these persons [i.e., the savers] would get a greater proportion of the total real income, they would have no reason" to consume the newly acquired capital (op. cit., p. 52). But it is not necessarily true that these persons will get a greater *proportion* of the total real income, and if the fall in the rate of interest is large enough they will get a smaller proportion; and anyhow it is difficult to see how the *proportion* of total income which falls to them can be relevant to the "decisions of individuals". Dr. Hayek, who extols the imaginary achievements of the "subjective method" in economics, often succeeds in making patent nonsense of it.

[14]Op. cit., p. 53.

When the robbery comes to an end, it is clear that the victims cannot possibly consume the capital which is now well out of their reach. If they are wage-earners, who have all the time consumed every penny of their income, they have no wherewithal to expand consumption. And if they are capitalists, who have not shared in the plunder, they may indeed be induced to consume now a part of their capital by the fall in the rate of interest; but not more so than if the rate had been lowered by the "voluntary savings" of other people.

We should expect that Dr. Hayek, having satisfied himself that the "artificial stimulant" of inflation in the shape of producers' credits cannot do any good and cause an accumulation of capital, would conclude that in its opposite form of consumers' credits it is equally incapable of doing harm by preventing voluntary accumulation. But now that he sees his chance he cannot resist the temptation and must let the damned thing run its full course of destruction.

Accordingly, in his next case he finds that if, when the consumers decide to save, additional money is issued through consumers' credits to the extent required for re-establishing the former proportion between the demand for consumers' goods and the demand for producers' goods, "the only effect of such an increase of consumers' money incomes would be to frustrate the effect of saving".[15] And from this it follows that inflation through consumers' credits, when no voluntary savings were being made, *would* be effective in decreasing capital. Thus Dr. Hayek will have it both ways.

If this were not sufficient to show that Dr. Hayek's discussion is utterly irrelevant to money and to inflation, one or two further cases which he has overlooked might be considered. Thus, on his assumptions, if the banks increased the circulation but apportioned the additional money between consumers' and producers' credits so as not to disturb the initial "proportions", nothing would happen. And, on the other hand, if, as their outstanding loans fall due, they changed the "proportions" by increasing the quantity of producers' credits to the same extent as they decreased the quantity of consumers' credits, the effects would be the same as in the case of the "inflation" effected through producers' credits although the circulation would remain unchanged; and conversely for consumers' credits.

What has happened is simply that, since money has been thoroughly "neutralised" from the start, whether its quantity rises, falls, or is kept steady, makes not the slightest difference; at the same time an extraneous element, in the shape of the supposed power of the banks to settle

---

[15]Op. cit., p. 57.

the way in which money is spent, has crept into the argument and has done all the work. As Voltaire says, you can kill a flock of sheep by incantations, plus a little poison.

Dr. Hayek's theory of the relation of money to the rate of interest is mainly given by the way of criticism and development of the theory of Wicksell. He states his own position as far as it agrees with Wicksell's as follows: "In a money economy, the actual or money rate of interest may differ from the equilibrium or natural rate, because the demand for and the supply of capital do not meet in their natural form but in the form of money, the quantity of which available for capital purposes may be arbitrarily changed by the banks."[16]

An essential confusion, which appears clearly from this statement, is the belief that the divergence of rates is a characteristic of a money economy: and the confusion is implied in the very terminology adopted, which identifies the "actual" with the "money" rate, and the "equilibrium" with the "natural" rate. If money did not exist, and loans were made in terms of all sorts of commodities, there would be a single rate which satisfies the conditions of equilibrium, but there might be at any one moment as many "natural" rates of interest as there are commodities, though they would not be "equilibrium" rates. The "arbitrary" action of the banks is by no means a necessary condition for the divergence; if loans were made in wheat and farmers (or for that matter the weather) "arbitrarily changed" the quantity of wheat produced, the actual rate of interest on loans in terms of wheat would diverge from the rate on other commodities and there would be no single equilibrium rate.

In order to realize this we need not stretch our imagination and think of an organised loan market amongst savages bartering deer for beavers. Loans are currently made in the present world in terms of every commodity for which there is a forward market. When a cotton spinner borrows a sum of money for three months and uses the proceeds to purchase spot, a quantity of raw cotton which he simultaneously sells three months forward, he is actually "borrowing cotton" for that period. The rate of interest which he pays, per hundred bales of cotton, is the number of bales that can be purchased with the following sum of money: the interest on the money required to buy spot 100 bales, plus the excess (or minus the deficiency) of the spot over the forward prices of the 100 bales.

In equilibrium the spot and forward price coincide, for cotton as for any other commodity; and all the "natural" or commodity rates are equal

---

[16]Pp. 20–21. "Equilibrium rate" is the term Dr. Hayek proposes to substitute for Wicksell's "natural rate".

to one another, and to the money rate. But if, for any reason, the supply and the demand for a commodity are not in equilibrium (i.e., its market price exceeds or falls short of its cost of production), its spot and forward prices diverge, and the "natural" rate of interest on that commodity diverges from the "natural" rates on other commodities. Suppose there is a change in the distribution of demand between various commodities; immediately some will rise in price, and others will fall; the market will expect that, after a certain time, the supply of the former will increase, and the supply of the latter fall, and accordingly the forward price, for the date on which equilibrium is expected to be restored, will be below the spot price in the case of the former and above it in the case of the latter; in other words, the rate of interest on the former will be higher than on the latter. It is only one step to pass from this to the case of a non-money economy, and to see that when equilibrium is disturbed, and during the time of the transition, the "natural" rates of interest on loans in terms of the commodities the output of which is increasing must be higher, to various extents, than the "natural" rates on the commodities the output of which is falling; and that there may be as many "natural" rates as there are commodities.[17] It will be noticed that, under free competition, this divergence of rates is as essential to the effecting of the transition as is the divergence of prices from the costs of production; it is, in fact, another aspect of the same thing.

This applies as much to an increase of saving, which Dr. Hayek regards as equivalent to a shift in demand from consumers' to producers' goods, as to changes in the demand for or the supply of any other commodities. In criticising Wicksell for having prescribed as the criterion of "neutral" money the incompatible aims of a stable price-level and of equality of the money rate with the natural rate, he says that in a society in which there are additions to the supply of savings, "to keep the money rate of interest at the level of the equilibrium rate would mean that in times of expansion of production the price-level would fall. To keep the general price-level steady would mean, in similar circumstances, that the loan rate of interest would have to be lowered below the equilibrium rate. The consequences would be what they always are when the rate of investment exceeds the rate of saving".[18]

But in times of expansion of production, due to additions to savings, there is no such thing as an equilibrium (or unique natural) rate of interest, so that the money rate can neither be equal to, nor lower than

---

[17]And, for each commodity, there will be different rates for loans of different lengths.
[18]Op. cit., p. 24.

it: The "natural" rate of interest on producers' goods, the demand for which has relatively increased, is higher than the "natural" rate on consumers' goods, the demand for which has relatively fallen. This, however, though it meets, I think, Dr. Hayek's criticism, is not in itself a criticism of Wicksell. For there is a "natural" rate of interest which, if adopted as bank-rate, will stabilize a price-level (i.e., the price of a composite commodity): It is an average of the "natural" rates of the commodities entering into the price-level, weighted in the same way as they are in the price-level itself. What can be objected to Wicksell is that such a price-level is not unique, and for *any* composite commodity arbitrarily selected there is a corresponding rate that will equalise the purchasing power, in terms of that composite commodity, of the money saved and of the additional money borrowed for investment. Each of these monetary policies will give the same results in regard to saving and borrowing as a particular non-monetary economy—that is to say, an economy in which the selected composite commodity is used as the standard of deferred payments. It appears, therefore, that these non-monetary economies retain the essential feature of money, the singleness of the standard; and we are not much the wiser when we have been shown that a monetary policy is "neutral" in the sense of being equivalent to a non-monetary economy which differs from it almost only by name.

As for the other conceivable and more truly non-monetary economies, in which different transactions are fixed in terms of different standards, there are no monetary policies which can exactly reproduce their results. Which perhaps matters very little, since the essential consequence of a divergence between the demand and the supply of consumption goods is common to monetary and non-monetary economies. In so far as the consumption goods saved are perishable, they must be consumed by somebody or go entirely to waste; and in so far as they are durable, and can be stored up, they are partly wasted for a time and partly consumed by others than the savers (since their spot price must fall to make storing worth while). With or without money, if investment and saving have not been planned to match, an increase of saving must prove to a large extent "abortive". On the other hand, the conception underlying the inquiry into neutral money appears to be this: When savings take place in a non-monetary economy a stream of finished goods, which might be consumed, is diverted from consumption into investment—the problem is to find a monetary policy which does not interfere with the stream. But the stream is a delusion. When it flows safely into investment, it has never flown out of the savers' hands in the shape of consumers' goods—production must have been so planned ahead as not to produce the unwanted goods; and when the saved goods flow out of the consumers' hands, they do not reach investment unimpaired. Thus, to borrow a distinction due to Mr. Robertson, savings may be the "inducement" but cannot in general be the "source" of investment.

Dr. Hayek's own solution of the problem as opposed to that of Wicksell is contained in the following passage, which should be read keeping in mind that by "supply of capital" he means "voluntary saving", and that "amount of the circulation" is an abbreviation for amount multiplied by the velocity of circulation. "It is perfectly clear that, in order that the supply and demand for real capital should be equalised, the banks must not lend more or less than has been deposited with them as savings. And this means naturally that they must never change the amount of their circulation".[19]

We are kept languishing for the clue to this "perfectly clear" mystery until, at the very end of the book, it flashes upon us in Dr. Hayek's definition of real capital: "'*Real* capital' stands here as the only short (but probably misleading) expression which I can find for that part of the total *money*-stream which is available for the purchase of producers' goods" (p. 108, my italics).[20] Misleading indeed! The epithets *money* and *real* (applied to wages, costs, incomes, etc.) having always been used as opposites, Dr. Hayek coolly "defines" them as synonyms. And he is the first to be misled, for he uses this argument as a criticism of Wicksell, who by real capital means real capital and not money capital. And he is also misled into believing that he has proved something about "neutral" money, when he is far away from the barter economy in which real capital can be anything but a quantity of money.

His statement might now be translated back into ordinary language as follows: "In order that the sum of money borrowed for investment should be equal to the sum of money saved, bank loans must increase neither more nor less than the amount that is deposited with them as savings". And finally, to complete the picture, we should add two modifications which Dr. Hayek has introduced in the (later) German version of his book.[21] The first is an exception: The banks must not lend more than has been deposited with them as savings "or at most such amounts in addition which, though saved, have not been invested".[22] The second is a new definition of savings: When some firms are making

[19]Op. cit., p. 23.

[20]*Ibid.*, p. 108, my italics. The doubt that the definition may apply only to a different context is dispelled by its occurring in a footnote attached to the following text: "The 'natural' or equilibrium rate of interest which would exclude all demands for capital which exceed the supply of real capital...."

[21]*Preise und Produktion*, op. cit.

[22]*Ibid.*, p. 26.

losses, "only the excess of savings over the amount necessary to balance these losses, or *net savings*, can be regarded as an increase of the demand for means of production; and when in what follows we speak of savings we mean always and exclusively savings in this sense".[23]

Thus defined and transformed this will not sound unfamiliar to readers of Mr. Keynes's *Treatise on Money*; in effect, it appears that Dr. Hayek in running away from his problem of neutral money has landed himself right in the middle of Mr. Keynes's theory. And here this review must stop, for space does not allow of an adequate criticism of the new and rather unexpected position taken up by Dr. Hayek.

[23] *Ibid.*, p. 49.

EIGHT

MONEY AND CAPITAL: A REPLY[1]

1. With an article devoted to a critical discussion of my *Prices and Production*, Mr. Sraffa has recently entered the arena of monetary controversy.[2] There is no denying the fact that reviewing books on money, at a time when monetary theory is in a state of violent fermentation, is not an easy, and perhaps not even a pleasant, task. I can easily understand Mr. Sraffa being a little upset at having spent so much time on a work from which he has obviously derived no profit and which appears to him merely to add to the prevailing confusion of thought on the subject. But it seems to me that, in expressing indignation without making his own position quite clear, he has run the risk of doing himself less than justice and of taking up a position which is, to say the least, somewhat confused. I am not anxious to indulge in controversy for its own sake. But it seems to me that, in replying to Mr. Sraffa's strictures, I may be able not only to defend myself against what appear to me to be needless misunderstandings but also to make clearer certain matters which do present, to use Mr. Robertson's phrase, "appalling intellectual difficulty".[3] Hence I have asked the Editors of this journal to give me space for reply.

Mr. Sraffa objects that I tried to say too much in four lectures, but his criticism really demands that I should have said a great deal more. In fact, many of his objections concern points which are implied rather than specifically developed in *Prices and Production*, this being partly due to the fact that I had discussed them in some detail elsewhere and partly to the fact that I thought that they must be sufficiently clear to an economist without further elaboration. In a short reply it is obviously impossible to discuss the relation between the general theory of

---

[1][F. A. Hayek, "Money and Capital: A Reply", *Economic Journal*, vol. 42, June 1932, pp. 237–249. —Ed.]

[2]See his article, "Dr. Hayek on Money and Capital", *Economic Journal*, vol. 42, no. 165, March 1932, pp. 42ff. [Reprinted as chapter 7, this volume. Hayek refers to his *Prices and Production*, 1931, op. cit. —Ed.]

[3][Robertson referred to monetary theory as "a field of appalling intellectual difficulty" in his article, "Mr. Keynes's Theory of Money", op. cit., p. 395. —Ed.]

equilibrium and the theory of money—one of the points on which Mr. Sraffa disagrees with my method of approach. Fortunately, however, a translation of my earlier treatment[4] of these prolegomena to a discussion of the role of money in the theory of industrial fluctuations has just been completed, and will be published before very long; so that I hope I may be permitted to refer Mr. Sraffa to this book for a reply to his methodological criticisms, and to ask him to return to the points which I do not discuss here should he still feel dissatisfied.

If he does so, I should also like to ask him to define his own attitude to these problems more clearly than he has yet done. From his article one gains the impression that his attitude is a curious mixture of, on the one hand, an extreme theoretical nihilism which denies that existing theories of equilibrium provide any useful description of the non-monetary forces at work; and, on the other hand, of an ultracon-servatism which resents any attempt to show that the differences between a monetary and a non-monetary economy are not only, and not even mainly, "those characteristics which are set forth at the beginning of every textbook on money". I am, however, not quite sure whether Mr. Sraffa has perceived that the refutation of this idea is one of the central theses of my book. What he certainly has not seen—though I should have thought that this was a rather obvious point—is where the essential differences between monetary and a non-monetary economy are to be sought. I have been assuming that the body of existing pure economic theory demonstrates that so long as we neglect monetary factors, there is an inherent tendency towards an equilibrium of the economic system; and what I tried to do in *Prices and Production*, and in certain earlier publications, was to show that monetary factors may bring about a kind of disequilibrium in the economic system—which could not be explained without recourse to these monetary factors. I do not quite understand whether Mr. Sraffa thinks that, in order to show this, it would have been necessary first to restate the whole of equilibrium economics. I thought that this was not only impossible within the limits of a small book, but also quite unnecessary.

Mr. Sraffa's suggestion that I am surreptitiously shifting my position from the theoretical analysis of "neutral" money to the defence of one particular maxim of monetary policy is entirely due to his misunder-standing of this point.[5] I am, indeed, assuming that it is generally thought desirable to avert any developments which lead the system away from an equilibrium position, and which, therefore, make a revulsion inevitable sooner or later. But there is no justification for the suggestion

[4]F. A. Hayek, *Geldtheorie und Konjunkturtheorie*, op. cit. [Published in English as *Monetary Theory and the Trade Cycle*, op. cit. —Ed.]

[5]Sraffa, op. cit., p. 43. [See this volume, chapter 7, pp. 198–199. —Ed.]

that after this, my exposition illegitimately takes certain aims of economic policy for granted—which I assume "will be found desirable by every right-thinking person".[6] However, I must not devote too much space to these general methodological questions, but must turn now to Mr. Sraffa's criticism of more specific points in my theory.

2. It is against two cardinal points in my theory that Mr. Sraffa directs most of his criticism: One being the concept of a money rate of interest which is different from the "equilibrium" rate—a concept which it has in common with the theories of a number of other contemporary writers, the other being the tendency for capital accumulated by "forced saving" to be, at least partly, dissipated as soon as the cause of the "forced saving" disappears. This latter point is, in a certain sense, a peculiar characteristic of my own theory of the credit cycle, since it has, so far as I know, never been as explicitly stated before; and it is upon the truth of this point that my theory stands or falls. Following the order of Mr. Sraffa's criticism, I shall deal with this latter point first.

Before it is possible to reach the central point, however, it will be necessary to discuss two closely related questions which are essential to the understanding of the main problem—in spite of the fact that Mr. Sraffa considers them to belong to the "preliminaries" which he thinks "so utterly irrelevant" that he relegates them to two footnotes.[7] In *Prices and Production* I have used the concept of the proportion between the demand for consumers' goods and the demand for producers' goods in two senses—a "real" and a monetary one. This procedure was justified by a special simplifying assumption, on which the greater part of the argument was based, and which made the two proportions identical. In the *real* sense, the concept of this proportion corresponds[8] to the concept of the average investment period, as is easily seen when we regard all goods and services which are already within a unit period of time of becoming ripe for consumption, as consumers' goods; and all other unfinished goods and services as producers' goods. Then the proportion between the amount of consumers' goods and the amount of producers' goods existing at a moment of time (required in order to continue production by the same method) will correspond (except for a small difference which stands in a definite relationship to the arbitrary unit period chosen) to the average investment period measured in the

[6]*Ibid.*, p. 43. [See this volume, chapter 7, p. 199. —Ed.]

[7]Sraffa, op. cit., pp. 45, 46. [This volume, chapter 7, notes 9, 10. —Ed.]

[8]This is strictly true only if the proportion is expressed not as a simple algebraical expression, but as a differential quotient of the function expressing the rate at which the original factors are applied during the production period. Cf. the German edition of the book in question: *Preise und Produktion*, op. cit., p. 39.

same units. The proportion between the demand for both types of goods and services, as exercised in the form of *money* offered for them, will correspond to the real proportion *only* under the special assumption made for convenience of exposition in the earlier parts of *Prices and Production*, viz., that all goods and services used in the process of production are exchanged against money every time they advance one unit period of time nearer to the consumption stage. That this is a case which is hardly ever likely to occur in the real world is obvious from the fact that it could never occur where any of the durable goods used last for more than one unit period of time. And I think that I have amply indicated in *Prices and Production* that, in the real world, the monetary proportion will be very different from the real proportion.[9]

But the first essential point which Mr. Sraffa seems to have overlooked is that there is some relation between the monetary and the real proportion in the sense that a change in the former will tend to bring about a like change in the latter. Of the fact that, when once this simplifying assumption, made in the earlier part of *Prices and Production*, is dropped, this relation becomes extremely complex, nobody could be more conscious than I am. But how Mr. Sraffa, in view of the discussion of this point on pp. 104–106 of *Prices and Production*, could suggest that I have overlooked it, is beyond my comprehension. In any case, it is the demand as expressed in money which determines the prices of goods in the successive stages of production, and it is these relative prices which determine the physical quantities of goods directed to the several stages.

The second essential point on which Mr. Sraffa has obviously misunderstood me concerns the reasons why these proportions (in the first instance the monetary proportion—which will lead to a similar change in the real proportion) may alter. The monetary proportion (for the system as a whole) is the proportion between the sum of the amounts spent by individuals on consumers' goods and the sum of the amounts spent by them on producers' goods; and it may therefore alter *either* in consequence of a change in the proportion of their income which individuals devote to each of these objects of expenditure, *or* in consequence of a change in the relative amount which the different individuals have to divide, i.e., a change in the distribution of purchasing power. Mr. Sraffa must have overlooked this when he accused me

---

[9]Cf. pp. 42, 63, 105. I should like to take this opportunity of particularly stressing the importance of the qualifications introduced in lecture 4 of *Prices and Production* which Mr. Sraffa has entirely neglected; for, if these qualifications are overlooked, the argument of the earlier lectures, which was based on highly simplified assumptions, must of necessity seem somewhat unrealistic.

of making contradictory statements in connection with the questions as to whether it is the decisions of entrepreneurs or those of consumers (or both) which determine the changes in the proportion.[10] In fact, of course, entrepreneurs are also consumers—though not all consumers are entrepreneurs—and individuals of both groups may change their proportions[11] (by saving or consuming capital); but the social proportion may be affected not only by the decisions of individuals, but also by changes in the buying power of different groups of individuals—due to additions of new money. Now the essential point to note here is that the additional money is, in the normal course of things, lent to somebody who, at that lower rate of interest, is willing to invest more money than before—and to borrow for this purpose.[12] As I think I have sufficiently emphasized in *Prices and Production*,[13] it is the fact that, when additional money is lent at interest to the highest bidder we are able to draw certain general conclusions as to where it will be used, which enables us to analyse the effects of the increase of money beyond mere generalities. If it is used—and in this case there is every likelihood that it will be so used—to purchase more producers' goods, a further train of effects will inevitably follow, which may be summarised as temporary forced saving, with a subsequent destruction of at least part of the capital so accumulated; or as a misdirection of production with a consequent crisis.

3. To simplify matters for the analysis of the process of "forced saving", it is expedient to start from a situation where no new savings are accumulated and where, therefore, the proportion is entirely determined by what is necessary to maintain the existing capital. This means that persons who possess capital must consume only their net income from that capital, and re-invest such parts of their gross receipts

---

[10]See footnote, p. 45. [This volume, chapter 7, note 9. —Ed.]

[11]I do not understand why Mr. Sraffa should suggest that a consumer who is not an entrepreneur will not affect the proportion between the demand for consumers' goods and the demand for producers' goods by his decision to save. It is certain that when he invests his savings by lending them out at interest he is instrumental in directing part of his money income to the purchase of producers' goods, without himself becoming an entrepreneur.

[12]I do not suggest, and my argument does not rest on the assumption, as Mr. Sraffa believes, that the banks have "the power to settle the way in which money is spent" (op. cit., p. 49). The only essential assumption which I actually make is that money lent at interest will normally, for the reasons discussed in the text, go to the purchase of producers' goods. It is, however, possible that the loans are made in such a way that they are used to increase the demand for consumers' goods; e.g. when they are made to the government in order to increase the salaries of civil servants. That I do discuss the case of consumers' credits separately is due to the fact that it has actually been suggested that we should "maintain purchasing power" by financing consumption in this way.

[13]See, for example, op. cit., p. 11.

as are necessary to keep the capital intact. Now if, through a relative lowering of the money rate of interest, people who find it profitable to invest at that rate borrow additional money from the banks (i.e., money which has not been saved but which is the product of credit expansion), then the proportion of expenditure on producers' goods to the expenditure on consumption goods will be raised, prices of producers' goods will rise and their production will increase relative to that of consumers' goods.

Every individual entrepreneur can increase his real capital only by spending more on capital goods and less on labour[14] used in current production (or, what amounts to the same thing, more on labour which is invested for a relatively long period). He can, however, spend more on capital goods than on wages only so long as wages have not risen in proportion to the additional money which has become available for investment. Ultimately, incomes must rise in that proportion, since even the money used for the purchase of new capital goods must ultimately be paid out to the factors which make these new capital goods.[15] But they will rise to the full extent only when all the new money has passed backwards through the successive stages of production until it is finally paid out to the factors. There will, therefore, always be a considerable lag between the increase in the money used for productive purposes and the corresponding increase in the incomes of the factors—and consequent increase in the demand for consumers' goods. And, so long as money keeps on increasing (and for some time afterwards—because of this lag), the demand for producers' goods will be increased relative to the demand for consumers' goods. But as the effect of this rise in wages is no longer compensated by new money becoming available for investment, a point must come when the proportion of his money receipts which is left to every individual entrepreneur to spend on capital goods is no greater than before.

This is modified only to the extent that entrepreneurs may not consume part of the extra profit made during that period, but may invest it. In such a case, the shift of incomes from a class less inclined to save to a class more so inclined will ultimately have produced some real saving. But, as Mr. Sraffa rightly remarks, it is not necessarily true that the persons who now possess more capital will, in consequence, get

[14]The term "wages" is used throughout this discussion as a short term for the remuneration of all the original factors of production used.

[15]Except for such amounts as may be absorbed in cash holdings in any additional stages of production.

a greater *proportion* of the total real income,[16] and, in any case, the effect of this can hardly ever be sufficient to prevent any increase in the relative demand for consumers' goods.

Now, before wages rose in proportion to the increase in money (and, therefore, all the time when money kept on increasing at a constant or increasing rate), although the increased amount of money capital in the hands of entrepreneurs had put them in a position to buy (or produce) more capital goods than before, and so to increase their equipment and stocks; yet as soon as the competition of entrepreneurs for the factors of production has driven up wages in proportion to the increase in money, and no additional credits are forthcoming, the proportion which they are able to spend on capital goods must fall. This means, however, not only that they must stop adding to the existing capital, but also that they will be unable to maintain and replace all the capital which is the product of the forced saving. Except in so far as they are able, and find it profitable, to make up for this at the expense of their own increased income,[17] they will be able to replace their capital only at the same rate as before the forced saving took place, and their capital will, therefore, be gradually worn down to something approaching its former state.

To describe in detail the process by which the additional capital is consumed would be a lengthy task, which I hope to undertake soon in another place. Here it must suffice to point out that if entrepreneurs in one stage of production find it impossible or unprofitable to replace for example their machines, then this will cause the capital instruments which are devoted to the production of these machines to lose their value. That the physical quantity of these capital goods will, for some time, continue to exist unchanged does not mean that their owners have not lost the greater part, or all, of their capital. It is of very little use for the machine manufacturer to hold on tight to his capital goods when the producer who used to buy the machines is either unable, or finds it unprofitable at the higher rate of interest, to do so now. Whether he likes it or not, the actions of other people have destroyed his capital.[18]

It is a surprisingly superficial objection to this analysis to say simply that "one class has, for a time, robbed another class of a part of their incomes; and has saved the plunder. When the robbery comes to an end, it is clear that the victims cannot possibly consume the capital

---

[16]See footnote, p. 47. [This volume, chapter 7, note 12. —Ed.]

[17]See p. 215.

[18]He does not, of course, necessarily lose all of it. So far as he has definitely committed his capital to the purpose in question, he will write off part of it and will go on producing and selling below cost, thus transferring part of the loss to his competitors who, perhaps, have not profited from the inflation.

which is now well out of their reach".[19] Is Mr. Sraffa really unfamiliar with the fact that capital sometimes falls in value because the running costs of the plant have risen; or does he belong to the sect which believes in curing such a situation by stimulating consumption? And would he really deny that, by a sudden relative increase in the demand for consumers' goods, capital may be destroyed against the will of its owners? Surely the case which we are discussing is just the same: As incomes rise in consequence of the preceding credit expansion and the mass of consumers, who under our assumption spend all their income on consumption goods, increase their expenditure accordingly, while the money available for investment in capital goods does not increase any longer, the value of some capital goods produced under the inducement of a relatively stronger demand for such goods will fall below their cost of production.

It is difficult to understand why Mr. Sraffa thinks that it is a contradiction to say that an inflation for productive purposes will cause little *permanent*[20] increase of capital, while an inflation for consumptive purposes will actually cause a consumption of capital. The fact is simply this, that any increase of incomes used for consumptive purposes relatively to the sums available for productive purposes, will tend to decrease the "purchasing power" of these sums (i.e., the purchasing power of money-capital); and that, whereas in the former case, where the relative rise of incomes follows only a preceding relative rise in the demand for capital goods, only part of the capital created by the inflation is destroyed again, in the latter case, the destruction of capital is not offset by any preceding gain.

Finally, Mr. Sraffa levels against this part of my argument the further objection that "if the banks increased the circulation but apportioned the additional money between consumers' and producers' credits so as not to disturb the initial proportions, nothing would happen".[21] I wonder whether this curious "objection" is not the product of an unconscious recollection from the German edition of *Prices and Production,* of which Mr. Sraffa has made so ingenious a use at the end of his article. There I have stated explicitly that a stabilization of incomes "without causing a misdirection of production, could be effectual only if it were possible to inject the additional quantities of money required for that purpose

[19]Sraffa, op. cit., p. 48 [This volume, p. 204. —Ed.]

[20]I have, of course, never said, as Mr. Sraffa suggests here—thus contradicting his earlier, more correct, interpretation—that the banks cannot cause *any* accumulation of capital.

[21]Sraffa, op. cit., p. 48. [This volume, p. 204. —Ed.]

into the economic system in such a way that no change in the proportion between the demand for consumers' goods and the demand for producers' goods would be brought about".[22] In any case, I welcome Mr. Sraffa's endorsement of one of the obvious corollaries of my theory of the influence of the money stream on the structure of production. But if he accepts this, how can he reject the other corollary, that if the increase in circulation is not so distributed then changes in the time structure will result? And how can he ignore the fact that an expansion of credit via the Bank Rate mechanism will *not* "apportion to the additional money between consumers and producers so as not to disturb the initial proportions", but will certainly favour the "higher" stages at the expense of the "lower".[23]

4. I have occupied a relatively large amount of space in demonstrating the way in which at least part of the forced savings are lost because, as I have already stated, this point seems to me to be the most fundamental. I can, however, deal much more briefly with the second main point raised by Mr. Sraffa, since his confusion here must have been obvious to most readers. Mr. Sraffa denies that the possibility of a divergence between the equilibrium rate of interest and the actual rate is a peculiar characteristic of a money economy. And he thinks that "if money did not exist, and loans were made in terms of all sorts of commodities, there would be a single rate which satisfies the conditions of equilibrium, but there might, at any moment, be as many 'natural' rates of interest as there are commodities, though they would not be 'equilibrium' rates."[24] I think it would be truer to say that, in this situation, there would be *no single rate* which, applied to all commodities, would satisfy the conditions of equilibrium rates, but there might, at any moment, be as many "natural" rates of interest as there are commodities, *all* of which would be *equilibrium rates*; and which would all be the combined result of the factors affecting the present and future supply of the individual commodities, and of the factors usually regarded as determining the rate of interest. There can, for example, be very little doubt that the "natural" rate of interest on a loan of strawberries from July to January will even be negative, while for loans of most other commodities over the same period it will be positive.

---

[22]*Preise und Produktion*, op. cit., p. 100.

[23]That the second case which Mr. Sraffa mentions in this connection (pp. 204–205) is not analogous to a case of inflation, but to a case of saving will, I think, be obvious. Certainly, a man who repays a consumer's credit performs saving.

[24]Sraffa, op. cit., p. 49. [This volume, p. 205. —Ed.]

The interrelation between these different rates of interest is far too complicated to allow of detailed discussion within the compass of this reply. It becomes particularly complex when we take into account the fact that—as Mr. Sraffa points out—any single one of these rates may be out of equilibrium, just as any price may be out of equilibrium. But the only essential point at issue here is whether the fact that any of these "natural" rates, in terms of a single commodity, may be out of equilibrium in consequence of a disparity between the supply of and demand for this particular commodity can have effects which are anything like those of a divergence between the actual money rate and the equilibrium rate which is due to an increase in the quantity of money. I certainly believe that it is possible in this case to change "artificially" the rate of interest in a sense in which this (with the exception of one particular case which I shall mention) cannot be said of any commodity.

Let us take Mr. Sraffa's case in which the farmers "arbitrarily changed" the quantity of wheat produced—which I understand, from what follows, to mean that they, for example, so increased the supply of wheat that its price fell below its cost of production and, as a consequence of its temporary abundance, loans of wheat were made at a much lower rate of interest than loans of other commodities. But would that fall in the rate of interest on wheat-loans cause anyone to start roundabout processes of production for which the available subsistence fund is not sufficient? There is no reason whatever to assume this. In so far as people live on wheat, they will actually be provided with food for a longer period; and in so far as the lower price of wheat will induce people to eat more of it—instead of something else—these other goods will also be available for a longer period of time, and interest in terms of these goods will also fall. The effects will be just the same as if a corresponding amount of wheat had been saved, and when, as a consequence of the fall in the price of wheat, its output falls again, the accumulation of capital made possible by the surplus of wheat will simply cease.[25]

The case would, however, be different if the actual supply of wheat were not changed, but if, under the mistaken impression that the supply of wheat would greatly increase, wheat dealers sold *short* greater quantities of future wheat than they will actually be able to supply. This is the only case I can think of where, in a barter economy, anything corresponding to the deviation of the money rate from the equilibrium

[25]That large fluctuations in the rate of saving may have effects similar to those of changes in the quantity of money, I have already pointed out in *Geldtheorie und Konjunkturtheorie*, op. cit., p. 120.

rate could possibly occur. And if we assume that, in the community where this happens, wheat is the most important consumption good, then the consequences might be similar to those which occur when the money rate is below the equilibrium rate. The relatively low price at which (for example, in terms of machines) consumers' goods are offered for the immediate future will, in this case, make it worthwhile to secure sufficient supplies of them to start longer processes of production. But a time must come when the error is noticed, prices of consumers' goods rise, and it becomes obvious that it is not possible to wait as long as had at first seemed practicable for the product of the investment. Although I am tempted to follow this example further, I must leave it here, and trust that this sketchy outline will be sufficient to show the main differences between this and the former case.

If we generalise this second case, and assume that it is not the promise of a particular kind of consumers' good, but the claim on present goods in general which is offered in exchange for promises of future goods in excess of present goods available for that purpose, then we have the case of an increase of money by means of additional loans for investment purposes. Investment will exceed saving; i.e., processes of production will be started which will be longer than is justified by the available subsistence fund, and which must, therefore, be discontinued as soon as consumers in general are no longer "robbed" by means of more and more issues of new money. The further effects of such a process have already been discussed in the preceding section.

Mr. Sraffa, it appears, sees no reason why the demand for new capital should be limited to the amount provided by saving, and he obviously sees only one reason why the rate of interest should not be lowered to zero—viz., the danger of a general rise of prices. But this is not surprising as coming from an author who considers a discussion of the real aspects of the capitalistic structure of production as being "utterly irrelevant" to the problems of money and inflation.

5. So far, Mr. Sraffa's criticisms, although they seem to me to be based upon a misconception of the problems at issue, are fairly intelligible. But in the last paragraphs of his article he adds some remarks which I confess I find it more difficult to follow. They begin with the paragraph at the bottom of p. 52,[26] where Mr. Sraffa tries to make use of the fact that, at one part of my exposition, I use—for want of a better expression—the phrase "supply of real capital" for that part of the total money stream available for investment which comes from real sources (saving or the amortisation of existing capital), and not from additional credits,

[26][This volume, p. 208. —Ed.]

in order to prove that I confound, or define as synonymous, real capital and money capital. He does so in spite of the fact that, at the point at which I do this, a footnote expressly warns the reader that "'real capital' stands here as the only short (but probably misleading) expression which I can find for that part of the money stream which is available for the purchase of producers' goods *and which is composed of the regular receipts of the turnover of the existing producers' goods (i.e., in the case of durable goods, the reserves accumulated to make up for depreciation) plus new savings*".[27] Mr. Sraffa quotes part of this footnote. But he omits the essential part, which I have italicized here, and thus makes my use of the term look entirely silly, though the term "real", in this connection, has a perfectly definite—even if not quite usual—meaning. I cannot believe that Mr. Sraffa wants to misrepresent me, but I confess I find it difficult to understand the state of mind in which he singles out this footnote and then leaves out the qualifying phrase, the inclusion of which would deprive his criticism of its point. Can it be that Mr. Sraffa does not understand that that part of the money stream I thus single out must necessarily have a special economic significance? Certain of his remarks about forced saving lead me to suspect that this may be the case.[28]

But in the spectacular conclusion of his article Mr. Sraffa makes an even more absurd suggestion. In the discussion which followed the delivery of my English lectures, I became aware that, obviously owing to the influence of Mr. Keynes, the term "saving" was frequently understood in a sense different from the one in which I employed it. As a consequence, when, a few months later, I prepared for the press the German edition of *Prices and Production*, I inserted, among other additions which were intended to clear up the more difficult points, a paragraph which, I hoped, would mark off my concept of saving from, for example, that used by Mr. Keynes. Nothing could have surprised me more than that this attempt to make the difference between Mr. Keynes's theory and my own more clear should be interpreted by anyone as "landing me right in the middle of Mr. Keynes's theory". (That I meant it in this sense is obvious from the fact that I quoted this paragraph against Mr. Keynes in my Rejoinder to his Reply to my criticism of his *Treatise*.[29]) I venture to believe that Mr. Keynes would

---

[27][*Prices and Production*, op. cit., p. 108. —Ed.]

[28]I need not go into the other supposed 'modification' of my theory which Mr. Sraffa mentions in this connection, as it ought to be obvious that the case in which the amounts saved are not invested is a case of a change in the velocity of circulation; i.e., a case which, in the English edition of *Prices and Production*, I had already expressly stated to be an exception to the general rule.

[29]See "Rejoinder", op. cit., p. 402n. [This volume, chapter 5, note 12. —Ed.]

fully agree with me in refuting Mr. Sraffa's suggestion. That Mr. Sraffa should have made such a suggestion, indeed, seems to me only to indicate the new and rather unexpected fact that he has understood Mr. Keynes's theory even less than he has my own.[30]

---

[30][With Professor Hayek's permission I should like to say that, to the best of my comprehension, Mr. Sraffa has understood my theory accurately. —J. M. Keynes.] [This last note was added by Keynes, who was at that time an editor of the *Economic Journal*. —Ed.]

NINE

A REJOINDER[1]
by Piero Sraffa

This specimen of Dr. Hayek's manner of arguing is by itself such an eloquent illustration of my review that I am reluctant to spoil it by comments. I shall therefore confine my reply to the two "cardinal" questions, whilst for the other points referring the patient reader (if there be any) to my previous contribution.

The first question is whether, as Dr. Hayek asserts, the capital accumulated by "forced saving" will be, "at least partly", dissipated as soon as inflation comes to an end: "It is upon the truth of this point that my [Dr. H.'s] theory stands or falls".[2] My simple-minded objection was that forced saving being a misnomer for spoliation, if those who had gained by the inflation chose to save the spoils, they had no reason at a later stage to revise the decision; and at any rate those on whom forced saving had been inflicted would have no say in the matter. This appeal to common sense has not shaken Dr. Hayek: he describes it as "surprisingly superficial", though unfortunately he forgets to tell me where it is wrong. I must therefore make another attempt to follow him a little way into "profundity".

I shall take up his argument at the point where the inflation which has caused the accumulation of capital comes to an end. In order that the case may be comparable with Dr. Hayek's case of "voluntary saving", inflation must have proceeded at a gradually decreasing rate until it ends just when the longest among the newly started processes of production begin to yield consumable products: From that moment onwards the entrepreneurs will be able to meet their outgoings for current production and for maintenance of the increased capital entirely out of their receipts from sales, without need of any additional inflationary money. This, of course, as Dr. Hayek says, is possible "only so long as wages [i.e., incomes] have not risen in proportion to the additional money which has become available for investment."[3] And now we reach the point of the dispute: "Ultimately, incomes must rise in that

---

[1] [Piero Sraffa, "A Rejoinder", *Economic Journal*, vol. 42, June 1932, pp. 249–251. —Ed.]
[2] "Money and Capital: A Reply", op. cit., p. 239. [This volume, p. 212. —Ed.]
[3] Op. cit., p. 242. [This volume, p. 215. —Ed.]

proportion, since even the money used for the purchase of capital goods must ultimately be paid out to the factors which make these new capital goods".[4] I contend that this will not happen. Once more Dr. Hayek himself provides me with the argument against his theory, by appending here this footnote: "Except for such amounts as may be absorbed in cash holdings in any additional stages of production".[5] Exactly; and if Dr. Hayek had taken as much pains in writing his book as his reviewer has taken in reading it he would remember that under his assumptions such cash holdings will absorb not merely certain exceptional amounts, but *the whole* of the additional money issued during the inflation; that consequently incomes cannot rise at all, and there will be no occasion for any dissipation of capital. Let me remind him that he has assumed in his book that capital will be accumulated in proportion to the quantity of money issued in the form of loans to producers; that the number of stages of production will increase in proportion to the quantity of capital; that the quantity of payments to be made will increase in proportion to the number of stages: As a result, the quantity of payments to be made increases in proportion to the quantity of money, and the whole of the additional money is absorbed in cash holdings for performing such payments.

It may be noticed as a curiosity that in the world assumed by Dr. Hayek, inflation through credits to producers, while it leaves money incomes unchanged, brings about a positive *fall* in the prices of consumers' goods. (As this may sound incredible, perhaps even to Dr. Hayek, compare in *Prices and Production* figure 2, p. 40, which represents the initial position, with figure 4, page 50, which represents the situation at the end of the inflation: The aggregate money value of the mass of consumers' goods is unchanged, but their quantity being larger after the inflation, prices per unit must be lower. See also pp. 51–52.)

After this Dr. Hayek will allow me not to take seriously his questions as to what I "really believe". Nobody could believe that anything that logically follows from such fantastic assumptions is true in reality. But I admit the abstract possibility that conclusions deduced from them by faulty reasoning may, by lucky accident, prove quite plausible.

I have only a few words to add on the second cardinal question, that of the "money" and the "natural" rates of interest. Dr. Hayek's ideal maxim for monetary policy, like that of Wicksell, was that banks should adopt the "natural" rate as their "money" rate for loans: The only obstacle which he saw was the difficulty of ascertaining in practice the

[4] *Ibid.*
[5] *Ibid.*

level of the "natural" rate.[6] I pointed out that only under conditions of equilibrium would there be a single rate; and that when saving was in progress there would at any one moment be many "natural" rates, possibly as many as there are commodities; so that it would be not merely difficult in practice, but altogether inconceivable, that the money rate should be equal to "the" natural rate. And whilst Wicksell might fall back, for the criterion of his "money" rate, upon an average of the "natural" rates weighted in the same way as the index number of prices which he chose to stabilise, this way of escape was not open to Dr. Hayek, for he had emphatically repudiated the use of averages. Dr. Hayek now acknowledges the multiplicity of the "natural" rates, but he has nothing more to say on this specific point than that they "all would be equilibrium rates". The only meaning (if it be a meaning) I can attach to this is that his maxim of policy now requires that the money rate should be equal to all these divergent natural rates.

[6]Op. cit., p. 108.

PART III

ESSAYS ON KEYNES

TEN

REVIEW OF HARROD'S
LIFE OF J. M. KEYNES[1]

As a biography of a contemporary figure published within five years of his death, this monumental life of Lord Keynes is a remarkable achievement. Written by one of his closest friends and most fervent admirers, it gives a sympathetic, yet unsparingly honest, picture of one of the most influential and colorful minds of his generation. It is based on a thorough examination of the great mass of private and official documents which are available and gives a vivid picture of the background against which the career of Keynes must be seen.

The profound influence which Keynes exercised on the development of ideas, the role he played in English public life, and the part he took in his last years in Anglo-American relations make the book a major contribution to the history of our time. The almost unbelievable variety of Keynes's activities and interests made such a biography a task of unusual difficulty. But R. F. Harrod was in most respects almost ideally qualified for it. He shared many of Keynes's interests, had followed him both in his theoretical work and in some of his more practical activities, and had personally known most of the circles in which Keynes had moved even in his earlier years. He writes an easy and lucid style and succeeds in making intelligible even to the layman some of the intricacies of Keynes's contributions to economic theory. In places one might wish that there were less argument or fewer attempts to defend and justify and more of Keynes's own informal accounts of the working of his mind. But, although Harrod reproduces parts of many interesting letters which whet the appetite for more, one gathers that the greater part of Keynes's correspondence will not be suitable for publication during the lifetime of his contemporaries.

Whatever one may think of Keynes as an economist, nobody who knew him will deny that he was one of the outstanding Englishmen of his generation. Indeed, the magnitude of his influence as an economist is

---

[1][F. A. Hayek, Review of R. F. Harrod's *The Life of John Maynard Keynes* (New York: Harcourt Brace, 1951; reprinted, New York: Norton, 1982), in *The Journal of Modern History*, vol. 24, no. 2, June 1952, pp. 195–198. See page 57, note 26, for more on Harrod. —Ed.]

probably at least as much due to the impressiveness of the man, the universality of his interests, and the power and persuasive charm of his personality as to the originality or theoretical soundness of his contribution to economics. He owed his success largely to a rare combination of brilliance and quickness of mind with a mastery of the English language in which few contemporaries could rival him and—what is not mentioned in the *Life* but to me seemed always one of his strongest assets—a voice of bewitching persuasiveness. As a scholar he was incisive rather than profound and thorough, guided by strong intuition which would make him try to prove the same point again and again by different routes. It is not surprising that a man who at one stage was able to divide his time between teaching economics and conducting a ballet [company], financial speculation and collecting pictures, running an investment trust and directing the finances of a Cambridge college, acting as the director of an insurance company and practically running the Cambridge Arts Theatre and attending there to such details as the food and wine served in its restaurant, should show sometimes surprising lack of knowledge on subjects where his predominantly aesthetic sympathies had not been aroused. While, for instance, his book-collecting activities had given him a considerable knowledge of the intellectual history of the seventeenth and eighteenth centuries, his knowledge of nineteenth-century history and even of the economic literature of that period was somewhat meager. He was able to master the essential outlines of a new subject in a remarkably short time; indeed, he seems to have turned himself into an economist, after a university course in mathematics, in the course of little more than two years filled with many other activities. The result of this, however, was that the scope of his knowledge remained always not only somewhat insular but distinctly "Cambridge". He had been unusually fortunate in his background, his early associates, and the group with which he spent his formative years. And he seems to the end of his life to have regarded the views and the outlook of that particular set as the highest flower of civilization.

Although by disposition the young Keynes was a characteristically rationalist radical of his generation, the kind who felt that it was their vocation to judge all things anew",[2] a member of a group who were convinced that only they knew the rudiments of a true theory of ethics",[3] and who in 1918 described himself as a bolshevik who was not sorry to watch the disappearance of the social order as we have known it

---

[2]Harrod, op. cit., p. 77.
[3]*Ibid.*, p. 114.

hitherto—[4] as an economist he was, even at the time when he achieved international fame, still an old-fashioned liberal. In his celebrated articles in the *Manchester Guardian Commercial* in 1921 and 1922 he still believed in free trade, the international gold standard, and the need for more saving.[5] There is some reason to doubt whether he ever fully understood the classical theory of international trade on which that position was largely based (even Harrod has to admit, in another connection that "he was himself in some confusion about what the classical position really was"[6]), and it would probably be possible to trace much of his later development from certain questionable arguments which he had effectively employed in this field in a good cause in his *Economic Consequences of the Peace Treaty*.[7] The great change came before the Great Depression, about the time of Great Britain's return to the gold standard in 1925. His own explanation of why he had become convinced of "the end of laissez-faire"[8] are, as Harrod also seems to feel, really surprisingly thin and flimsy. But there can be little doubt that, with his new beliefs in a managed currency, in controlled investment, and in cartels, he became, together with his great antagonist, David Lloyd George, the main author of the conversion of the British Liberal party to the semi-socialist program expounded in the "Liberal Yellow Book".[9]

Harrod takes some pains to defend Keynes against the charge of inconsistency. In this he seems to me not to be very successful. There was, undoubtedly, a continuity of development and a persistence of ultimate aim. But there was also in Keynes a certain puckish delight in shocking his contemporaries, a tendency to overstate his disagreements with current views, and a fondness for stressing his broadminded understanding of the more revolutionary attitudes which are not very compatible with consistency. Again and again he would surprise his friends by an argument which did not seem to agree with his public pronouncements. I remember particularly one occasion which well

[4]*Ibid.*, p. 223.

[5][The articles from the *Manchester Guardian Commercial* formed the basis for Keynes's *A Tract on Monetary Reform*, op. cit.. For the names and dates of the articles, see *ibid.*, "Note to the Reader", p. xii. —Ed.]

[6]Harrod, op. cit., p. 453.

[7][J. M. Keynes, *The Economic Consequences of the Peace*, op. cit. —Ed.]

[8][J. M. Keynes, "The End of Laissez-faire" [1926], reprinted in *Essays in Persuasion*, op. cit., pp. 272–294. —Ed.]

[9]*Britain's Industrial Future* (London: Benn, 1928), pp. 392–393. [Keynes contributed substantially to Book 2 and to parts of Book 5 of this publication, soon nicknamed "The Yellow Book". Prior to the 1929 General Election, the Liberal politician David Lloyd George (1863–1945) offered the pamphlet *We Can Conquer Unemployment*, in which he echoed many of the proposals found in "The Yellow Book". —Ed.]

illustrates this. He had not long before coined the phrase of the "euthanasia of the *rentier*",[10] and in a deliberate attempt to draw him out I took the next opportunity to stress in conversation the importance which the man of independent means had had in the English political tradition. Far from contradicting me, this made Keynes launch out into a long eulogy of the role played by the propertied class in which he gave many illustrations of their indispensability for the preservation of a decent civilization. Perhaps it was his gift for phrasemaking which made him so often overstate his point. Certainly, such phrases as the "humbug of finance", "the end of laissez faire", and "in the long run we are all dead" must often have recoiled against their author when he was in a more conservative mood.[11] And even his greatest admirers must have winced a little when in 1933 he chose a German periodical to praise "National self-sufficiency",[12] and one can only wonder what he can have meant when, three years later in his preface to the German translation of *The General Theory of Employment, Interest, and Money*, he commended the book to its readers on the ground that "the theory of production as a whole which is the goal of this book can much more easily be adapted to the conditions of a total state" than is true of the competitive theory.[13] Harrod stresses that toward the end of his life there

[10][Keynes speaks of the "euthanasia of the *rentier*" in *The General Theory of Employment, Interest and Money*, op. cit., p. 376. —Ed.]

[11][Keynes offers the famous observation that "*In the long run* we are all dead" in *A Tract on Monetary Reform*, op. cit., p. 65. After a lengthy search and much consultation, I was unable to locate the phrase "humbug of finance" in any of Keynes's writings. Donald Moggridge, who was particularly helpful in the search, suggested that Keynes may have used the phrase in some of their conversations. —Ed.]

[12][J. M. Keynes, "Nationale Selbstgenügsamkeit", *Schmoller's Jahrbuch für Gesetzgebung, Verwaltung und Volkswirtschaft im Deutschen Reiche*, vol. 57, no. 4, 1933, pp. 77–86. The English version of "National Self-Sufficiency" appears in *Activities 1931–9: World Crises and Policies in Britain and America*, ed. Donald Moggeridge, vol. 21 (1982) of *The Collected Writings of John Maynard Keynes*, op. cit., pp. 233–246. The German version was heavily censored, with passages that would be offensive to National Socialism altered or removed. Keynes initially objected to the editing, but ultimately acquiesced in what a later writer would characterize as "a remarkable example of scholar[ly] 'self-censorship'". See Knut Borchardt, "Keynes's 'Nationale Selbstgenügsamkeit' von 1933: Ein Fall von kooperativer Selbstzensur", *Zeitschrift für Wirtschafts- und Sozialwissenschaften*, vol. 108, 1988, pp. 271–284; quotation on p. 283. —Ed.]

[13][J. M. Keynes, *Allgemeine Theorie der Beschäftigung, des Zinses, und des Geldes*, trans. Fritz Waeger (Munich and Leipzig: Duncker & Humblot, 1936). The English version of the Preface to the German edition is reprinted in *The General Theory of Employment, Interest, and Money*, op. cit., pp. xxv–xxvii. It differs slightly from what actually appeared in German. There is a puzzle about how the exact contents of the German Preface came to be written; see Bertram Schefold, "The General Theory for a Totalitarian State? A Note on Keynes's Preface to the German Edition of 1936", *Cambridge Journal of Economics*, vol. 4, June 1980,

was some return to free-trade views, and some of his occasional utterances seem to suggest this. But as late as October 1943 he had still stressed that the future seemed to him to lie with "(i) State trading for commodities; (ii) International cartels for necessary manufactures; and (iii) Quantitative import restrictions for non-essential manufactures".[14]

It is perhaps significant that Keynes hated to be addressed as "professor" (he never had that title). He was not primarily a scholar. He was a great amateur in many fields of knowledge and the arts; he had all the gifts of a great politician and a political pamphleteer; and he knew that "the ideas of economists and political philosophers, both when they are right and when they are wrong, are more powerful than is generally understood. Indeed the world is ruled by little else".[15] And as he had a mind capable of recasting, in the intervals of his other occupations, the body of current economic theory, he more than any of his compeers had come to affect current thought. Whether it was he who was right or wrong, only the future will show. There are some who fear that if Lenin's statement is correct that the best way to destroy the capitalist system is to debauch the currency, of which Keynes himself has reminded us,[16] it will be largely due to Keynes's influence if this prescription is followed.

Harrod is very frank about Keynes's temperamental shortcomings, not only "his minor failings—impetuosity, change of view, speaking beyond his book"[17] but also about his strong propensity to gamble, his ruthlessness and occasional rudeness in discussion ("all seemed fair to him in controversial warfare"),[18] his tendency to "cultivate the appearance of omniscience"[19] and of "always being ready to guess a figure to illustrate a point".[20] It may be doubted whether "his flair for 'global' estimates"[21] which, not least due to his influence, has now become the fashion, and his general habit of thinking in terms of aggregates and averages, have been beneficial to the understanding of economic phenomena. Economic activity is not guided by such totals but always by relations between different magnitudes, and the practice of always thinking in

---

pp. 175–176. —Ed.]

[14]Harrod, op. cit., p. 568.

[15]J. M. Keynes, *The General Theory of Employment, Interest, and Money*, op. cit., p. 338. [*The General Theory of Employment, Interest, and Money*, op. cit., p. 383. —Ed.]

[16]Harrod, op. cit., p. 273.

[17]*Ibid.*, p. 373.

[18]*Ibid*, p. 359.

[19]*Ibid.*, p. 468.

[20]*Ibid.*, p. 507.

[21]*Ibid.*, p. 229.

"global" totals can be most misleading. In at least one instance his later arguments against orthodoxy were largely directed against a view which few reputable economists except he himself had ever advocated: against the demand for an all-around cut of wages and salaries to meet unemployment.[22] Much of the confusion about the effects of wage reductions has been caused by the fact that Keynes himself was always thinking in terms of a general wage cut, while the argument of his opponents was in favour of allowing some wages to fall.

Perhaps the explanation of much that is puzzling about Keynes's mind lies in the supreme confidence he had acquired in his power to play on public opinion as a supreme master plays on his instrument. He loved to pose in the role of a Cassandra whose warnings were not listened to.[23] But, in fact, his early success in swinging round public opinion about the peace treaties had given him probably even an exaggerated estimate of his powers. I shall never forget one occasion—I believe the last time that I met him—when he startled me by an uncommonly frank expression of this. It was early in 1946, shortly after he had returned from the strenuous and exhausting negotiations in Washington on the British loan. Earlier in the evening he had fascinated the company by a detailed account of the American market for Elizabethan books which in any other man would have given the impression that he had devoted most of his time in the United States to that subject. Later, a turn in the conversation made me ask him whether he was not concerned about what some of his disciples were making of his theories. After a not very complimentary remark about the persons concerned, he proceeded to reassure me by explaining that those ideas had been badly needed at the time he had launched them. He continued by indicating that I need not be alarmed; if they should ever become dangerous I could rely upon him again quickly to swing round public opinion—and he indicated by a quick movement of his hand how rapidly that would be done. But three months later he was dead.

---

[22] *Ibid.*, pp. 361–362.

[23] [The first sentence of Keynes's Preface to *Essays in Persuasion*, op. cit., reads "Here are the collected croakings of twelve years—the croakings of a Cassandra who could never influence the course of events in time" (p. xvii). —Ed.]

Addendum: Hayek on Beveridge[24]

If the present concern with full employment were the result of a belated recognition of the urgency of the problem, we should have much reason to be ashamed of the past and to congratulate ourselves on the new resolution. But this is not the position.

In England, in particular, unemployment has for nearly a generation been the burning problem that constantly occupied statesmen and economists. The reasons for the intensified agitation must be sought elsewhere. The fact is that the remedies proposed by the economists had been persistently disregarded because they were of a kind that hurt in the application.

Then Lord Keynes assured us that we had all been mistaken and that the cure could be painless and even pleasant: all that was needed to maintain employment permanently at a maximum was to secure an adequate volume of spending of some kind. The argument was not less effective because it was couched in highly technical language. It gave the support of the highest scientific authority to what had always been the popular belief, and the new view gained ground rapidly.

It is the great merit of democracy that the demand for the cure of a widely felt evil can find expression in an organized movement. That popular pressure might become canalized in support of particular theories that sound plausible to the ordinary man is one of its dangers. But it was almost inevitable that some gifted man should see the opportunity and try to ride into political power on the wave of support that could be created for some such scheme. This is what Sir William Beveridge is attempting. His *Full Employment in a Free Society*[25] is as much a political manifesto as a handbook of economic policy. Its appearance coincides with the author's entry into Parliament, and together with his earlier report on social security constitutes his program of action.[26]

---

[24] [F. A. Hayek, "Review of Sir William Beveridge's *Full Employment in a Free Society*" (London: G. Allen and Unwin, 1944; New York: Norton, 1945; 2nd edition, 1960) in *Fortune*, vol. 31, no. 3, March 1945, pp. 204–206. Sir William Beveridge (1879–1963) was the Director of the LSE from 1919 to 1937; see chapter 1, note 9, for more on him. Hayek was blunt in his assessment: "As for Beveridge, he was completely ignorant of any economics whatever". The quotation is from *Hayek on Hayek*, op. cit., p. 83. This autobiographical volume contains some additional, and very revealing, reminiscences about Beveridge and the LSE. —Ed.]

[25] William Beveridge, *Full Employment in a Free Society: A Report* (New York: Norton, 1945).

[26] [Hayek refers to *Social Insurance and Allied Services* (London: HMSO, 1942), a report prepared during the war at the request of the government. Soon known as the Beveridge Report, the document proposed the institution of a nationwide social welfare system and formed the basis for such post-war legislation as the Family Allowances Act of 1945 and the National Health Service and National Insurance Acts of 1946. In this earlier report Beveridge had mentioned employment policy as another area in which legislation was needed, and *Full Employment in a Free Society*, op. cit., which he published on his own, was intended to fill the gap. It was there that full employment was identified with a three per cent rate of unemployment. —Ed.]

This is not to say that Sir William does not bring special qualifications to the task. But they are not mainly those of the economist. Himself a brilliant expositor who earned his spurs as a leader-writer on one of London's big dailies, a successful administrator with the essential skill of tapping other people's brains, and an acute student of unemployment statistics, he has called in the assistance of a group of younger economists for the more theoretical parts of the book.[27] Its strength and its weakness reflect this origin. The clear exposition and the stress on some important facts that are not always recognised are Sir William at his best, and the great interest in changes in government machinery equally characteristic.

But the theoretical framework is that of Lord Keynes as seen by his younger disciples and familiar to American readers mainly through the writings of Professor A. H. Hansen.[28] Only one of Sir William's collaborators, N. Kaldor, appears by name as the author of a highly ingenious appendix, which to the economist is the most interesting part of the book and supplies the foundation for much of it.[29]

It is open to question whether the attempt to combine Sir William's characteristic views with the fashionable Keynesian doctrines has made the book more valuable, though it will certainly make it more acceptable to many of the younger economists. Although Sir William is confident that his own approach and "the revolution of economic thought effected by J. M. Keynes" are "not contradictory but complementary", the book leaves many inconsistences unresolved.[30] One of Sir William's most valuable contributions, for example, is the emphasis on the extreme diversity of the extent of unemployment from industry to industry and from place to place, which certainly throws much doubt on the adequacy of an explanation in terms of a general deficiency of demand; yet he swallows the demand-deficiency theory lock, stock, and barrel.

Equally important is Sir William's stress on the close connection in Great Britain between unemployment and foreign trade. Yet his remedies are almost entirely of a domestic nature. Indeed, though he realizes that hardly any of the imports of Great Britain before the war "can be described as luxuries", he

---

[27][In addition to being Director of the LSE, Beveridge had served for a time as the lead writer for *The Morning Post*. A second edition of his book on employment, *Unemployment: A Problem of Industry* (London: Longmans, 1909), was released under the title *Unemployment: A Problem of Industry, 1909 and 1930* (London: Longmans, 1930). —Ed.]

[28][Alvin Hansen (1887–1975) was the leading American expositor of Keynes's ideas; see chapter 2, note 35, for more on Hansen. —Ed.]

[29][Nicholas Kaldor (1908–1986) was a Hungarian-born economist who taught at both the LSE and Cambridge; see this volume, chapter 1, note 23. According to Hayek, Kaldor essentially wrote Beveridge's entire book and thus can be credited with spreading the Keynesian revolution in England. "I have reason to say that it probably should be called a Kaldorian revolution, not for anything which is connected with Kaldor's name, but what spread it was really Lord Beveridge's book on full employment, and that was written by Kaldor and not by Beveridge, because Lord Beveridge never understood any economics". F. A. Hayek, *Hayek on Hayek*, op. cit., p. 96. —Ed.]

[30][Beveridge, *Full Employment in a Free Society*, op. cit., pp. 106 and 107. —Ed.]

suggests as a way out "the alternative of cutting down imports and becoming more independent" because "the stability of international trade is as important as its scale".[31] The former champion of free trade has traveled far!

Perhaps most surprising of all is that, while Sir William admits that "a policy of outlay for full employment, however vigorously it is pursued by the State, will fail to cure unemployment. . . if, with peace, industrial demarcations with all the restrictive tendencies and customs of the past return in full force",[32] these factors have no place in his diagnosis of the causes of unemployment. One wonders to what conclusions the author would have been led had they been given their proper place in the analysis and not merely added as an afterthought.

One of the main differences between Sir William's proposals and the British White paper[33] on employment policy is that Sir William refuses to accept the fact that private investment tends to fluctuate, and to confine himself to compensating measures. As an out-and-out planner, in the modern sense of the term, he proposes to deal with this difficulty by abolishing private investment as we knew it: that is, by subjecting all private investment to the direction of a National Investment Board. It is mainly here that apprehensions must arise against which the second half of the title of the book is meant to reassure us. Sir William endeavours to show that, despite all the controls he wishes to impose, "essential liberties" will be preserved. But private ownership of the means of production is, in his opinion, "not an essential liberty in Britain, because it is not and never has been enjoyed by more than a very small proportion of the British people".[34]

It is surprising that he should not yet have learned that private ownership of the means of production is important to most people not because they hope to own such property, but because only such private ownership gives them the choice of competing employers and protects them from being at the mercy of the most complete monopolist ever conceived.

However interesting the points of detail on which Sir William differs from the current Keynes-Hansen theory, much the most important fact about his book is that he lends the weight of his prestige in support of this view. If all the conclusions he draws do not necessarily follow from it, they certainly stand and fall with the belief that a deficiency of final demand is the initial cause of cyclical unemployment.

This theory holds that as employment increases a progressively increasing share of the new income created will not be spent but will be saved. This, it is suggested, must sooner or later produce a situation in which final demand is

---

[31][*Ibid.*, pp. 213, 267, and 268. Beveridge had headed the group of economists who published *Tariffs: The Case Examined* (London: Longmans, 1931). The book was aimed in part at Keynes's endorsement of protectionist measures in 1930–31. In the book, Keynes's earlier writings in favour of free trade were cited in making the case against him. —Ed.]

[32][Beveridge, *Full Employment in a Free Society*, op. cit., pp. 173–174. —Ed.]

[33][A government White Paper on employment policy was published on May 26, 1944. Beveridge's book contains a postscript that compares the government's policies with his own proposals. —Ed.]

[34][Beveridge, *Full Employment in a Free Society*, op. cit., pp. 21–23. —Ed.]

insufficient to take the output of consumers' goods off the market at remunerative prices. One may grant the first statement and yet deny that the alleged consequences are at all likely to follow. The larger share that is saved out of the additional income would necessarily lead to an insufficiency of final demand only if the additional output contained as large a proportion of consumers' goods as total output.

This assumption seems highly implausible, however. Along with all other students of these matters Sir William stresses that unemployment during a depression is very much greater in the industries making capital goods than in the others. An approach to full employment therefore increases the output of capital goods proportionally much more than the output of consumers' goods. And if no larger proportion of the additional income were saved than was saved out of the smaller income, final demand would grow much faster than the supply of consumers' goods.

As a matter of fact, it seems highly unlikely that the share saved out of additional income during a recovery will be even as big as the share of the additional output that is in the form of capital goods. What then becomes of the case that depressions are brought on by oversaving and underconsumption? Of course, we can assume that the decline of investment in a slump *must* be due to an initial deficiency of final demand. This, however, is simply reasoning in a circle.

The cause of the decline of the demand for capital goods must, therefore, be sought elsewhere than in a deficiency of final demand, and may even be an excessive final demand. All the fashionable remedies, including Sir William's, not only fail to touch the root of the matter but may even aggravate the problem. Of course, once final demand shrinks on the scale that will occur as a result of extensive unemployment in the capital-goods industries, this will start the vicious spiral of contraction. But the crucial question is: What causes the initial decline of the capital-goods industries?

If, as is more than likely, it is that they tend to overgrow during the boom, all attempts to maintain activity in them at the maximum will only perpetuate the causes of instability.

ELEVEN

SYMPOSIUM ON KEYNES: WHY?[1]

It would be unfair to blame Lord Keynes too much for the undoubted harm his theories have done, for I am convinced from personal knowledge that had he lived he would have been one of the leaders in the fight against the postwar inflation. Yet he bears in a great measure the responsibility for it.

His great gifts have made it possible for his theories to exercise during the past twenty-five years an immediate and pervading influence which is unique in the history of economic thought.

[1][Nate White et. al., "Symposium on Keynes: Why?", *The Christian Science Monitor*, September 11, 1959, vol. 51, p. 13. Nate White was the Business and Financial Editor of *The Christian Science Monitor*. The other contributors to the Symposium included: Adolf A. Berle, Jr. (1895–1971), American lawyer, economist, and member of Franklin D. Roosevelt's "brain trust", whose book with Gardiner Means, *The Modern Corporation and Private Property* [1932], revised edition (New York: Harcourt Brace & World, 1968), analysed the implications of the separation of management from ownership in large American corporations; Arthur F. Burns (1904–1987), Austrian-born economist who became a major force in American economic policy, becoming chairman of the Council of Economic Advisors under Eisenhower, president of the National Bureau of Economic Research (1957–67), and chairman of the Board of Governors of the Federal Reserve System (1970–78); Canadian-born Harvard economist John Kenneth Galbraith (1908–), who argued in such books as *The Affluent Society* (Boston: Houghton Mifflin, 1958) and *The New Industrial State* (Boston: Houghton Mifflin, 1967) that the atomistic free market system is a myth, that large and contending "countervailing powers" actually determine the progress of the economy and distribution of goods, and that an insufficient amount of public goods are produced under such a system; Seymour E. Harris (1897–1975), Galbraith's colleague at both the Office of Price Administration and as chair of the Harvard Economics Department, who was a tireless promulgator of the 'Keynesian' revolution in books like Harris, ed., *The New Economics: Keynes's Influence on Theory and Public Policy*, op. cit.; Calvin B. Hoover (1897–1974), American economist and civil servant; Henry Hazlitt (1894–1993), American financial journalist and Keynesian critic in such books as *Economics in One Lesson* [1946], revised edition (New York: Manor Books, 1975), and *The Failure of the 'New Economics': An Analysis of the Keynesian Fallacies* (Princeton: Van Nostrand, 1959); Neil H. Jacoby (1909–1979), Canadian-born American economist who served on Eisenhower's Council of Economic Advisors; Ludwig von Mises (1881–1973), Hayek's mentor and author of *Human Action: A Treatise on Economics* [1949], 3rd revised edition (Chicago: Contemporary Books, 1966); and Sumner H. Slichter (1892–1959), American economist and industrial relations scholar, whose article "The Passing of Keynesian Economics", *Atlantic Monthly*, vol. 200, no. 5, November 1957, pp. 141–146, together with Hazlitt's *The Failure of the 'New Economics'*, op. cit., helped set the stage for the symposium. —Ed.]

Yet these gifts were not mainly those of an economic theorist, and, though his ideas seemed to constitute a revolution to the generation which they captivated, they will probably appear as no more than a passing phase in the history of economic thought.

The main reproach to which Keynes laid himself open was that he presented as a "General Theory" what was essentially a tract for his times.

It was the successful one of repeated attempts he made to justify his practical inclinations by theoretical argument. It succeeded partly because it provided a highly sophisticated support for demands which are always popular in times of depression and partly because it was expressed in a form congenial to the scientific fashions of the moment.

Yet it was based on assumptions even more unrealistic than those Keynes ascribed to what he called classical economics. If it was a defect of the latter that it assumed for a first approach that there existed no reserves of unused resources, Keynes was even more unrealistic in assuming that there existed always ample reserves of all resources.

In short he assumed away that scarcity of resources which is the root of all our economic problems. In consequence, while of doubtful application even in times of depression, his original theory is entirely inapplicable in times of prosperity.

Keynes's disciples have since succeeded in purging the original version of most of its unrealistic assumptions and internal inconsistencies and developed it into a formal apparatus of analysis, which is largely neutral in policy applications.

It continues to enjoy popularity because it is more in accord with current methodological fashions than the classical approach. It is used by many who do not draw the conclusions Keynes drew from it. Yet I doubt whether even this will prove to be a permanent contribution to economics.

But apart from Keynes's peculiar factual assumptions it does not lead to conclusions essentially different from classical analysis. The most significant of those assumptions was that workers will resist a lowering of their money wages but will put up with a reduction of their real wages brought about by a fall in the value of money.

Indeed the ultimate motive of Keynes's efforts was to find a round-about method of reducing wages too high to allow employment of all seeking jobs. We now know better than to believe that workers will long allow themselves to be deceived in this way. This, however, was the most distinctive element of the Keynesian views of the 1930s.

It was this argument which broke down the intellectual resistance to ever-present tendencies toward progressive inflation. Yet this crucial element has by now lost all plausibility.

If one may judge from the first accounts of the latest programmatic document on British monetary policy, the recently published "Radcliffe Report",[2] Keynesianism in its original sense seems to have lost its appeal even more in its country of origin than elsewhere.

[2][A report published in August 1959 on British monetary policy by the Committee on the Working of the Monetary System, headed by Lord Radcliffe. The report advanced the claim that monetary policy was ineffective (due to the endogeneity of the money supply) as a tool of stabilization policy. Hayek also emphasized the difficulty of controlling the money supply. There was a difference in conclusions, however: British Keynesians used the finding to justify a more activist pursuit of fiscal and incomes policies. For an enthusiastic history see Nicholas Kaldor, "The Radcliffe Report and Monetary Policy", in *The Scourge of Monetarism* (Oxford: Oxford University Press, 1982), pp. 2–36. —Ed.]

TWELVE

PERSONAL RECOLLECTIONS OF KEYNES AND THE 'KEYNESIAN REVOLUTION'[1]

Even to those who knew Keynes but could never bring themselves to accept his monetary theories, and at times thought his pronouncements irresponsible, the personal impression of the man remains unforgettable. And especially to my generation (he was my senior by sixteen years), he was a hero long before he achieved real fame as an economic theorist. Was he not the man who had had the courage to protest against the economic clauses of the peace treaties of 1919?[2] We admired the brilliantly written books for their outspokenness and independence of thought, even though some older and more acute thinkers at once pointed out certain theoretical flaws in his argument. And those of us who had the good fortune to meet him personally soon experienced the magnetism of the brilliant conversationalist with his wide range of interests and his bewitching voice.

I met him first in 1928 in London at some meeting of institutes of business cycle research, and though we had at once our first strong disagreement on some point of interest theory, we remained thereafter friends who had many interests in common, although we rarely could agree on economics. He had a somewhat intimidating manner in which he would try to ride roughshod over the objections of a younger man, but if someone stood up to him he would respect him forever afterwards even if he disagreed. After I moved from Vienna to London in 1931 we had much occasion for discussion both orally and by correspondence.

I had undertaken to review for *Economica* his *Treatise on Money*[3] which had then just appeared, and I put a great deal of work into two long articles on it. To the first of these he replied by a counterattack on my

[1] [F. A. Hayek, "Personal Recollections of Keynes and the 'Keynesian Revolution'", *The Oriental Economist*, vol. 34, no. 663, January 1966, pp. 78–80; reprinted in F. A. Hayek, *New Studies in Philosophy, Politics, Economics and the History of Ideas* (Chicago: University of Chicago Press, 1978), pp. 283–289. —Ed.]

[2] [J. M. Keynes, *The Economic Consequences of the Peace*, op. cit. —Ed.]

[3] [J. M. Keynes, *A Treatise on Money*, op. cit. —Ed.]

Prices and Production.[4] I felt that I had largely demolished his theoretical scheme (essentially volume 1), though I had great admiration for the many profound but unsystematical insights contained in volume 2 of the work. Great was my disappointment when all this effort seemed wasted because after the appearance of the second part of my article he told me that he had in the meantime changed his mind and no longer believed what he had said in that work.

This was one of the reasons why I did not return to the attack when he published his now famous *General Theory*[5]—a fact for which I later much blamed myself. But I feared that before I had completed my analysis he would again have changed his mind. Though he had called it a 'general' theory, it was to me too obviously another tract for the times, conditioned by what he thought were the momentary needs of policy. But there was also another reason which I then only dimly felt but which in retrospect appears to me the decisive one: My disagreement with that book did not refer so much to any detail of the analysis as to the general approach followed in the whole work. The real issue was the validity of what we now call macroanalysis, and I feel now that in a long-run perspective the chief significance of the *General Theory* will appear that more than any other single work it decisively furthered the ascendancy of macroeconomics and the temporary decline of microeconomic theory.

I shall later explain why I think that this development is fundamentally mistaken. But first I want to say that it is rather an irony of fate that Keynes should have become responsible for this swing to macrotheory, because he thought in fact rather little of the kind of econometrics which was just then becoming popular, and I do not think that he owes any stimulus to it. His ideas were rooted entirely in Marshallian economics, which was in fact the only economics he knew. Widely read as Keynes was in many fields, his education in economics was somewhat narrow. He did not read any foreign language except French—or, as he once said of himself, in German he could understand only what he knew already.[6] It is a curious fact that before the First World War he had reviewed L. von Mises's *Theory of Money*[7] for the *Economic Journal* (just as A. C. Pigou had a little earlier reviewed Wicksell) without in any way profiting from it.[8] I fear it must be admitted that before he started to

---

[4][See this volume, chapters 3–6, for the reviews and responses. —Ed.]

[5][J. M. Keynes, *The General Theory of Employment, Interest and Money*, op. cit. —Ed.]

[6][Keynes's disclosure is in his *A Treatise on Money*, op. cit., vol. 5, p. 178, n. 2. —Ed.]

[7][Ludwig von Mises, *Theorie des Geldes und der Umlaufsmittel*, op. cit. —Ed.]

[8][J. M. Keynes, "Review of Ludwig von Mises's *Theorie des Geldes und der Umlaufsmittel*", op. cit.; A. C. Pigou, "Review of Knut Wicksell's *Vorlesungen über Nationalökonomie*", op. cit.

develop his own theories, Keynes was not a highly trained or a very sophisticated economic theorist. He started from a rather elementary Marshallian economics and what had been achieved by Walras and Pareto, the Austrians and the Swedes, was very much a closed book to him. I have reason to doubt whether he ever fully mastered the theory of international trade; I don't think he had ever thought systematically on the theory of capital, and even in the theory of the value of money his starting point—and later the object of his criticism—appears to have been a very simple, equation-of-exchange-type of the quantity theory rather than the much more sophisticated cash-balances approach of Alfred Marshall.

He certainly from the beginning was much given to thinking in aggregates and always had a *faible* for (sometimes very tenuous) global estimates. Already in discussion of the 1920s arising out of Great Britain's return to the gold standard his argument had been couched entirely in terms of price- and wage-levels, in practically complete disregard of the structure of relative prices and wages, and later the belief that, because they were statistically measurable, such averages and the various aggregates were also causally of central importance appears to have gained increasing hold upon him. His final conceptions rest entirely on the belief that there exist relatively simple and constant functional relationships between such 'measurable' aggregates as total demand, investment, or output, and that empirically established values of these presumed 'constants' would enable us to make valid predictions.

There seems to me, however, not only to exist no reason whatever to assume that these 'functions' will remain constant, but I believe that microtheory had demonstrated long before Keynes that they cannot be constant but will change over time not only in quantity but even in direction. What these relationships will be, which all macroeconomics must treat as quasi-constant, depends indeed on the microeconomic structure, especially on the relations between different prices which macroeconomics systematically disregards. They may change very rapidly as a result of changes in the microeconomic structure, and conclusions based on the assumption that they are constant are bound to be very misleading.

Let me use as an illustration the relation between the demand for consumers' goods and the volume of investment. There are undoubtedly certain conditions in which an increase of the demand for consumers' goods *will* lead to an increase in investment. But Keynes assumes that

See this volume, chapter 1, note 18, for more on the reviews. —Ed.]

this will always be the case. It can easily be demonstrated, however, that this cannot be so and that in some circumstances an increase of the demand for final products must lead to a *decrease* of investment. The first will generally be true only if, as Keynes generally assumes, there exist unemployed reserves of all factors of production and of the various kinds of commodities. In such circumstances it is possible at the same time to increase the production of consumers' goods and the production of capital goods.

The position is altogether different, however, if the economic system is in a state of full or nearly full employment. Then it is possible to increase the output of investment goods only by at least temporarily reducing the output of consumers' goods, because, to increase the production of the former, factors will have to be shifted to it from the production of consumers' goods. And it will be some time before the additional investment helps to increase the flow of consumers' goods.

Keynes appears to have been misled here by a mistake opposite to that of which he accused the classical economists. He alleged, with only partial justification, that the classics had based their argument on the assumption of full employment, and he based his own argument on what may be called the assumption of full unemployment, i.e., the assumption that there normally exist unused reserves of *all* factors and commodities. But the latter assumption is not only at least as unlikely to be true in fact as the former; it is also much more misleading. An analysis on the assumption of full employment, even if the assumption is only partially valid, at least helps us to understand the functioning of the price mechanism, the significance of the relations between different prices and of the factors which lead to a change in these relations. But the assumption that all goods and factors are available in excess makes the whole price system redundant, undetermined and unintelligible. Indeed, some of the most orthodox disciples of Keynes appear consistently to have thrown overboard all the traditional theory of price determination and of distribution, all that used to be the backbone of economic theory, and in consequence, in my opinion, to have ceased to understand any economics.

It is easy to see how such belief, according to which the creation of additional money will lead to the creation of a corresponding amount of goods, was bound to lead to a revival of the more naive inflationist fallacies which we thought economics had once and for all exterminated. And I have little doubt that we owe much of the post-war inflation to the great influence of such over-simplified Keynesianism. Not that Keynes himself would have approved of this. Indeed, I am fairly certain that if he had lived he would in that period have been one of the most determined fighters against inflation. About the last time I saw him, a few weeks before his death, he more or less plainly told me so. As his remark on that occasion is illuminating in other respects, it is worth repeating. I had asked him whether he was not getting alarmed by the use to which some of his disciples were putting his theories. His reply was that these theories had been greatly needed in the 1930s; but if these theories should ever become harmful, I could be assured that he would quickly bring about a change in public opinion. What I blame him for is that he had called such a tract for the times the *General Theory*.

The fact is that, although he liked to pose as the Cassandra whose dire predictions were not listened to, he was really supremely confident of his powers of persuasion and believed that he could play on public opinion as a virtuoso plays on his instrument. He was, by gift and temperament, more an artist and politician than a scholar or student. Though endowed with supreme mental powers, his thinking was as much influenced by aesthetic and intuitive as by purely rational factors. Knowledge came easily to him and he possessed a remarkable memory. But the intuition which made him sure of the results before he had demonstrated them, and led him to justify the same policies in turn by very different theoretical arguments, made him rather impatient of the slow, painstaking intellectual work by which knowledge is normally advanced.

He was so many-sided that when one came to estimate him as a man it seemed almost irrelevant that one thought his economics to be both false and dangerous. If one considers how small a share of his time and energy he gave to economics, his influence on economics and the fact that he will be remembered chiefly as an economist is both miraculous and tragic. He would have been remembered as a great man by all who knew him even if he had never written on economics.

I cannot from personal knowledge speak of his services to his country during the last five or six years of his life when, already a sick man, he gave all his strength to public service. Yet it was during those years that I saw most of him and came to know him fairly well. The London School of Economics had at the outbreak of the war been moved to Cambridge, and when it became necessary in 1940 for me to live wholly at Cambridge, he found quarters for me at his college. On the weekends for which, so far as possible, he sought the quiet of Cambridge, I then saw a fair amount of him and came to know him otherwise than merely professionally. Perhaps it was because he was seeking relief from his arduous duties, or because all that concerned his official work was secret, that all his other interests then came out most clearly. Though he had before the war reduced his business connections and given up the bursarship of his college, the interests and activities he still actively pursued besides his official duties would have taxed the whole strength of most other men. He kept as informed on artistic, literary, and scientific matters as in normal times, and always his strong personal likes and dislikes came through.

I remember particularly one occasion which now seems to me characteristic of many. The war was over and Keynes had just returned from an official mission to Washington on a matter of the greatest consequence which one would have assumed had absorbed all his energy. Yet he entertained a group of us for part of the evening with details about the state of the collection of Elizabethan books in the United States as if the study of this had been the sole purpose of his visit. He was himself a distinguished collector in this field, as of manuscripts of about the same period, and of modern paintings.

As I mentioned before, his intellectual interests were also largely determined by aesthetic predilections. This applied as much to literature and history as to other fields. Both the sixteenth and seventeenth centuries greatly appealed to him, and his knowledge, at least in selected parts, was that of an expert. But he much disliked the nineteenth century and would occasionally show a lack of knowledge of its economic history and even the history of its economics which was somewhat surprising in an economist.

I cannot in this short essay attempt even to sketch the general philosophy and outline on life which guided Keynes's thinking. It is a task which has yet to be attempted, because on this the otherwise brilliant and remarkably frank biography by Sir Roy Harrod is hardly sufficient—perhaps because he so completely shared and therefore took for granted the peculiar brand of rationalism which dominated Keynes's generation. Those who want to learn more about this I would strongly advise to read Keynes's own essay "My Early Beliefs" which was published in a little volume entitled *Two Memoirs*.[9]

In conclusion I want to say a few words about the future of Keynesian theory. Perhaps it will be evident from what I have already said that I believe that this will be decided not by any future discussion of his special theorems but rather by the future development of views on the appropriate method of the social sciences. Keynes's theories will appear merely as the most prominent and influential instance of a general approach the philosophical justification of which seems to be highly questionable. Though with its reliance on apparently measurable magnitude it *appears* at first more scientific than the older microtheory,

---

[9][J. M. Keynes, *Two Memoirs* [1949], reprinted in *Essays in Biography*, op. cit., pp. 387–450. The memoirs did not appear in the 1933 version of the *Essays*. —Ed.]

it seems to me that it has achieved this pseudo-exactness at the price of disregarding the relationships which really govern the economic system. Even though the schemata of microeconomics do not claim to achieve those quantitative predictions at which the ambitions of macroeconomics aim, I believe by learning to content ourselves with the more modest aims of the former, we shall gain more insight into at least the principle on which the complex order of economic life operates, than by the artificial simplification necessary for macrotheory which tends to conceal nearly all that really matters. I venture to predict that once this problem of method is settled, the 'Keynesian Revolution' will appear as an episode during which erroneous conceptions of the appropriate scientific method led to the temporary obliteration of many important insights which we had already achieved and which we shall then have painfully to regain.

THIRTEEN

THE KEYNES CENTENARY:
THE AUSTRIAN CRITIQUE[1]

It will not be easy for future historians to account for the fact that, for a generation after the untimely death of Maynard Keynes, opinion was so completely under the sway of what was regarded as Keynesianism, in a way that no single man had ever before dominated economic policy and development. Nor will it be easy to explain why these ideas rather suddenly went out of fashion, leaving behind a somewhat bewildered community of economists who had forgotten much that had been fairly well understood before the "Keynesian Revolution". There can be no doubt that it was in Keynes's name and on the basis of his theoretical work that the modern world has experienced the longest period of general inflation, and has now again to pay for it by a widespread and severe depression. Yet it is more than doubtful whether Keynes himself would have approved of the policies pursued in his name.

It was Keynes who had told us in 1919[2] that

> There is no subtler, no surer means of overturning the existing basis of society than to debauch the currency. The process engages all the hidden forces of economic law on the side of destruction, and does it in a manner which not one man in a million is able to diagnose.

It was Keynes who alleged that Lenin had concluded that "the best way to destroy the capitalist system was to debauch the currency".[3]

During this crucial period I could watch much of this development and occasionally discuss the decisive issues with Keynes, whom I in many ways much admired and still regard as one of the most remarkable men I have known. He was certainly one of the most powerful thinkers and expositors of his generation. But, paradoxical as this may sound, he was neither a highly trained economist nor even centrally concerned with the

---

[1][F. A. Hayek, "The Keynes Centenary: The Austrian Critique", *The Economist*, June 11, 1983, pp. 45–48. —Ed.]

[2][J. M. Keynes, *The Economic Consequences of the Peace*, op. cit. The quotation appears on p. 149. Though it would have made for a nice story, Lenin never said it. See Donald Moggridge, *Maynard Keynes: An Economist's Biography* (London: Routledge, 1992), pp. 332–333. —Ed.]

[3][Keynes, *The Economic Consequences of the Peace*, op. cit., p. 148. —Ed.]

development of economics as a science. In the last resort he did not even think much of economics as a science, tending to regard his superior capacity for providing theoretical justifications as a legitimate tool for persuading the public to pursue the policies which his intuition told him were required at the moment.

The question of Keynes's role in history is essentially one of how his teaching could succeed once more in opening the floodgates of inflation after it had become generally recognized that the temporary gain in employment achieved by credit expansion had necessarily to be paid for by even more severe unemployment at a later stage. This old truth is now being rediscovered. Bitter experience has again shown that the acceleration of inflation, which alone can preserve the kinds of jobs that have been created by inflation, cannot be indefinitely continued.

Keynes never recognized that progressive inflation was needed in order that any growth in monetary demand could lastingly increase the employment of labour. He was thoroughly aware of the danger of growing monetary demand degenerating into progressive inflation, and towards the end of his life greatly concerned that this might happen. It was not the living Keynes but the continuing influence of his theories that determined what did happen. I can report from firsthand knowledge that, on the last occasion I discussed these matters with him, he was seriously alarmed by the agitation for credit expansion by some of his closest associates. He went so far as to assure me that if his theories, which had been badly needed in the deflation of the 1930s, should ever produce dangerous effects he would rapidly change public opinion in the right direction. A few weeks later he was dead and could not do it.

Yet it is undeniable that inflationary conclusions could in good faith be drawn from his teaching. This suggests that his theories must have suffered from a serious defect and raises the central question—whether the great influence that his views have had on professional opinion was due to a real advance of our understanding or to some definite error. Special circumstances made me from the very beginning regard his whole analysis as based on a crucial error.

I am afraid this obliges me to say frankly that I still have no doubt that Maynard Keynes was neither a full master of the body of economic theory then available, nor really cared to acquaint himself with any development which lay outside the Marshallian tradition which he had learnt during the second half of his undergraduate years at Cambridge. His main aim was always to influence current policy, and economic theory was for him simply a tool for this purpose. He trusted his intellectual powers readily to produce a better theory for this purpose, and tried to do so in several different forms.

In these theoretical efforts he was guided by one central idea—which in conversation he once described to me as an "axiom which only half-wits could question"—namely, that general employment was always positively correlated with the aggregate demand for consumer goods. This made him feel that there was more truth in that underconsumption theory preached by a long row of radicals and cranks for generations but by relatively few academic economists. It was his revival of this underconsumption approach which made his theories so attractive to the Left. John Stuart Mill's profound insight that demand for commodities is not demand for labour, which Leslie Stephen could in 1876[4] still describe as the doctrine whose "complete apprehension is, perhaps, the best test of a sound economist", re- mained for Keynes an incomprehensible absurdity.

The Role of Investment

In the Cambridge tradition that governed Keynes's brief study of economics, the Mill-Jevons theory of capital, later developed by Böhm-Bawerk and Wicksell, was not seriously considered. By about 1930 these ideas had been largely forgotten in the English-speaking world. Along with most of my professional colleagues, I might also have readily accepted Keynes's elaboration of the commonsense belief of a direct dependence of employment on aggregate demand. However, not only had I been brought up in the Böhm-Bawerk-Wicksell tradition but, just before Keynes's *Treatise on Money*[5] appeared, I had also spent much time analyzing a somewhat similar but much cruder American effort to develop a monetary theory of the causes of 'underconsumption'.[6] For this purpose I had already developed a little further the Wicksell-Mises theory of monetary overstimulation of investment which, I felt, refuted the naive assumption of a direct dependence of investment on final demand from which Keynes had started.

In the course of the years I had several occasions to discuss these issues with Keynes. It became quite clear that our differences rested

---

[4][Sir Leslie Stephen, *History of English Thought in the Eighteenth Century* (London: Smith, Elder, 1876), vol. 2, chapter 11, p. 297. Stephen's two daughters by his second wife, Vanessa (who married Clive Bell) and Virginia (who married Leonard Woolf), were central figures in the Bloomsbury Group, Keynes's closest associates in the years between the university and his marriage in 1925 to Lydia Lopokova. —Ed.]

[5][J. M. Keynes, *A Treatise on Money*, op. cit. —Ed.]

[6][His efforts resulted in the paper, "The 'Paradox' of Saving", reprinted as chapter 2, this volume. —Ed.]

wholly on his refusal to question that assumption. On one occasion I succeeded in making him admit, with evident surprise, that in certain circumstances, preceding investment might cause an increase in the demand for capital. But when on a later occasion I had got him momentarily interested in the possibility that a fall in product prices might lead to investment in order to reduce units costs, he soon dismissed this brusquely as nonsense!

Since the determinants of employment other than final demand are the factors which Keynesian macroeconomics so fatally neglects, an assessment of its historical role must attempt to bring this aspect of economics briefly back to mind. It is helpful to conceive of the continuous flow of production as a great river that may, independently of the suction from its mouth, swell or shrink in its different parts as its countless tributaries further upstream add more or less to its volume. Fluctuations in investment and replacement will cause the stream to increase or reduce the volume in its upper reaches with consequent changes in employment, as occurs in the course of industrial fluctuations. There is no necessary correspondence between the volume (or even the direction of the change) of the sale of final products during a period and that of employment during that period.

The volume of investment is far from moving proportionally to final demand. Not only the rate of interest but also the relative prices of the different factors of production and particularly of the different kinds of labour will affect it, apart from technological change. Investment will depend on the volume of the different parts of the stream, whether at any one moment total employment of factors of production will be greater or smaller than the effective demand for final products. The immediate determinants directing the tributaries to the main stream will not be final demand but the structure of relative prices of the different factors of production: the different kinds of labour, semi-finished products, raw materials and, of course, rates of interest.

When, as directed by these relative prices, the whole stream changes its shape, employment is bound to change at its different stages at very different rates: Sometimes the whole stream will, as it were, happily stretch itself, providing additional jobs, while sometimes it will shrink. This may cause strong fluctuations in the volume of employment, particularly in the 'heavy' industries and in building, without any changes of consumer demand in the same direction. It is a well-known historical fact that in a slump the revival of final demand is generally an effect rather than a cause of the revival in the upper reaches of the stream of production—activities generated by savings seeking investment and by the necessity of making up for postponed renewals and replacements.

The important point is that those independent swellings and shrinkings of the different reaches of the stream of production are caused by the changes in the relative prices of different factors: some being drawn by higher prices to earlier stages of the process or vice versa. This constant reallocation of resources is wholly concealed by the analysis Keynes chose to adopt and which has since come to be known as 'macroeconomics': an analysis in terms of the relations between various aggregates or averages, such as aggregate demand or supply, average prices etc. This approach obscures the character of the mechanism by which the demand for the different kinds of activities is determined.

The Myth of Measurement

The hope of becoming more 'empirical' by becoming more macro-economic is bound to be disappointed, because these statistical magnitudes—which are alone ascertainable by 'measurement'—do not also make them significant as the cause of actions of individuals who do not know them. Economic phenomena are not mass phenomena of the kind to which statistical theory is applicable. They belong to that intermediate sphere that lies between the simple phenomena of which people can ascertain all the relevant data and the true mass phenomena where one must rely on probabilities.

It cannot seriously be denied that monetary causes exert important effects on the order of the world of real goods, or that these effects were largely neglected by Keynes. Yet the purely monetary approach he had adopted created considerable difficulties for criticism by an opponent who felt that Keynes had missed the crucial issues. I ought to explain why I failed to return to the charge after I had devoted much time to a careful analysis of his writings—a failure for which I have reproached myself ever since. It was not merely (as I have occasionally claimed) the inevitable disappointment of a young man when told by the famous author that his objections did not matter since Keynes no longer believed in his own arguments. Nor was it really that I became aware that an effective refutation of Keynes's conclusions would have to deal with the whole macroeconomic approach. It was rather that his disregard of what seemed to me the crucial problems made me recognize that a proper critique would have to deal more with what Keynes had not gone into than with what he had discussed, and that in consequence an elaboration of the still inadequately developed theory of capital was a prerequisite for a thorough disposal of Keynes's argument.

So I started on this task intending it to lead to a discussion of the determinants of investment in a monetary system. But the preliminary 'pure' part of this work proved to be much more difficult, and took me very much longer, than I had expected. When war broke out, making it doubtful that publication of such a voluminous work would be possible, I put out as a separate book what had been meant as a first step of an analysis of the Keynesian weaknesses, which itself was indefinitely postponed.[7]

The main cause of this postponement was that I soon found myself supporting Keynes in his struggle against wartime inflation, and at that time wished nothing less than to weaken his authority. Although I regard Keynes's theories as chiefly responsible for the inflation of the past quarter of a century, I am convinced that this was a development which he did not intend and which he would have endeavoured with all his strength to prevent. I am not sure he could have succeeded because he had never seen clearly that only accelerating inflation could lastingly secure a high level of employment.

Deviating Disciples

Towards the end of his life Keynes was certainly not happy about the direction of the efforts of his closest associates. I can well believe his saying that, just as Marx was never a Marxist, so he was never a Keynesian. We have it also, on the authority of Professor Joan Robinson, that "there were moments when we had trouble in getting Maynard to see what the point of his revolution really was, but when he came to sum it up after the book was published he got it into focus".[8] It was, in fact, the group of younger Keynesian doctrinaires whose ideas guided the inflationary 'full-employment' policy for the next thirty years, not only of Britain but for most of the rest of the world.[9]

I am fully aware that, in effect, I am claiming that perhaps the most impressive intellectual figure I have ever encountered and whose general intellectual superiority I have readily acknowledged was wholly wrong in the scientific work for which he is chiefly known. But I must add that I am convinced that he owed his extraordinary influence in this field,

---

[7][F. A. Hayek, *The Pure Theory of Capital*, op. cit. —Ed.]

[8][Joan Robinson, "What Has Become of the Keynesian Revolution?", presidential address, British Association, 1972, in her *Collected Economic Papers*, volume 5 (Cambridge, Mass.: MIT Press, 1980), p. 170. —Ed.]

[9][See this volume, Addendum to chapter 10, for more on this episode. —Ed.]

to which he gave only a small part of his energy, to an almost unique combination of other gifts. Irrespective of whether he was right or wrong, those gifts made him one of the outstanding figures of his age. He will in future appear as representative of his time as some of the famous Renaissance figures now appear to us. I am not contending that his influence in other fields was necessarily more beneficial. Indeed I am convinced that, through his denial of conventional morals[10] and his haughty "in the long run we are all dead" approach, his influence was disastrous.

Yet it was his great gifts which made it so difficult to escape his influence and to resist being drawn into his way of thinking. He not only possessed an incredible variety of intellectual interests but was perhaps even more drawn to the arts. He was also a great patriot, if that is the right word for a profound believer in the superiority of British civilisation. That his intellectual efforts were largely dominated by his aesthetic feelings was one of his strongest characteristics, and chief source of the personal fascination he exercised.

Alpha Plus

A little episode on the same last occasion when I met him at dinner at King's College may give an idea of the amazing richness of his mind. In the later years of the war he had been regularly sending me the American *Journal of the History of Ideas* to which he subscribed and which I found difficult to obtain. Two or three weeks before the dinner at King's he had sent me the latest issue; it happened that I had read in it the same morning an article on the circumstances of the posthumous publication of the second work of Copernicus. At coffee I sat opposite the College astronomer, who had not yet seen the article, so it provided a welcome topic of conversation.

Keynes, sitting a little further up the table and engaged in another conversation, was evidently at the same time following my account of the affair. He suddenly interrupted me in the rendering of a complicated detail with "You are wrong, Hayek". He then gave a much fuller and more accurate account of the circumstances, although it must have been

---

[10][For Keynes's views on ethics and morality, see his essay "My Early Beliefs", op. cit., pp. 433–450. For the importance of the paper in understanding Keynes's thought, see Robert Skidelsky, *John Maynard Keynes: Volume One, Hopes Betrayed 1883–1920* (New York: Viking, 1983), chapter 6. —Ed.]

two or three weeks since he had seen what I had read a few hours before.

I have confined myself here to the distinctive contributions Keynes made to economic theory. But his great influence far exceeded and also antedated the hopes this technical work held out of lastingly full employment. He had gained the ear of the "advanced" thinkers much earlier and greatly contributed to a trend very much in conflict with his own classical liberal beginnings. The time when he had become the idol of the leftish intellectuals was in fact when in 1933 he had shocked many of his earlier admirers by an essay on "National Self-Sufficiency" in the *New Statesman and Nation*[11] (reprinted with equal enthusiasm by the *Yale Review*,[12] the communist *Science and Society*,[13] and the national-socialist *Schmoller's Jahrbuch*[14]). In the essay he proclaimed that "The decadent international but individualistic capitalism, in the hands of which we found ourselves after the war, is not a success. It is not intelligent, it is not beautiful, it is not just, it is not virtuous—and it does not deliver the goods. In short, we dislike it and are beginning to despise it".[15] Later, still in the same mood, in his preface to the German translation of *The General Theory*,[16] he frankly recommended his policy proposals as being more easily adapted to the conditions of a totalitarian state than those in which production is guided by free competition.

No wonder his disciples were shocked when, long after his death, it became known that less than a decade later he had, in a private letter, said of my book, *The Road to Serfdom*,[17] that "morally and philosophically [he found himself] in agreement with virtually the whole of it; and not

[11] [*The New Statesman and Nation*, July 8, 1933, pp. 36–37, and July 15, 1933, pp. 65–67. Reprinted in *Activities 1931–9: World Crises and Policies in Britain and America*, op. cit., pp. 233–246. —Ed.]

[12] [*The Yale Review*, vol. 22, no. 4, summer 1933, pp. 755–769. —Ed.]

[13] [There is no mention in the General Index of the Marxist periodical *Science and Society* that Keynes's article was ever reprinted there. —Ed.]

[14] ["Nationale Selbstgenügsamkeit", *Schmoller's Jahrbuch für Gesetzgebung, Verwaltung und Volkswirtschaft im Deutschen Reiche*, op. cit. —Ed.]

[15] ["National Self-Sufficiency", op. cit., p. 239. —Ed.]

[16] [J. M. Keynes, *Allgemeine Theorie der Beschäftigung, des Zinses, und des Geldes*, op. cit. The Preface to the German edition is reprinted in *The General Theory of Employment, Interest and Money*, op. cit., pp. xxv–xxvii. The relevant passage reads: "[T]he theory of output as a whole, which is what the following book purports to provide, is much more easily adapted to the conditions of a totalitarian state, than is the theory of production and distribution of a given output produced under conditions of free competition and a large measure of laissez-faire" (p. xxvi). —Ed.]

[17] [F. A. Hayek, *The Road to Serfdom*, op. cit. —Ed.]

only in agreement with it, but in a deeply moved agreement".[18] He qualified this approval by the curious belief that "dangerous acts can be done safely in a country which thinks rightly, which could be the way to hell if they were executed by those who feel wrongly".

Inspired geniuses possessing a great power of conviction are not necessarily a blessing for the society in which they spring up. John Maynard Keynes was undoubtedly one of the great men of his age, in some respects representative and in others revolutionary, but hardly the great scientist whose growing insight moves along a single path. His *Collected Writings*, "chiefly in the field of economics" and now approaching the thirtieth volume, are certainly a most revealing documentation of the intellectual movements of his time. But an economist may feel some doubt whether this distinction, for which Newton, Darwin, and the great British philosophers all still have to wait, is not rather a token of the idolatry he enjoyed among his personal admirers than proportionate to his contribution to the advance of scientific knowledge.

---

[18][Letter of June 28, 1944, reprinted in *Activities 1940–6: Shaping the Post-War World—Employment and Commodities*, op. cit., p. 385. —Ed.]

EDITOR'S ACKNOWLEDGEMENTS

I received numerous comments on earlier drafts of the Introduction from Donald Moggridge, Brad Bateman, Bob Coats, Mark Blaug, Dan Hammond, Stephan Boehm, and Stephen Kresge. Their close readings revealed an embarrassingly large number of errors of fact and infelicities of style, and I thank them all for saving me from a more public airing of my limitations. None is to be blamed for remaining errors. I also thank Donald Moggridge, Mark Blaug, and Jack Birner for helping me to track down some of the more obscure citations to be found in the footnotes. I finally would like to thank my graduate research assistants Reggie Harris and Faye Newton for their contributions to this project, and Stephen Kresge for his sound guidance and advice in his role as series general editor.

Bruce Caldwell
Greensboro, North Carolina
September 1994

INDEX

Abbati, Alfred H., 193 & n
Adams, Arthur B., 85n, 85, 100,
104, 110n, 114n, 119n
Aggregates, use of, 17, 33, 42–3,
60–1, 128, 150n, 167, 231–3, 238,
241–2, 245–6, 250–1
Allen, R. G. D., 56–7 & n
American Economic Association, 85
Arrow, Kenneth, 56n
Austria, 2, 9–11, 18, 69

Bailey, Samuel, 54 & n
Bamberger, Ludwig, 112n
Bank of England, 3, 5, 8
Bank of International Settlements,
94n
Bank Rate, 3, 188, 218; Keynes's
theory of, 142, 146, 174–9
Banking system; Cannan's views
on, 29–31, 71–2; in Foster and
Catchings's model, 83; in Hayek's
exchange with Sraffa, 199, 204–5,
208–9, 214–18; in Keynes's *Trea-
tise on Money*, 26, 136, 141–3,
148, 151–3, 161–2, 174–6, 181,
186–90, 195; in trade cycle in
Austrian theory, 15 & n, 16, 29,
195–7, 215, 218
Barber, William J., 34n
Barter economy, 77, 124, 156, 199,
209, 220
Bartley, III, W. W., 58n
Bateman, Bradley, 44n
Batson, H. E., 10n
Bean, Charles, 47n
Beckhart, B. H., 10
Bell, Clive, 249n
Bell, Vanessa, 249n

Bendixen, Friedrich, 55n
Benham, Frederic, 56 & n
Berle, Jr., Adolf A., 237n
Beveridge, Sir William, 19, 36 & n,
52 & n, 62, 233–5 & n, 236; and
LSE, 19, 52 & n, 233n–234n
Bickerdike, C. F., 85n
Blaug, Mark 31 & n, 32n
Bloomsbury group, 249n
Boehm, Stephan, 36n, 100n
Böhm-Bawerk, Eugen, 15 & n, 42,
44n, 50n, 58n, 94, 106n, 113 &
n, 130–1 & n, 155, 163, 169, 249
Borchardt, Knut, 230n
Bowley, A. L., 64n
Bryce, R. B., 34
Burns, Arthur F., 237n
Business cycle, *see* trade cycle

Caine, Sir Sidney, 51n
Caldwell, Bruce, 17n, 32n, 43n,
62n
Cambridge, 2, 5n, 19, 23–4, 26,
31, 34–7, 45–6, 50 & n, 51, 55,
57n, 59 & n, 63, 72n, 112n, 121,
150, 228, 234n, 244, 248–9, 253
Cambridge Circus, 23 & n, 24, 35,
39, 57n, 59n
Cannan, Edwin, 19–20, 51 & n,
52–3, 55 & n, 56, 64–8 & n, 69 &
n, 70, 71–2 & n, 73, 92n; and his
approach to economic theory,
55–6, 65–8, 71–2; and LSE, 19,
51 & n–53, 55 & n–56, 64–73
Capital, accumulation of, 202–4,
212, 217n, 220, 223; consumption of, 182, 204, 214, 216; circulating and fixed, in Hayek's cri-

INDEX

Monetary Theory and the Trade Cycle
(F. A. Hayek), 14n, 17 & n, 29 &
n, 36–8, 56n, 102n, 145n, 211n,
220n
Morgenstern, Oskar, 18, 37
Mummery, A. F., 75n
Myrdal, Gunnar, 26n, 36

Nasse, Erwin, 112n
National Bureau of Economic Re-
search, 84n, 93n, 237n
National Investment Board, 235
National Labor Relations Board,
89n

Neisser, H., 85n
'Neutral' money, *see* monetary the-
ory
New York University, 10
Newton, Sir Isaac, 255
Nicholson, Joseph Shield, 69 & n,
71
Novogilov, Victor Valentinovitch,
85n, 85, 91n

O'Brien, D. P., 36n
O'Driscoll, Gerald, 31n
Olmsted, Frederick Law, 85n, 93n
Oxford University, 7, 19, 24, 51,
55 & n, 57 & n, 65, 72n

Pantaleoni, Maffeo, 50 & n
"'Paradox' of Saving, The" (F. A.
Hayek), 17–19, chapter 2 *passim*,
194n
Pareto, Vilfredo, 50 & n, 67 & n,
242
Paris Peace Conference, 2, 41, 240
Patinkin, Don, 24n, 26n
Pattern prediction, 44
Persons, Warren Milton, 89 & n
Pierson, Nikolaas G., 112 & n

Pigou, A. C., 2, 20, 28 & n, 50–1n,
53n, 55 & n, 112 & n, 150n, 166,
241 & n
Plant, Arnold, 56 & n
Pollack Foundation for Economic
Research, 76 & n, 78n, 193n
Presley, John, 36n
Prices and Production (F. A. Hayek),
14n, 21, 25, 27, 29–30, 35, 37 &
n, 44, 58 & n, 59, 97n, 122n,
163n, 168–9, 180n, 194n, chapters 7–9 *passim*, 241; Hayek's response to Sraffa's review of, 37–9,
172, chapter 8; Keynes's references to, 148 & n, 149 & n, 151
& n, 152 & n, 153 & n, 154, 155,
156 & n; Sraffa's review of, 37–9,
172, chapters 7, 9
Prices, 13–15; and aggregate price
indices, 17, 60–1, 87–8, 123,
150n; controls on, 45, 70; in
Hayek's exchange with Sraffa,
198, 200, 206–7, 225; in Keynes's
Treatise on Money, 123, 134–5n,
138, 142–5, 148, 150n, 153,
156–7, 174, 176, 180, 182, 188n,
192–3; relative, 13–15, 43–5, 60,
128, 138, 140, 198, 242–3, 250–1;
rising, as a stage in Hayek's theory of trade cycle, 12, 17, 24, 38,
182; spot vs. forward, 206, 208;
stabilization of, as a goal of policy, 5, 13, 16–17, 58–59n, 98,
113, 118–19, 225; stable, in Wicksell, 176, 207, 225
Production, 57, 61; "average period of", 15, 42, 44n, 94–8, 131,
168–9, 195, 212 & n, 213; effect
of savings on, in Hayek's model,
14–16, 91–8, 107–11, 201–2, 215
& n-19; in Hayek's exchange
with Sraffa, 38, 198–202, 207,

INDEX

INDEX